Experiment:

conversations in

art and science

Edited by Bergit Arends and Davina Thackara

Preface / Introduction   **7/9**
Ken Arnold / Bergit Arends

Medusae   **16**
Marina Warner / Dorothy Cross / Tom Cross

How To Live   **62**
Jeni Walwin / Bobby Baker / Richard Hallam

Red and Wet on the Iron Air   **96**
Bergit Arends / Tony Holder

Soundless Music   **132**
Susan Hallam / Sarah Angliss / GéNIA / Ciarán O'Keeffe /
Richard Wiseman / Richard Lord

Navigating Memories   172
Colette Conroy / Jennie Pedley / Laura Camfield / Nigel Foreman

Viewing the Instruments   **236**
Brian Hurwitz / Jane Wildgoose / Philip Parr / Peter Isaacs

Baby Epsilons   **274**
Luke Wilson / Sean Gandini / Norihide Tokushige

Projects 2000 – 2002 / Biographies   **308/342**

Preface

Ken Arnold

The intermingling of practices from the arts and sciences, a taste of which is presented in this volume, has prompted much questioning. What is it about science that attracts artists? Is it the richness of its subject matter, the moral vibrancy of the issues it raises, or the compelling strength of its methodology? On the other side, what does science gain from these encounters? Visually compelling parades of its results; easier ways of understanding difficult ideas; an opportunity to gain greater public trust; or perhaps a different way of thinking about science and the world? And does this integration of methodologies and backgrounds represent something genuinely new, or is it simply a fashionable repackaging of the already familiar? This book is offered less by way of answers to these questions, and more as a source of rich evidence on which to base further thought and discussion.

The Wellcome Trust is an independent research-funding charity that has as its mission to foster and promote research with the aim of improving human and animal health. Scientific research is undertaken within broader social and cultural contexts, which the Trust is also committed to exploring and understanding. As part of this effort, the Trust started funding arts schemes in the mid-1990s. Almost a decade later, after supporting more than 50 science and art projects, this publication is a gesture towards what has cumulatively become a rich strand in its work to raise awareness of the historical, ethical, social and cultural aspects of biomedical science.

Introduction

Bergit Arends

Despite technological advances, biologists' laboratory benches continue to be stocked with bottles, pipettes and petri dishes. This seemingly chaotic arrangement has its own logic that ensures a structured and systematic approach to the testing of cells and tissues. A setting of this kind was once the scene of an accident – one in a long and distinguished line of serendipitous moments in science. As a result of a labelling mix-up in an experiment conducted by Sir Alan Parkes, glycerol was used in place of lactose in the preparation of sperm for freezing. The glycerol performed impressively and, in time, this chance discovery led to the routine preservation of tissues and cells at low temperature. Without this fortuitous event, an important advance that altered the whole field of reproductive biology might never have occurred.

i Schaffer S (1996) Making up discovery. In Boden MA (ed.) Dimensions of creativity. Cambridge, MA: MIT Press

The story highlights the significance of randomness in scientific method. It would be easy to overstate the contribution of chance to science,[i] but it is easier still to deny its occurrence in favour of the myth of an entirely prescribed methodology. Science is hypothesis driven – an idea is conceived, tested, discussed, peer reviewed and, possibly, published. If the results are reliable or, better still, unforeseen, the publication is likely to be cited, perhaps even become famous. But the first step on this journey, namely the generation of the hypothesis itself, is rarely discussed. Mere observation of phenomena is obviously not sufficient, for if it were, it is difficult to see why hypothesizing should be so difficult.

As physicist and feline gambler Erwin Schrödinger put it, "The task is not to see what has never been seen before, but to think what has never been thought before about what you see every day". This early and ill-described stage entails a 'methodology gap'. It is at this messy and amorphous juncture, where the creation of knowledge starts, that scientists must find their inspiration. It is an opening that offers opportunities to collaborations between art and science.

Artists' productivity, like scientists', comes from an attitude of curiosity, an urge to find out. However, in artistic endeavour, it is the methodology gaps, rather than the methodology itself, that are often most evident. In recent years artists have increasingly been encouraged to undertake research within academic institutions and art schools, and to pursue higher degrees in subjects such as 'Fine Art Practice'; but the necessity and the shape of this development is much debated. Methodologically prescribed research is something of an anathema to the eclecticism of most artistic practice and its procedures remain poorly defined.

Experiment: conversations in art and science presents a number of recent research projects between scientists and artists that have taken place in different subject areas and media. The purpose of the publication is to lay bare the collaborative research process. Its chapters are not exercises in critical analysis, but first-hand accounts of the development of ideas, cooperative working processes, deployment of information, and the emergence of new knowledge through transdisciplinarity. Their authors have not sought to deliver answers on the relationship between art and science, but rather to intrigue and captivate through narratives that combine method and rigour with quirkiness and poetry.

A difficulty of the publication was to find an appropriate aesthetic and linguistic form in which to present the diversity of material involved without compromising artistic and, in particular, scientific information. Scientists accustomed to publishing accounts of their work tend to adopt a specialized and technical style, suited to their (largely professional) audience. One of the editorial challenges was to adapt this style in the service of a more general readership. In making these editorial decisions, we trust that we have not infringed upon the credibility of scientific data and narrative.

In recognition of the diversity of the projects and their range of imagery, each chapter has been given a different visual treatment, taking its inspiration from the aesthetic character and working processes of the collaboration it describes. In several cases the device of the diary, the dialogue, and the sketchbook has been used, as reflected in the book's subtitle, as a way of emphasizing the duality of the relationship and the ongoing nature of the research.

A particularly distinctive chapter is *Viewing the Instruments*. An eighteenth-century score for bass viol written by the composer Marin Marais illustrating lithotomy (the surgical removal of a stone from the urinary system), led the project team to investigate historic and contemporary surgical techniques, and patients' responses to the operating environment then and now.

The rich and fascinating historic imagery presented in this chapter invites a host of new insights, including a fresh interpretation of the gaze on the male body as it undergoes surgical intervention. There are resonances here with artworks of our own era that explore the interior of the body for metaphorical purposes, as well as with analogies that have been made at various times between medicine and music. Terms such as tone, tonic and temperance, which have their origin in music, are still applied in medicine today. In Pythagorean philosophy the body itself was viewed as a kind of musical instrument, with strings that required the right tension and balance. The research has resulted in a complex piece of performance presenting music, imagery and patients' testimonies in a dramatic format.

In a very different kind of musical investigation characterized by its oxy-moronic title, *Soundless Music* revels in the eccentric and bizarre. This unique experiment with live infrasound delves into the murky science of frequencies and parapsychology, provoking challenging and unorthodox considerations of music, not only for musicians, but also for engineers, psychologists and physicists. Experimental psychology also features in the dogmatic-sounding *How To Live*, devised by performance artist Bobby Baker and psychologist and therapist Richard Hallam. The collaborators have united in an attempt to bring greater equality and transparency to a therapy system that would normally categorize them as 'user' and 'provider'. Taking a highly unconven-tional approach to the training video, the artist successfully assimilates and subverts, while the scientist looks for new ways forward for a society in need of taming its emotions.

Navigating Memories describes how young adults with disabilities learned to represent their autobiographies through stories and drawing, translated into virtual 3D environments in which they, and not their disabilities, take centre stage. In a series of intense workshops these young people, at the cusp of leaving the care system, worked with an anthropologist, a psychologist and an artist on the verbal and visual tracing of key life experiences that are told with courage and humour. We are privileged to be able to publish these unaffected, yet affecting, stories and drawings alongside a more dispassionate description of the process by which they were obtained.

Natural science is represented by two projects, one celebrating the wonder of the animal world, another highlighting the havoc that micro-organisms continue to wreak with human life. In *Medusae,* brother and sister, Tom and Dorothy Cross, have engaged in a dialogue around the strangeness and beauty of jellyfish. As a team they have woven together many disparate threads: natural history, genetics, design, the role of women in nineteenth-century science and exploration, and the evolution of scientific working methods across time. The reader also becomes witness here to the life of amateur scientist Maude Delap. It was Delap's passion for the study of jellyfish along the Irish coast that awoke Tom Cross's curiosity to study the biomechanics of box jellyfish, the most venomous species found in Australian waters.

Two videos, a film, a digital sequence of jellyfish movement and a radio programme have all emerged from this multilayered, creative partnership.

Red and Wet on the Iron Air, undertaken between an artist working in photography and a molecular biologist, describes a search, in the form of a journey, to uncover the biological, social and environmental links responsible for the spread of malaria. The project demonstrates the often inconclusive nature of research and the many uncertainties that can come with interdisciplinary experimentation. Unusually, in this chapter, it is the scientist's voice alone that speaks; the artist has chosen to keep her material under wraps until the work in progress becomes more tangible.

Our book ends on a celebratory as well as a deliberately ambiguous note. *Baby Epsilons* outlines the mathematical basis for a series of siteswap juggling patterns. Used in mathematics to denote small quantities, the Greek letter *epsilon* represented a small child to the Hungarian mathematician Paul Erdös. Juggling being a medium of motion, considerable emphasis is given in this chapter to the vibrancy and exuberance of image sequences as the principal language in which the work of practitioner and theoretician is expressed. The final image of juggling clubs raining down and sprawled in confusion on the floor invites us to toss the elements back into the air once more, to search for new relationships and to re-write the rules.

It would be fatuous to think that art is like science or vice versa, or that the combination of the two could create a new academic discipline. Equally, it would be short-sighted to assume that the two disciplines cannot engage in a meaningful and productive debate. The research that follows offers ample evidence that mutual inspiration can generate new transdisciplinary knowledge and that fresh perspectives have the potential to invigorate creativity in both domains.

The projects presented in this publication all received funding through the sciart programme while under the auspices of the Consortium (2000–2002). In its three years of operation the Consortium made a significant contribution to the funding landscape of collaborative research. The publication seeks to acknowledge this achievement and to make its outcomes more widely known. For the sake of historic completeness, all projects supported through the scheme are documented. Some have already been publicized and a number have even resulted in their own publications. In making selections for this anthology we have tried to avoid duplicating previous exposure. Those projects not included in the main chapters are summarized in a separate section at the end.

We would like to thank all the authors for their generous contributions to this book and for their patience throughout the editorial process. We are also grateful to our designers for their sensitive handling of each chapter and for creating a coherent whole. Finally, we would like to express our gratitude to all the teams involved in the sciart programme for their creative energy and enthusiasm that have made this experiment such a rewarding and stimulating process.

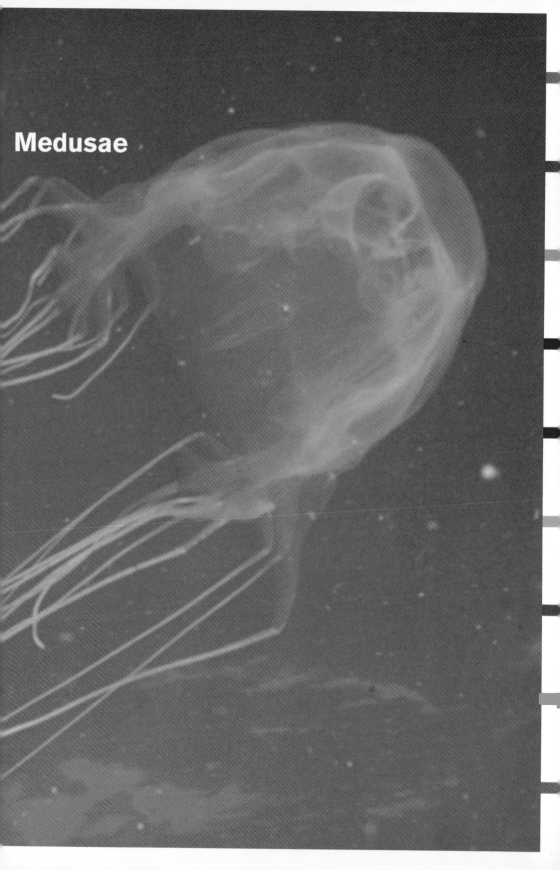

Medusae

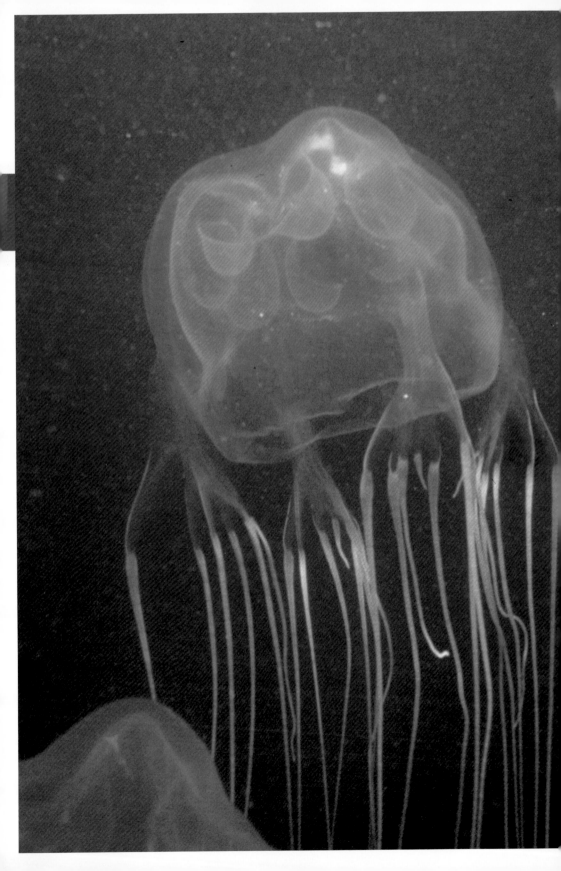

Medusae was a collaboration between sister and brother, artist Dorothy Cross and zoologist Professor Tom Cross, which focused on jellyfish. While Tom examined the biomechanics of *Chironex fleckeri* – a deadly and fast-moving Australian species – Dorothy explored the life and work of Maude Delap, an amateur naturalist who bred jellyfish at her home in Ireland in the early years of the twentieth century.

The research resulted in a diverse collection of moving images: a digital analysis of the swimming movements of *C. fleckeri* and a related species, and two work-in-progress videos, *Come into the garden Maude* and *Jellyfish Lake*. The main output of the research is a film, *Medusae*, that combines aspects from both sides of the project. The film received its first public screening on Valentia Island, Ireland, in April 2003.

Introduction

In her film, *Eyemaker*, Dorothy Cross shows a craftsman creating an eye out of a bulb of molten glass, blowing it into a fragile sphere, and gradually detailing it to resemble the human organ. In the last frames of the film, he breaks his handiwork, and his near perfect imitation of an eye falls into splinters.

The work comments on vision itself, on its fragility and limits, and it illuminates Dorothy's concerns, for she extends the usual scope of art far beyond the visual field into wider, multiple layers of sensation, physical and emotional. She doesn't restrict herself to the faculty of sight, but registers the experience of all her senses (touch above all), and then communicates with us, with our whole sensory range as well. Earlier sculptures using cowhides, their udders in evidence, aroused strong, strange, shivery-pleasurable, deep and old memories of contact, smell and taste as they confronted the animal in the human. Now, with *Medusae*, an ambitious, highly original, deeply layered, composite piece, made in collaboration with her biologist brother, Tom, she has chosen to work with another animal, one of the strangest and most ancient in nature, the jellyfish, a creature that provokes horror and fear at the thought of contact. While jellyfish are "overwhelmingly beautiful", they are, as Dorothy also says, "terribly alien", with their viscous, trailing, slimy shapelessness, their sometimes ferocious sting, their seemingly monstrous lack of brain or faculties, or eyes or face. *Smogairle róin* is the Irish word for a jellyfish and it means, 'spit of the seal'.

Jellyfish were called *medusae* in Latin by Linnaeus, after one of the three Gorgons, who was afflicted with snakes for hair and given the baneful power of turning to stone all who looked at her. In the Renaissance, Medusa's severed head symbolized the defeat of unruly, discordant rebellion, political unrest taking the form of a female monster. The Grand Duke Cosimo de' Medici commissioned Benvenuto Cellini to make the sculpture of Perseus trampling her mangled body as he holds up her head in trophy. The statue still stands in the Loggia dei Lanzi in Florence; it constitutes the Duke's response to the Michelangelo *David*: princely supreme justice overtaking

Michelangelo Merisi da
Caravaggio (1571–1610),
Medusa, painted on a
leather jousting shield,
16th century.

Republican virtue. Caravaggio's *Medusa*, with the blood splashing up from her neck and screaming in agony as if at the very moment of death, is painted on a shield, where she acts as a defensive emblem, like the demonic guardian of a threshold, repelling anyone who approaches.

The Medusa's repugnance has above all strongly sexual associations. Sigmund Freud famously interpreted Medusa's petrifying powers as phallic and placed her image at the centre of his castration theory. Her head, he explained, symbolizes the mother's lack of a penis; her private parts, beheld by the male child, stiffen him with terror that the same misfortune will overtake him. However fantastic this seems, the theory gives an insight into the fearful associations of jellyfish. The surrealist philosopher and naturalist Roger Caillois, in a 1973 essay, *La Pieuvre* (French for octopus), argued that some phenomena – tentacular, buggy, creepy-crawly, primordial things like squid and spiders and crabs and jellyfish – are intrinsically *foyers de songe* (dream hearths), incubating fantasies, and belong in an instinctive, universal, symbolic lexicon, across time and culture.

In a sense, jellyfish have petrified any possible students to such an extent that the story of these extraordinary creatures still remains untold. Yet they number among the oldest and most remarkable organisms in the world, coeval with sponges, and, as Tom Cross has uncovered so richly here, perform all kinds of feats of skill, especially in the manner and efficiency of their swimming – their pumping action even promising medical insights into the human heart. But Tom and Dorothy's *Medusae* does more than explore and record their findings: *Medusae* refashions and transvalues an animal body and its processes, as it journeys through the cycle from spawning to decay. The word *istoria* in Greek means 'inquiry', and both Tom and Dorothy have embarked on a passionate inquiry into the very nature of these mysterious animals. Dorothy's quest took her in one direction, to tell the story of Maude Delap, a highly gifted, amateur naturalist on the island of Valentia, off the west coast of Ireland. Meanwhile, Tom began examining the biomechanics of swimming in *C. fleckeri*, the deadliest jellyfish of all, responsible for more deaths in Australia than sharks or crocodiles.

Both Tom and Dorothy are excellent swimmers, and Tom coached Dorothy when she swam on the Irish team, so together they were able to experiment at close quarters with their subjects. It is breathtaking to watch Dorothy swimming through galaxies of *Aurelia aurita* and *Mastigias* jellyfish in Palau, Micronesia, in her earlier work, *Jellyfish Lake*. But the contact Dorothy and Tom made with their subject goes far deeper than the mermaid-like vision of her streaming through galactic shoals of gently pulsing, frilled jellyfish. Moving so gracefully, unharmed through their glinting, winking bells and fronds, she brings about one of those transformations of sensibility: the creature still belongs, according to Caillois' logic of the imaginary, to the category of disturbing things, but she has unsettled our response and changed the story. *Medusae* tackles the hierarchy of inherited values, about beauty, about animals, about pleasure and disgust. Dorothy is insisting in this work on her own creatureliness, and the creatureliness of the human; she is refusing to shudder at any living thing. She is recovering an aesthetic of wonder before the assumed vile body of the jellyfish, while Tom is studying jellyfish swimming techniques and examining how they function.

In another, yet more profound way, the communion of medusae, artist and scientist strikes at conventional aesthetics, especially sculptural. For jellyfish are loose, fluid, invertebrate, informe; these carnally rebarbative

phenomena are, paradoxically, nearly disincarnate: 98 per cent water, only
2 per cent animal, and they shrink in size all over, rather than lose weight in
particular areas when they starve or fail to thrive. They have no being outside
their element, and so exist in harmony with the sea, almost emanations of
its currents and eddies. All this lightness makes them a sculptor's paradox;
sculpture here has done with the column and the skeleton, the scaffold and
the rock. They are consubstantial with water, and in this transparency and
elusiveness, medusae figure forth, for both Dorothy and Tom, the enigma
that still surrounds them, in the scant records of scientific inquiry, in their
troubled and fragmentary appearances in art's stories. Their two different
approaches meet as they both test the unknowability of the jellyfish and
yield before its resilient strangeness. *Medusae* does not unweave the
rainbow in this respect, as Keats famously complained Newton had done,
but effectively realigns our senses so we can share in Dorothy's and Tom's
knowledge, and experience with our own senses the re-enchantment of
these dreaded creatures.

Marina Warner

Fig. 1
Maude Delap c. 1950.

Medusae

Dorothy Cross, Tom Cross*

Dorothy Cross Tom and I decided to work together because of our common fascination with jellyfish, our sibling relationship, and our enthusiasm for water and swimming. Tom was national coach to Ireland for several years and coached me and our sister Jane on the Irish team. The common denominator of our practice is jellyfish. Medusae are the punctuation and pacing of the work. They also exert a universal fascination: their transparency and venom, their 'other' beauty and their separate realm. Structureless in air, they defy easy examination. Under water they are the most lyrical and graceful of sea animals.

I heard the story of Maude Delap from a friend, who knew that I would be amazed. → Fig. 1 I also knew that Maude Delap's scientific practice, her life and her passion for jellyfish would interest my brother. Tom is a Professor of Zoology, Ecology and Plant Science at the National University of Ireland, Cork. His speciality is molecular genetics, primarily of fish, but he also works with other animals such as badgers and golden eagles. He decided to focus on biomechanics due to his expertise in human biomechanics, and to work on *C. fleckeri*, the deadliest and fastest-swimming jellyfish in the ocean. It is an animal about which relatively little is known. I began to research and glean as much information as I could on the life of Maude Delap.

*with scientific input from Mark Shorten

25

Fig. 2
Maude (in the hat) with her
sisters, Reenellen c. 1894.

Maude Delap

Maude Delap was born in Donegal, Ireland, in1866 and died in 1953. She succeeded in breeding jellyfish in her father's house at the turn of the century. Through
a series of coincidences, I met her two octogenarian nephews who had spent
childhood summers with her on Valentia Island: John Barlee, an ornithologist living
in Devon, and Peter Delap, a doctor living in Cumbria. They responded to my
requests for information with great generosity and enthusiasm. Sadly, both men
died in 2002.

We also contacted Mick Delap, Maude's great-nephew, who has written
poetry about his great aunt and is familiar with Valentia. John and Peter were the
only people alive who had spent much time with Maude, but even their summer
stories contain big unanswerable gaps and variations in accounts that cannot
be answered. We have only fragments of her life to work with.

Of the ten children in the family, Maude was the fifth of six daughters. → Fig. 2
When she was eight, her family moved to Valentia Island in County Kerry,
where her father took up the ministry of the Church of Ireland in the village of
Knightstown. The children were brought up in the parsonage, later moving
to Reenellen, a fine house by the harbour, with a tangled garden that was once

Fig. 3
Reenellen House, 1907.

manicured and tended by Maude and her sisters. → **Fig. 3** It turned out that Reenellen is owned by Paudie Lynch, an islander married to a cousin of Tom's wife.

The children were educated at home with great emphasis on natural history and studying nature. Connie, Maude's sister, had an interest in birds, and Maude was enthralled by the sea. After their father died they were left with little to live on, so they grew flowers to sell – lilies and a small gladiolus known as 'the bride' – which they transported to Dublin, along with the marine specimens that Maude sent to the Natural History Museum there. They kept an ordered garden and grew peaches and grapes in the sheltered areas warmed by the Gulf Stream. Myfanwy, wife of nephew Peter, said of the garden, "There were so many butterflies you could sweep them off the bushes".

Maude began to look seriously at the sciences in the late 1800s. She proceeded to collect specimens and set up a laboratory in Reenellen, which the family called 'the department'. Peter Delap said it smelt of 'low tide' when one entered the house. In 1902 she succeeded in breeding the species *Cyanea lamarki*, in bell jars in her home. It is particularly difficult to breed jellyfish in captivity and to succeed in doing so in 1902, with little or no equipment or water circulation systems,

is extraordinary. When I asked Peter how Maude kept the water moving he said, "I expect with her finger".

Maude devised a net that she attached to the stern of her brown punt and rowed the harbour collecting plankton to feed the medusae. Weather was always a factor and she had to venture out in wild times. The landscape of the island is a mixture of green fields sweeping down to the calm harbour that runs between the mainland and the island, and the rugged ocean side of the island with cliffs of tumbling slate, giant sea arches and ledges full of screaming sea birds. Valentia was a centre of weather research. In 1895, Superintendent Mr J.E. Cullen, of the island observatory, introduced magnetic observations. Valentia was also the point where Marconi first cabled to the USA. It was a time of enterprise, inquisitiveness and adventure.

In 1898, a flora and fauna study team was sent from Britain to do a survey of Valentia. One of the zoologists was called Edward Browne. Maude fell in love with him but apparently her feelings were not reciprocated. She assisted Browne with her knowledge and led him to new species including one she discovered in the harbour – a small sea anemone later named *Edwardsia delapiae.* We know of only one photograph of Edward Browne with Maude. They are standing on

Fig. 6
Natural History Museum,
Dublin.

the pinnacle of the Great Skellig rock. → Fig. 4 On the reverse in Edward's
hand-writing, almost indecipherable, is the date and place with the initials, E.T.B.

Maude continued to write to Edward Browne until he died. She sent him
a box of wild violets on his birthday every year all the way to Plymouth. → Fig. 5
He would refer fleetingly to this gift, generally followed by a list of instructions for
her fieldwork. We know that Maude was offered a job at the University in Plymouth,
but her father, the Minister, said, "No unmarried daughter of mine will leave this
house". So she remained on the island and continued her independent research,
later publishing several scientific papers on medusae.

Maude maintained a correspondence with the directors of the Natural History
Museum in Dublin until 1949, four years before her death. Unidentified and
rare specimens of fish found in the sea around Valentia Island were donated to
the museum collection and sent by boat and train, a journey that at the time took
several days. → Figs 6–8 Her letters, hand-written in pencil on tiny sheets of paper,
are humorous and warm, the weather is always mentioned, and there are requests
for remuneration for the islanders who had brought the fish or animal to her:

Fig. 7
Cuvier whale skull donated
by Maude Delap to the
Natural History Museum,
Dublin.

Fig. 8
Cabinet with small turtle
sent by Maude to the
Natural History Museum.

I am sending by rail today a small turtle which was picked up some days
ago on the shore here. It is alive, and if it survives the journey, may be of
interest for the lab. I gave the finder 5/= [shillings] to encourage further
finds. He was not certain if it was a 'bird a fish or some sort of crab'.
I hope it is not delayed in transit.

Maude Delap to Dr Scharff, Director, 1949

Your turtle survived the journey but of course it had to be killed. We are
adding it to our collection of turtles.

Dr Scharff[i]

i Both extracts are held in
the archives of the Natural
History Museum, Dublin.

Fig. 9
True's whale being
decapitated prior to burial
in the asparagus patch
of Reenellen garden to
clean the bones.

Fig. 10
Whale on a table
in the garden after
exhumation and cleaning
prior to presentation
to the Natural History
Museum, 1940.

True's Beaked Whale being decapitated by 'Mike' and John Dore. Valentia Is. c.1940.

Notes on the rearing, in an aquarium, of Cyanea Lamarcki, Peron et Lesueur.

by M.J. Delap

ii Original text from
Department of Agriculture
and Technical Instruction
for Ireland, *Fisheries
Branch, Scientific
Investigations, 1902–1903.*
No I, 1905.

On September 1st, 1900, a large shoal of Cyanea Lamarcki appeared in Valencia Harbour. The medusae were of a very deep blue colour, which looked almost black in certain lights.

The upper parts of the oral arms were of a yellowish colour, shading off into white at the extremities. Several of the largest specimens measured nine inches in diameter.

One large specimen was placed for a short time in a tank, where it deposited thousands of eggs, which looked just like little yellow grains of sand. Three days later some of the eggs developed into ciliated planulae, and swam about in a most active manner.[ii]

Maude Delap's publications

1901 Notes on the rearing of *Chrysaora isosceles* in an aquarium. *Irish Naturalist* 10: 25–28

1902 *Colias medusa* in west Kerry. *Irish Naturalist* 11: 324

1904 Seal caught on a hand-line. *Irish Naturalist* 13: 49

1905 Birds of the Skelligs. *Irish Naturalist* 14: 134

1905 With Constance: Notes on the Plankton of Valencia Harbour, 1899–1901. *Annual Report on the Fisheries of Ireland 1902–03.* Part II. Appendix I

1905 Notes on the rearing in an aquarium of *Cyanae lamarcki Peron et Lesueur. Annual Report on the Fisheries of Ireland 1902–03.* Part II. Appendix I

1906 With Constance: Notes on the rearing in an aquarium of *Aurelisa aurita L* and *Pelagia perla* (Slabber). *Fisheries Ireland, Scientific Investigations 1906:* 7

1906 With Constance: Notes on the plankton of Valencia Harbour, 1902–05. *Fisheries Ireland, Scientific Investigations 1906:* 7

1906 New localities for *Geomaculus maculosus. Irish Naturalist* 15:190

1909 Early appearance of *Macroglossia stellaturum. Irish Naturalist* 18: 140

1911 Some Holy Wells in Valencia and Portmagee. *Kerry Archaeological Magazine* 7: 403–414

1921 Drift on the Kerry coast. *Irish Naturalist* 30: 40

1922 The Breeding of the fulmar petrel in Ireland. *Irish Naturalist* 31: 130

1922 Swans in Valentia Harbour. *Irish Naturalist* 31: 140

1924 Further notes on the plankton of Valentia Harbour. *Irish Naturalist* 33: 1–6

From Byrne A (1997) Untangling the medusa. In: *Stars, Shells and Bluebells. Women scientists and pioneers.* Women in Technology and Science (WITS). Ireland

Fig. 13
Scyphozoan *Mastigias*
under water.

Why *Cubomedusae*?

Tom Cross and Marc Shorten The intention of the scientific part of this project
was to study the biomechanics of swimming in medusae by digital analysis of
video sequences. A great deal of biomechanical work took place in the 1970s,
before the recent exponential expansion in computer technology. We felt that more
rapid and comprehensive analysis of swimming movements would now be possible. Our original plan was to work on the jellyfish that appear commonly in coastal
waters of the north-east Atlantic (species such as the moon jelly and compass
jellyfish of the class Scyphozoa). → Fig. 13

When the opportunity arose to work on the little-researched, tropical box
jellyfish in north east Australia during the summer of 2000 (the Austral winter), the
work plan was altered. Box jellyfish, also known as 'marine stingers' or 'sea wasps',
are of great interest. The group, known as Cubozoa by zoologists, contain some
of the most venomous animals on earth and appear to have been the object of very
little scientific study. → Fig. 14

Cubozoa differ from other medusae of the Phylum Cnidaria ('true jellyfish')
being far more substantial than animals of the classes Syphozoa or Hydrozoa.
Whereas both of the latter are extremely jelly-like in consistency, cubozoans are

Fig. 14
C. fleckeri in mid-water
(Digital Dimensions
tank).

more akin to polyurethane. They are roughly cubical – hence their vernacular name
'box jellyfish'. Accentuating the box-like appearance and distinguishing them from
the rest of the medusoid Cnidaria, are four tentacles or tentacle groups, each
borne on a blade- or spatula-like pedalium. The pedalia arise from just above the
bell-margin and are relatively tough compared with the rest of the bell. The form of
the pedalia and the number of tentacles per pedalium are diagnostic of the taxo-
nomic groupings within the cubozoa. There are two main groupings: Carybdeidae
and Chirodropidae, distinguishable by the fact that Carybdeidae have only one
tentacle per pedalium, and Chirodropidae have more than one. The pedalia are
thought to steer the medusae while swimming and are known to function in feeding. Both of the species we studied – *C. fleckeri* and *Chiropsalmus quadrigatus* –
are chirodropids. Mature cubozoan medusae vary from 2–25 cm in bell diameter.
C. fleckeri is the largest species of the class (averaging 25 cm diameter when
mature) and *C. quadrigatus* is about 4.5 cm in bell height and slightly smaller in
diameter. → **Fig. 15**

Fig. 15
Rear view of the bell
of *C. fleckeri* showing
prominent features.

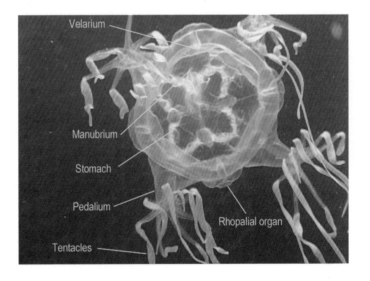

C. fleckeri and *C. quadrigatus*

In North Queensland *C. fleckeri* and *C. quadrigatus* are annual species. In
C. fleckeri (the life history of *C. quadrigatus* is less well known), the tiny fixed polyp
phase occurs in estuaries during the Austral winter (May to October). Planula
larvae are budded off, which give rise to the free-living medusa stage. These feed
and grow in coastal waters inside the Great Barrier Reef from November, then
return to spawn in estuaries, re-establishing the planula stage. Larger medusae
feed on prawns and small fish, and the highly toxic venom may have evolved to
capture these fast-moving prey species in open water. Once a prey item is caught
in the tentacles, they are retracted to bring the item towards the velarium, before
flexing one or more of the pedalia to feed the item to the manubrium (the animal's
mouth). They do not, of course, actively hunt humans but seek their natural prey
in shallow waters (often less than 1 m deep) over a sandy bottom. Thus they
are abundant off beaches during the Austral summer, when humans, particularly
children, run into the water and accidentally encounter them.

Between pairs of pedalia, Cubomedusans have organs called rhopalia on
which the balance organs (statoliths) and light-sensitive organs are located.
→ Fig. 16 In *C. fleckeri* there are three light-sensitive organs on each rhopalium

Fig. 16
Photomicrograph of a
rhopalium showing
balance organ or statolith
(top centre) and complex
eye (bottom centre).

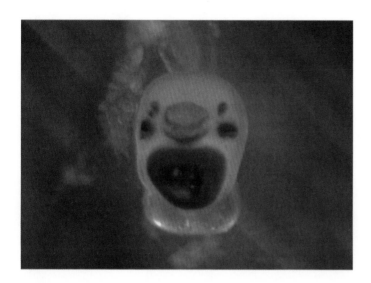

and at least one of these is a well developed eye with a lens and image-gathering neural retina. How the animal processes the images from these eyes, when it possesses only a simple nerve net instead of a brain, has been the topic of much debate.

C. fleckeri, which appears in northern Australia, Papua New Guinea and Indonesia, is the world's most venomous animal and resulted in at least 80 fatalities in Australia during the twentieth century. The venom is contained in millions of stinging cells called nematocysts, spread along the length of the highly muscular and contractile tentacles. → Figs 17, 18 These stinging cells contain a coiled and barbed microtubule and aliquot of venom. On physical or chemical stimulation, stinging cells are activated and microtubules are fired into the victim, releasing venom.

A single mature C. fleckeri has, in its tentacles, enough venom to kill 60 adult humans. In the southern hemisphere, chirodropid stings occur mainly in the Austral summer (November to May), but over a longer season in areas closer to the Equator. The database of the International Consortium of Jellyfish Stings has records of over 1100 individual cases of stings (some severe and fatal)

Fig. 17
Pedanum and tentacles
of *C. fleckeri*.

Fig. 18
Photomicrograph of
discharged stinging cell
(nematocyst) of *C. fleckeri*.

Fig. 19
Stinger exclusion nets
on a North Queensland
beach, designed to protect
swimmers.

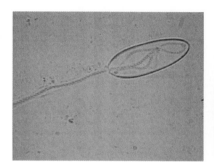 

from surf life-saving clubs in Queensland between 1990 and 1996. In a human
stinging incident, many thousands of nematocysts are activated. Vinegar is
available on north Queensland beaches as a first aid measure against stings.
The acidity of vinegar prevents additional stinging cells from firing but does nothing
to alleviate the effects of those that have already fired. When stinging does occur,
the most appropriate medical response, after flooding the wound with vinegar,
is rapid transport to a properly equipped intensive care unit, where the patient
is treated to reduce shock and, where necessary, artificially assisted in breathing.
An anti-venom agent against *C. fleckeri* stings has been developed by the
Australian Government laboratories and is issued to the emergency services
in the danger area.

It was discovered in Australia that a thin layer of synthetic material such
as polyester is largely protective, and thus the 'stinger suit' has evolved. Women
and children are more at risk because of lack of body hair, so nearly all children
on beaches are now equipped with these suits during the stinger season. During
the Austral summer areas of about 30m^2, enclosed by nets, are set up on popular
beaches to allow swimming. → Fig. 19 These stinger nets have a mesh size
designed to keep out all but the smallest box jellyfish (though broken-off tentacles,

Fig. 20
Wading with *Chironex*
nearby, Weipa, Australia.

which are still capable of delivering a nasty sting, can penetrate the nets).

C. quadrigatus is a less venomous species than *C. fleckeri,* but is very similar in appearance and exists within the same area (but with a much more restricted distribution). We reasoned that it might be easier, initially, to get suitable video sequences from this species because of its smaller size and less venomous nature. We were also interested in comparing the biomechanics of swimming in these two types.

Biomechanics of *C. fleckeri* and *C. quadrigatus*

Box jellyfish are active swimmers, whereas jellyfish of the class Scyphozoa, the common medusae in British and Irish waters, are feeble swimmers, largely at the mercy of the prevailing currents. There is a record from the Cairns area of Australia of *C. fleckeri* swimming at 3 knots (i.e. about 1.5 m / second, very little slower than an Olympic 1500 m swimmer) for 30 minutes. It is not known whether this was an accurate still-water speed, since simultaneous current measurements were not taken. In a later publication it has been reported that large *C. fleckeri* were

Fig. 21
Jamie Seymour holding
a large *C. fleckeri* and
being careful to avoid
contact with tentacles.

observed swimming at 10–20 cm / second in still water. Cubomedusans actively hunt, and exhibit a respiratory rate, on average, many times greater than Scyphozoan medusae.

Like other cubomedusan species, swimming in *C. fleckeri* and *C. quadrigatus* is by jet propulsion, and their speedy and graceful locomotion has provided a focus for aesthetic and scientific interest for well over a century. Writing about *Charybdea xaymacana* at the end of the nineteenth century, one author described their characteristic swimming movements:

> *Charybdea* is a strong and active swimmer, and presents a very beautiful appearance in its movements through the water, the quick, vigorous pulsations contrasting sharply with the sluggish contractions seen in most *Scyphomedusae.*
>
> Conant, 1898

Figs 22–27
Netting for box jellyfish
on Townsville beach
using a seine net.

Collecting box jellyfish

Dorothy Cross and Tom Cross In February 2001, we travelled to Australia
to work with Dr Jamie Seymour of James Cook University (JCU) on catching and
studying *C. fleckeri*. Jamie is an entomologist by training but now works on
box jellyfish, co-operating closely with medics on venom research. He was able
to assist us in numerous ways on the project since he knows where animals
are at different times of the day and year, where best to catch them and how to
handle them. → **Fig. 21**

We began by rising at dawn every morning to net box jellies on the shores just
north of Cairns. Jamie and his assistant, Teresa Carette, used a seine net approximately 4 ft × 40 ft stretched between two poles, which they 'walked' along the
shore where *Chironex* are known to feed. → **Figs 22–27** We netted every morning
for a week without success. The weather had turned unseasonably cold and
the storms had begun earlier than usual, so Jamie feared the animals might have
disappeared for the season. We then travelled south to Townsville to see if
we could catch some there … more empty nets. The nets were pulled in, catching
other things that we immediately released: barramundi, garfish, baby squid, man-
grove seed pods and a heavy, surprised, loggerhead turtle that fled at great speed.

The beaches of North Queensland are stunningly beautiful, immense and pure. Palm trees and wilderness run right down to the shoreline of turquoise water. The sounds are of exotic tropical birds and tree frogs. The presence of *C. fleckeri,* such a deadly invisible threat in the shallow waters of what appears as paradise, is strange. Little is spoken about the jellyfish, but stinger nets are put up to protect swimmers during the season from November to May.

Jamie has jellyfish watchers all along the coast and we heard that a large number of *Chiropsalmus* had arrived in Port Douglas, north of Cairns. We caught some animals there to bring back for filming in the laboratory tanks at JCU. → **Figs 29–32** Not finding the larger and deadlier *C. fleckeri* that season may have been fortuitous. We realized we would have to return the following year when they were again present, but in the meantime we could experiment with the logistics of netting, transport, grids and camera angles.

Videoing

In both 2001 and 2002, videoing was carried out using a digital camera running at 25 frames/second. In 2001, the camera was mounted 60 cm from a glass

aquarium, and a plastic mesh grid against a black background placed at the back of the aquarium to provide scale and contrast. Before filming, measurements of bell diameter based on inter-pedalial distance were taken from each individual.

In 2002 we returned to Australia several weeks earlier, in late January. The same process of netting began, first in Cairns and then in Townsville, 400 km to the south. In Cairns we caught many *Chiropsalmus* but no *Chironex*. In Townsville we managed to catch *Chironex* on our second day.

In catching *Chironex*, we found that their tentacles were getting torn off, which affected their swimming. With the aid of Polaroid glasses, Jamie succeeded in catching them by hand, holding them by their bell, which does not contain stinging cells, and placing them in buckets without tentacle damage. The animals are so transparent that their shadow on the sands is often seen before they are.

The *Chironex* were taken for videoing to a large, custom-built tank at Digital Dimensions Film Studio in Townsville, north Queensland. We used a digital video camera in an underwater housing mounted on a tripod. The tripod was set 70 cm from a perspex sheet, which in turn was placed 70 cm from the wall of the tank and fitted with a plastic grid to provide scale. The animals were introduced at one end and released to swim at right angles to the camera.

Figs 33–38
Filming *Chironex* at Digital
Dimensions Film Studios,
Townsville, 2002.

Biomechanical analysis

Tom Cross and Marc Shorten All footage from both years was reviewed
to assess its suitability for kinematic analysis and downloaded to computer. In
the best footage the line between any two neighbouring pedalia was either
parallel, or at 90° to the camera lens. Each sequence used contained at least
2.5 cycles (pulses) of movement.

Footage from both 2001 and 2002 sampling periods was run through
graphics packages to identify nodes on seven readily apparent body locations.
→ Figs 39–43 By using these superimposed coloured nodes on each frame,
we could plot mathematically the position of a particular body part at any given
time. The positions of these nodes were as follows:

Nodes 1 and 7 on the outside of the bell fall at the point where the base
of the pedalia and the velarium meet and describe inter-pedalial diameter.
Nodes 2 and 6 describe the midpoints between nodes 1 and 3, and 5
and 7, respectively.
Nodes 3 and 5 are found on opposite corners of the gastric pouches.
Node 4 gauges the distance covered in each frame, and thus characterizes
gait in terms of speed.

Figs 39–43
Video frames from two
locomotor cycles of
C. quadrigatus selected
at the points of maximum
circular muscle contraction
and relaxation, with position of landmarks used
in subsequent analysis
indicated.

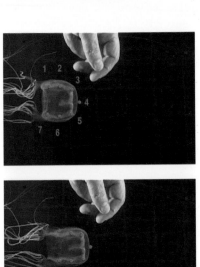

Fig. 44
Graphical representation
of node movements of
C. quadrigatus over time.

Distance from node one to node seven (mm) against time (s)

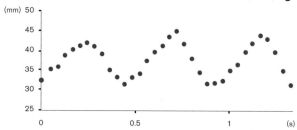

Bell volume (cubic mm) against time (s)

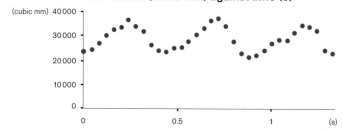

Speed in previous frame m/s

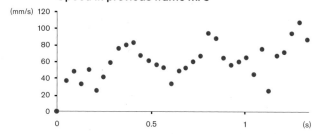

Figs 45–47
Video frames of dye
shedding and vortex
formation in *Chiropsalmus*.

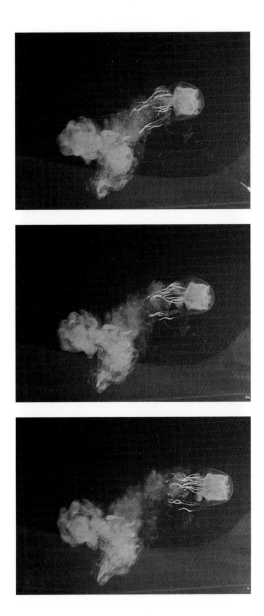

The x and y co-ordinates were determined in each frame and then transferred to a spreadsheet for geometrical interpretation. Graphs based on the co-ordinates of the nodes during locomotion allowed numerical description of gait. These graphs, on the same horizontal scale, display various parameters that change in the course of movement. → Fig. 44

Both species were seen to execute a 'pulse-and-coast' style of jet propulsion. One cycle (or pulse) of movement consisted of contraction of the bell, causing ejection of water through the velarium followed by eversion and reduced bell volume. The contraction stage was succeeded by a relaxation phase when the animal coasted, refilling the bell as the mesoglea returned to its original shape and the velarium was once more inverted.

Dye shedding and statistical analysis

To visualize the water currents produced during movement, the bright green dye, fluorescein, was injected into the bell, using a hypodermic syringe. At each contraction (jetting), a spurt of dye was observed moving out quickly through the velarium. When this aliquot of dye reached a certain distance behind the animal, it slowed down and rolled outwards into a ring structure orientated at right angles to the direction of movement. → Figs 45–47 Hydrodynamics specialists refer to such ring structures as 'vortices' and to their formation during motion as 'vortex shedding'.

Despite the general similarities of the gaits of the two species, it became clear that there were underlying differences between species, and even size classes within species. Statistical testing demonstrated that *C. quadrigatus* ejected a greater volume of water relative to bell size than *C. fleckeri*. There was also a significant correlation between relative body size and pulsation frequency within species, with smaller animals pulsing faster. The computer-based approach to statistical analyses of gait parameters used here has not, to our knowledge, been used previously in this biomechanical context. This investigation sets a framework for other researchers studying medusan locomotion and animal gait in general.

Fig. 48
Scyphozoan *Mastigias*
under water, Palau,
Micronesia.

Palau

Dorothy Cross In August 2001 I travelled to Palau, Micronesia, to film jellyfish in
the famous lakes there. Together with Loring McAlpin, an artist friend of mine,
we got permission from the Palau National Park Head Ranger, Mr Adalbert Eledui,
to enter several lakes and film the vast shoals of *Mastigias* jellyfish. → **Figs 48–51**
Only one lake is open to tourists but Mr Eledui allowed us access to several other
lakes because he loved the story of Maude Delap. We required good footage
of dense medusa shoals to use as a vein running through the stories of Maude and
the scientific research. During our filming, another art work emerged, which was
later titled *Jellyfish Lake*. Loring McAlpin filmed the animals swimming through my
hair and around my neck and shoulders from just below the surface of the water.
Scuba is not permitted in the lakes as the bubbles can get trapped in the jellyfish
bells, preventing them from descending.

Fig. 49
Dorothy snorkelling,
Jellyfish Lake, Palau.

Fig. 50
Jellyfish Lake, Palau,
Micronesia.

Fig. 51
Jellyfish Lake, Palau,
Micronesia.

 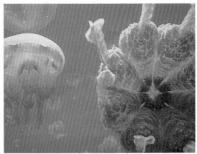

Tom Cross The archipelago of Palau was formed relatively recently, about
10–15 000 years ago. Layers of limestone were lifted up to form lakes. These lakes
provide a unique habitat where the two dominant species are *Mastigias* and
Aurelia jellyfish. In these relatively shallow seawater lakes, the community composition is much simpler than in more open ocean environments because of the long,
narrow tunnels that connect the lakes to the sea and prohibit colonization by
the majority of species. In addition, the lakes are stratified into two layers, with an
upper layer high in oxygen (required by most life forms) but very low in salinity and
nutrients. The lower layer, on the other hand, is rich in nutrients but low in oxygen,
and nutrient transfer is minimal and sporadic. These factors are unfavourable to
many oceanic animals. Apart from jellyfish, there are various plant plankton species
(phytoplankton), a tiny shrimp-like copepod, a small fish called the silverside, mus-
sel larvae and many types of bacteria. The biggest jellyfish present is *Mastigias*,
a relative of *Rhizostomum octopus*, which is found in British and Irish waters.
In Palaun *Mastigias* there are fewer stinging cells (the nematocysts) normally used
for capturing prey. Instead of feeding as predators, these jellyfish derive most of
their energy from the photosynthesis (conversion of sunlight into energy) of symbi-
otic bacteria abundant in their tissues. This is a mode of energy gathering that

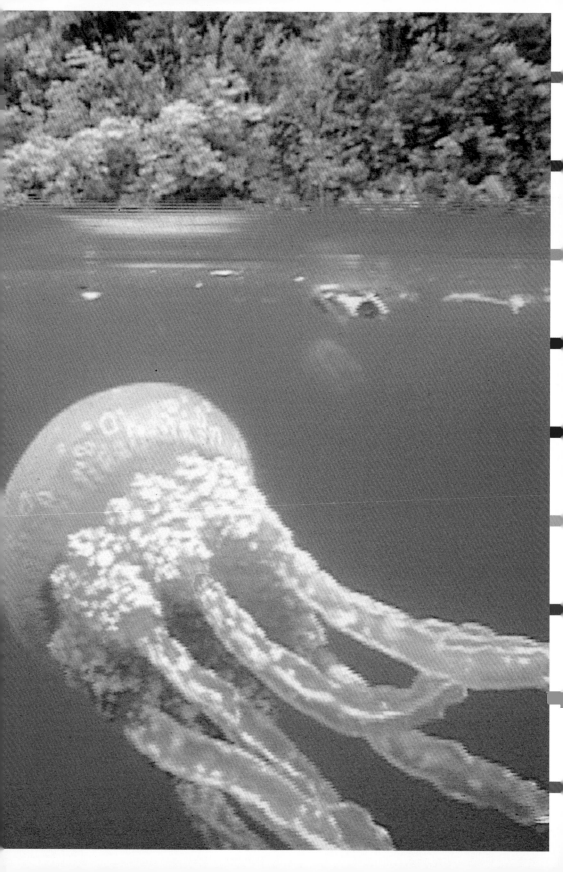

predominates in higher plants but which also occurs in reef-building corals and giant clams. It allows *Mastigias* to exist in huge numbers that move daily up and down the lakes, orientated in such a way as to obtain maximum sunlight.

Haeckel and the Blaschkas

Dorothy Cross Maude had contemporaries who were fascinated by jellyfish: Ernst Haeckel, a scientist from Jena, Germany, known as the Darwin of Germany; and Leopold and Rudolf Blaschka, a father and son team, who revolutionized glass-making, producing exquisite models of glass jellyfish.

Ernst Haeckel was born in 1834, two years after the death of his famous townsman, Goethe. I travelled to Villa Medusa in Jena, the home of Ernst Haeckel (now a museum), to see examples of ceilings, furniture and teacups, all decorated with jellyfish. → **Fig. 52** Haeckel's early years were spent gathering specimens of lower marine animals in the Mediterranean, collecting and describing more than 4000 species. He was the author and artist of *System der Medusen* (1880) and *Kunstform der Natur* (1899–1904). Other designs of his include the great lumière and glass lamps for the central room of the exquisite Musée d'Océanographique

in Monaco, built by Prince Albert I in 1899. → **Fig. 53** The central hall has a *Chrysoara* chandelier with four microscopic, radiolarian lamps made in coloured glass, floating like sputniks in the four corners. Haeckel travelled to Dublin in 1906, but never met Maude Delap.

At the Phyletisches Museum Jena, I met with Gerta Pouchert, a technician, who told me of paintings of jellyfish found under the false ceilings that were exposed when the East opened up ten years earlier. Gerta was breeding *Cassaeiopia* jellyfish in bowls in her office but had never seen the sea.

Leopold and Rudolf Blaschka became famous for fabricating extremely delicate marine invertebrates. It was the first time such animals were ever seen outside water. The Natural History Museum in Dublin has an excellent collection of Blaschkas, and there are several glass specimens in the National University of Ireland in Cork. → **Figs 54, 55** It is thought that Maude made only one visit to the Natural History Museum in Dublin in later life and met the director with whom she had corresponded for more than 50 years. In 1886 a professor from Harvard University travelled to Dresden and commissioned the Blaschkas to make some flowers, resulting in a collection of more than 800 plant specimens that are now in the Peabody Museum in Boston. Amongst them is a bunch of glass violets.

'Tentacular' projects

Dorothy Cross Several associated works have grown out of the *Medusae* project. In 2001 I was invited by Public Art Development Trust to make a video about Maude Delap for the 4th Wall series of projections on the Royal National Theatre in London; and by Kate Bland, of Just About Productions, to make a radio programme for the BBC Radio 3 series, Between the Ears.

Come into the garden Maude, a 43-minute film that wandered through the story of Maude Delap, was screened on the theatre's large south wall in November, 2001. → Fig. 56 Fragments of the story were spoken by the actor, Fiona Shaw, and music from Maude's lifetime was sung above and below water by the tenor, Eugene Ginty.

Sound became an important vehicle for the work. While researching tunes that would have been familiar to Maude, I worked with Eugene and asked him to sing underwater...words distort in water, but a hum transfers beautifully. Through experimentation we discovered that the most efficient way to record was with a hydrophone. Eugene dropped to the bottom of a swimming pool with a weighted belt to sing each phrase. Distortions and gaps for breath became major elements, as we were aware continuously of risking distortion in the life of Maude. I also asked Eugene if he could sing backwards. He picked up the music of *All things bright and beautiful*, and without missing a note, sang it perfectly, words and music in reverse.

Jellyfish was aired on BBC Radio 3 in September 2002. This included a mixture of information on jellyfish, descriptions of visits to Valentia and Maude's home, and alien sound by the musician, Alisdair Molloy, on glass harmonica and water phone, in which different versions of tunes were played with familiar and strange shifts in their timing. We particularly wanted sound that evoked the motion of medusae. A glass harmonica creates notes according to the proportion of liquid contained in different-sized glasses, with the sound made by running wet fingers around the rim. The water phone is a relatively recent instrument, introduced to us by Alisdair, which produces a sound like the call of a whale.

Molecular genetics

Tom Cross We also developed 'genetic fingerprinting' systems for the two jellyfish species in a spin-off project funded by Enterprise Ireland, undertaken largely by Dr Jamie Coughlan from the Department of Zoology, Ecology and Plant Science, National University of Ireland, Cork. Dr Seymour supplied tissue samples of *C. fleckeri* and *C. quadrigatus* to the molecular genetics laboratory in Cork for DNA extraction and development of microsatellite (genetic fingerprinting) primers. This process has not previously been attempted in *C. fleckeri* or, as far as we are aware, in any cubomedusan, and will therefore be a novel scientific development. Such probes will enable a genetic study of the *C. fleckeri* population throughout its range. → Fig. 57

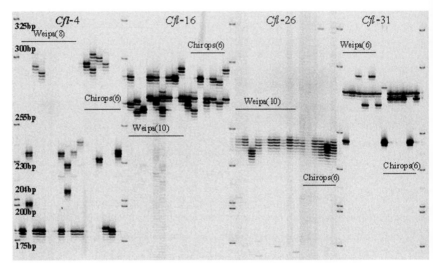

Conclusion

Dorothy Cross and Tom Cross As we write, *Medusae* has just been completed and shown for the first time. The stories of Maude and of jellyfish are still largely unknown. The work occurs at the point where both territories meet, like reflective opposites.

Essentially, there is little difference in the way we have approached our respective roles. It has been a triangle of activity: science, art and jellyfish, based on Tom's exploration of the swimming systems of *Chironex,* and Dorothy's visualization of Maude. Neither work is conclusive; more remains to be remembered and discovered, and *Medusae,* our film, is without a clear beginning or end.

Acknowledgements

sciart Consortium.

Mary Cross, Maud Cross, Dr Jamie Coughlan, Dr Emer Rogan, Professor John Davenport, Fiona Shaw, Eugene Ginty, Alisdair Molloy, Kieran and Vivien Guinness, Pat Hayes, Eamon de Buitleir. Cuan MacConghaile, and Valerie Connor.

Family: Mick Delap, John and Laura Barlee, and Peter and Myfanwy Delap.

Jena: Dr Erika Krause, and Gerta Puchert.

Monaco: Anne Toulemont.

Valentia Island: Paudie Lynch, Monica Gibson, Michael Egan, and Clare Ring.

Palau: Adalbert Eledui (Director State Rangers Palau National Park), Dr Mike Dawson, and Dr Laura Martin (Coral Reef Research Foundation Palau).

Australia: Dr Jamie Seymour and Teresa Canette, James Cook University; Richard Fitzpatrick, Warren Haydon, Adam Barnett, Brett Shorthouse and Dr Russell Kelly, Digital Dimensions; Paul Sutherland.

Mike Bohan and Declan O'Connell, Wildacre Productions. Robin Lydenberg, Niall MacMonagle, Loring McAlpin, Opera Theatre Company, Frith Street Gallery, London, Kerlin Gallery, Dublin, Traditional Music Archive, Dublin; Cian de Buitleir, Professor Patrick O'Sullivan and Dr Mark Holmes, Natural History Museum, Dublin; Willie Siddall, Gladys Gill (Scubadive West).

Fiach MacConghaile, Paul Johnson and Sandra Percival, PADT; Kate Bland and Susan Marling, Just About Productions.

References and further sources

Barnes JH (1965) *Chironex fleckeri* and *Chiropsalmus quadrigatus*: morphological distinctions. *North Queensland Naturalist* 32: 13–22

Berger EW (1900) The Cubomedusae including Dr F. S. Conant's notes on the physiology. *Memoirs of the John Hopkins Biological Laboratory* 4: 1–81

Bone Q, Trueman ER (1982) Jet propulsion of the calycophoran siphonophores *Chelophyes and Abylopsis*. *Journal of the Marine Biological Association of the United Kingdom* 62: 263–276

Conant FS (1898) The Cubomedusae. In: Brooks WK (ed.) *Memoirs from the Biological Laboratory of the John's Hopkins University IV*. Baltimore: John's Hopkins Press

Gillett K (1964) Queensland's deadly 'Sea Wasp' photographed alive. *Australian Natural History* (June): 312–313

Hamner WM, Jones MS, Hamner PP (1995) Swimming, feeding, circulation and vision in the Australian box jellyfish, *Chironex fleckeri* (Cnidaria: Cubozoa). *Marine and Freshwater Research* 46: 985–990

Rees WJ (1966) *The Cnidaria and Their Evolution*. London: The Zoological Society of London, Academic Press

Trueman ER (1980) Swimming by Jet Propulsion. In: Elder HY, Trueman ER (eds) *Aspects of Animal Movement*. Cambridge: Society for Experimental Biology, Seminar Series 5, Cambridge University Press

How To Live

Bobby Baker as Pea, 2002.

How To Live was an experiment to investigate
a cognitive behavioural therapy technique (CBT)
conducted by performance artist Bobby Baker
and psychologist Dr Richard Hallam. The project
set out to compare the influence of two videos,
one explaining a particular CBT technique,
the other a comparison condition, which were
screened to a group of participants before taking
part in a carefully staged tea party. The aim was
to assess reactions to an emotionally provocative
event and to gauge whether these had been
influenced by the technique suggested. *How To
Live* forms part of a larger project by Bobby Baker
due to be launched at the Barbican Centre,
London, in autumn 2004.

Introduction

i For a discussion of the ideas of Foucault and Lyotard, see Jan Verwoert (2002) Transdisciplinary Moves: basic ideas about the encounter between art and science. www.sciart.org/site/essay

At the forefront of much research and development across the professions, the value of working outside boundaries, and of unleashing moments that may be difficult to define or categorize, can no longer be considered a whimsical experiment. Both Jean-François Lyotard and Michel Foucault in their writings have spoken of 'transdisciplinarity' as a means of achieving new forms of knowledge.[i] This is the point at which people have the ability to move freely outside traditional disciplines and into others, engaging with new experiences and improvising unorthodox combinations of knowledge.

Bobby Baker is one of Britain's leading performance artists. Over the last 25 years in a series of performances that have been presented around the world, she has created opportunities to work with architects, photographers, composers, educators, theatre directors, filmmakers and writers. Her performances give creative force to the emotions and experiences associated with mundane daily tasks such as shopping, cooking and visiting the doctor. Baker has given these activities a poignant, sometimes witty, often ironic portrayal that allows us to appreciate them anew. The partnerships she has engendered with creative individuals from other sectors are crucial to this work. The contribution of collaborators is enmeshed into the heart of each project, yet the overriding force within each piece is always Baker's and they work to her agenda.

Richard Hallam has taught, researched and practised psychotherapy and published extensively in the field of CBT, specializing in anxiety and problems of hearing and balance. His career as a psychologist has involved collaborations with many different individuals from the worlds of anthropology, philosophy, medicine and psychiatry, and he has taken a particular interest in the influence of psychology on cultural practice.

Initially developed from the activities of faith healers and priests, therapy has been professionalized and theorized over time and its practitioners are now viewed as an élite specialist body. In the early 1970s, in an attempt to extend the range of therapy beyond the profession itself, Hallam helped to develop systems within the health service that would allow nurses to take on a more therapeutic role. More recently there has been a spectacular growth in self-analysis and self-management of psychological problems. He sees *How To Live* as an opportunity for further democratization of professional scientific practice.

As artist and therapist, respectively, Baker and Hallam have a common, as well as an individual, understanding of the project's central focus – CBT. Hallam sees CBT as a major example of the successful interface between science and cultural activity – the individual client is encouraged to model him or herself on the role of a working scientist, observing, monitoring and analysing their own behaviour. Baker's decision to move her artistic project into this shared territory, exploring the culture of self-help, is a natural extension of her work in performance and has often been triggered by personal experience. *Take A Peek* was produced as an uncanny response to the experience of visiting doctors' surgeries, and more recently, *Box Story* drew on autobiography and spiritual belief. In *How To Live* the scientific (in this instance, psychological) is also the personal in that Baker is a CBT user. The opportunities offered by this project have allowed Baker and Hallam to engage with another discipline in an entirely new way, enabling them to undertake a collaboration that has been mutual and equal.

At the end of the research period Hallam and Baker staged a one-day event for invited participants to reflect on the way we manage our emotions. Small groups of people watched a video in which Baker proposed countering various immediate feelings, such as anger or embarrassment, or even politeness, with their opposite emotion. Participants were then invited to take tea and make requests for helpings of cakes, sandwiches and meringues. Some guests were given plates loaded with mouth-watering food while others were left with plain dry biscuits. How the situation was managed varied from group to group. The point at which the arts and sciences seemed to join forces was most evident in participants' responses. Those who were used to attending Baker's performances (the arts audience) were expecting to be manipulated by her – to engage with the activity, but

Tea party experiment –
observers group.

to be witnessing an event over which she retained control. The image making remained the domain of the artist and the audience accepted the role of 'spectators', anticipating little influence over the outcome.

The scientists (mostly psychology students) on the other hand, undertook the task much as they would a training exercise – entering more wholeheartedly into the notion of experiment and attempting to deliver a considered response. They were generally less able to distance themselves from the action or to act as witness to the event, and their responses were more subjective and involved. But there was no hint that the outcome of the research had greater relevance for either the science or arts contingent. It appeared to rest somewhere in-between – neither a performance to be witnessed by spectators, nor a psychological training exercise aimed at therapists and clients.

In his introduction to this project Hallam describes how CBT routinely uses enactment and role-play to resolve problems. People's problems, he says, are intrinsically dramatic, and productive dialogue is at the root of all psychotherapy; to an extent, psychotherapy is theatre in miniature. The greatest potential for *How To Live* will be in its ability to go public, to perform and act out the same function as the therapy couch without the stigma of psychiatric labelling. If this can be achieved, then it will have succeeded in bringing science further into public consciousness via the very visible platform that the arts have already claimed as theirs.

Jeni Walwin

Fig. 1
Displaying the Sunday Dinner, Bobby Baker, 1998. The rituals surrounding buying and preparing food is a recurrent theme in Bobby Baker's work.

How To Live

Bobby Baker and Richard Hallam

Bobby Baker When I first got the idea for a show called *How To Live* in 1999 it came out of my then intense irritation with CBT and, in particular, the form of CBT that I was being treated with, namely dialectical behavioural therapy (DBT). I was puzzled by the psychologists I met, their peculiar language and set of assumptions that 'life-skills' and a variety of behaviour-changing techniques could have an impact, not only on my own mental health problems, but on society at large. Whilst I hugely appreciated the good intentions of these psychologists and their desire to help me, I felt the whole thing smacked of the 'thought police'. On top of that, the DBT training material that I was presented with was so bizarre and culturally specific to the USA that it grated on my European nerves.

As an artist I've always tried to make work that evades categorization, that questions received notions of thought and that stems from my own idiosyncratic, intuitive perception of the world. It was strange to be expected to buy into a new process of thinking that seemed to assume one would automatically conform to a given set of beliefs – ones that I had yet to be convinced by.

I then came up with the idea of inventing my own 'therapy', my own package of thoughts and beliefs that mimicked CBT/DBT. It would be called *How To Live*. I was inspired by the image of the exercise video with the 'trainer/life coach' prancing around with a group of people assiduously copying his or her actions. I decided to make myself the 'life coach' and thereby, as in my previous work, subvert, explore and call into question the very assumptions at the heart of the movement. I was fascinated by all the 'merchandising' material that seemed to be part of the treatment package. With the help of colleagues, I decided to create my own website, book, seminar, training videos and so on – in fact, to establish my own 'how to live' empire.

As I researched the area and my treatment progressed, I became increasingly aware of the level of sophistication these psychologists possessed, of the dialectics involved and of how clever and fascinating the processes were. What particularly interested me was the way in which CBT ideas had spread into so many sectors of society. Much of the self-help movement is an obvious offshoot, but there was plenty of other evidence of its impact on our lives. At that point I decided a more intense period of research into the whole field was called for before embarking on making the artwork. I established contact with Richard with a view to exploring our joint interests.

Richard Hallam I was introduced to Bobby through her therapist, a friend of mine, and the idea of working together appealed to me immediately. I was pleased to find that our interests coincided, sometimes in ways I had not anticipated. Ever since training as a clinical psychologist in the 1960s, I had practised, researched and written about the CBT approach to people's problems. Bobby is a 'user' in the present, preferred jargon, and I am a 'provider'. Users and providers hold a certain fascination for each other, held in check by some fairly rigid professional rules. Therapists are taught to reveal little or nothing about themselves, and their clients, in turn, are often left with a sense of unsatisfied curiosity. Of course, this artificial barrier did not exist between Bobby and myself except as a hangover we could discuss between us. I wanted to know how Bobby had experienced being on the receiving end of CBT. Perhaps we could begin to redefine the rules of the 'therapeutic relationship', to bring it into the twenty-first century.

I discovered that what Bobby and I share is, on the one hand, a general irreverence for received wisdom and, on the other, a respect, born of experience, for what CBT has to offer. Like Bobby, I am interested in the values that lie beneath this widely adopted method of working; it is, in fact, the most common form of psychological treatment offered by the National Health Service.

Perhaps a few words on the nature and development of CBT are in order here. The popularity of CBT has grown enormously in the last 50 years, but it has not done so in isolation from the wider cultural changes that have taken place over the last century. The behavioural dimension of CBT developed out of the movement in psychology that turned away from the study of consciousness to that of behaviour. J.B. Watson (1878–1958) is regarded as the American founder of this movement, although what he produced was an adaptation of a Russian import – the ideas of Ivan Pavlov. Watson argued that people could apply science to themselves, and by analysing the 'balance sheet of the self', choose to modify aspects of their behaviour in order to maximize return on 'investing in the self'. The idea of self-control was taken much further by B.F. Skinner (1904–1990) based on his research into how animals learn. It is hard to overestimate Skinner's influence, which extends to the notion of setting response criteria ('performance targets') and optimizing conditions and incentives to achieve them – ideas hardly foreign to present-day business people and politicians. The concept of 'skill' started to broaden out from its prosaic definition of manual dexterity and to be applied to all manner of human activities. Negotiating, coping, courting, praising and even punishing became teachable skills. As Skinner and his followers demonstrated, animals can be taught all sorts of complex and seemingly intelligent tasks just by breaking them down into single steps that are taught one at a time and then chained together. How much more then could people be taught!

CBT has taken on this pragmatic, no-nonsense, problem-solving approach and likes to see results from its efforts. It was always opposed to delving into the recesses of consciousness and had to do battle in its infancy with the prevailing ideas of Sigmund Freud. Andrew Salter, the originator of assertiveness training, began his 1952 book with this provocative sentence: "It is high time that psychoanalysis, like the elephant of the fable, dragged itself off to some distant jungle graveyard and died." (Needless to say, it has stubbornly refused to comply.)

Behaviourism *did* die in around 1965, although its legacy has persisted in a muted form. The mind was rediscovered – hence the cognitive side of CBT. But science remained victorious and so this was not a return to analysing consciousness. Clients were encouraged to see themselves as research students, forming theories about their feelings, thoughts and behaviour and then checking these out through deliberate actions. George Kelly (1955) and Aaron Beck (1976) can be understood as teaching clients a scientific methodology for learning how to profit from their own experience.

Bobby Baker I found these initial discussions very stimulating and they gave me the chance to gain some sort of perspective on the therapy movement and the focus on 'self'. I was particularly fascinated by what Nikolas Rose has to say in *Governing the soul: the shaping of the private self*:

> Behavioural techniques have associated themselves with the sterile atmos-
> phere of the laboratory, the rigour of experimental methods and advanced
> statistical techniques and the objectivity and neutrality of the white-coated
> psychologist. Yet they have played an important part in the extension of
> psycho-therapeutics to new problems and populations in the period since
> World War II, the diversification of therapeutic expertise, and the proliferation
> of sites for the practice of psychological engineers of the human soul. (1989)

I had the sense of going through a painful laboratory experiment in the process of being treated with DBT. → Fig. 2 Throughout the experience of researching behaviourism, therapy and the self, I found myself 'stepping outside' in my mind and becoming absorbed by images that corresponded to the theories we were discussing. I saw the 'self' represented as a single frozen pea. → Fig. 3 The image conveyed to me the vulnerability of the individual amidst the huge maelstrom of society. I imagined individual frozen peas suspended in various grand historical sites such as the pyramids, Westminster Hall and the Taj Mahal – images that appealed to me. How small and insignificant can we be in the face of the epic forces we face, how absurd, how banal, and how powerless?

Another compelling image was of ballroom dance steps, particularly the diagrams drawn of footmarks numbered and organized into sequences to be

Fig. 2
Me, experiencing DBT.
2002.

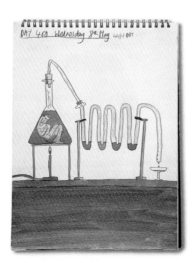

laboriously learned until the dance is achieved with grace and fluidity. These steps repeat themselves, form complex patterns and shapes, and control our behaviour. The dance teacher, the choreographer, corresponds in my mind to the psychologist. Although in CBT we are, in a sense, 'self-engineers', we are also given directions, movements, 'skills' that will help us fit into society as comfortable peas in a pod. My ambivalence about CBT and feelings of being manipulated were balanced by the idea that it's useful to be able to dance well, though I still liked the idea of inventing a challenging new dance of my own.

Richard Hallam CBT, and especially the earlier behavioural therapies, were criticized for being overly mechanistic, of treating people not as self-aware and self-determining, but as objects to be manipulated. Some of these criticisms were justified, and perhaps still are, but it is not my experience of CBT in practice. In my opinion, CBT practitioners are far more respectful of clients' attempts to understand where they are coming from and of what they want to achieve than many other therapists. The essence of the relationship is a collaborative one of sharing a problem. Of course, the therapist does not take responsibility for the problem or direct the client towards fixed goals. But psychology can offer some useful techniques for helping a person discover what their problem is, what is setting it off, what is maintaining it, and how to go about changing it. The humanist's emphasis on self-determination and authenticity is all very well, but we could not

ii Dr Hans J Eysenck
(1916–1997) was a found-
ing figure in clinical
psychology in post-war
Britain. His research
ranged from questions
of personality and intelligence to behavioural
genetics and therapy.

find an answer to many problems without falling back on some basic habitual resources, learned the hard way through constant practice. Even Leonardo da Vinci and Beethoven started out with fumbling efforts.

Bobby Baker I loved this quote by Hans Eysenck (1916–1997):[ii]

> [B]ehavioural methods [behaviour therapy, behaviour modification, conditioning treatment] have been shown to be effective, quick and appro-priate…we may be able within a measurable time to wipe out disabling fears, obsessive-compulsive behaviours, and many other serious neurotic disorders, possibly by sending around the country mobile treatment trucks fitted out as clinics, and staffed by clinical psychologists. These so-called 'minor' psychiatric troubles have caused much individual pain and sorrow; it is time an onslaught were made on them commensurate with the toll they take of human happiness. (1975)

Whilst enjoying the oddness of the concept of trucks trawling the streets searching for disordered individuals, I acknowledge with respect the urge to take action that will impact upon pain. I know full well how CBT techniques work for me.

Richard Hallam This quote from Hans Eysenck disturbs me with its missionary tone. The statement is one more missile in a long campaign against psychoanalysis (and any other 'unproven' therapy) that Eysenck had been conducting since the 1940s. Eysenck never practised therapy himself and his medical language (of 'neurotic disorders' and 'psychiatric troubles'), which still, unfortunately, permeates much CBT literature, betrays a certain amount of ignorance of the reality of thera-peutic work. However, as an intellect and effective advocate, he towers above most of his contemporaries and can be credited with fostering the birth and devel-opment of CBT therapies in the UK (at the Maudsley Hospital in London) in the 1950s. CBT has progressed considerably since 1975, when this quotation was written, but modesty must prevail. There are no sure-fire technical fixes to human

Fig. 3
Bobby Baker as Pea, 2002.

problems. An interesting feature of CBT is that it doesn't really possess any unchallengeable dogma except perhaps the aim of applying scientifically validated ideas from general psychology; however, these too can be discarded if they prove not to be fruitful in practice.

Bobby Baker It struck me that many of the procedures or therapeutic techniques that Eysenck championed corresponded to religious or ethical codes of behaviour, or sets of beliefs, that have governed societies through the ages. This particular DBT 'package' was just the latest thing but, in response to the times, it had taken on the guise of applied science. The decline of religion as a mainstay of western life leaves us open to a search for guidance from other sources. This time, however, it was scientists/behaviourists who were coming up with the principles. The self-help movement – in some ways a virtual cult – is largely based on CBT principles. In the National Health Service a person has to be counted as being in some way 'disordered' to receive CBT treatment. Looking around, I felt that society itself could be seen as 'disordered' and that perhaps these techniques could be applied to society at large, even to allegedly 'ordered' people. Could DBT be some form of evolutionary response to social problems? I was keen to see how ordinary members of the public responded to learning some of the techniques.

We talked very specifically about the various 'skills' that were part of the DBT package (a version of CBT), but the one that fascinated me most was that of

iii Dr Marsha Linehan (1993) Skills training manual for treating personality disorder. New York: Guilford Press.

'acting opposite to the emotion'.[iii] I'd explored the notion of controlling emotions in my show *Pull Yourself Together* (2000), when I toured the streets of London strapped to the back of a truck, yelling through a megaphone at passers-by to "pull yourselves together". This event was staged as part of Mental Health Action Week and was in response to having been brought up in a culture in which showing emotions was considered a sign of weakness – hence *Pull Yourself Together*. But there was also the Christian notion of turning the other cheek when attacked. A quote from an early Quaker, James Naylor (who was so persecuted for his beliefs that he had H for heretic branded on his forehead) – "There is a spirit which I feel that delights to do no evil nor to revenge any wrong." – manifests an extreme form of cheek turning. To what extent might 'acting opposite to the emotion' be seen as another expression of our system of cultural values?

What I began to realize through this period of the research was that we were embarking on a truly collaborative enterprise; I was not the dance teacher any more than Richard. Although I collaborate with many people I usually decide the main 'story', but in this instance Richard and I were both exploring CBT from different perspectives. What the final outcome would be, was, at this stage, unclear.

Richard Hallam As Bobby indicates, we eventually focused on emotions and how we manage them. Some CBT techniques specifically address the problem of unwanted, distressing emotions. In fact, to suffer extreme emotions – fear, sadness or anxiety – is probably the most common reason for seeking psychological help. People's attitudes towards emotion, even the concept of emotion itself, have had an interesting history in our culture. One tradition has it that emotions represent the primitive, animal part of ourselves, to be kept firmly in check by reason. To be overcome by emotion is to show weakness and a reversion to impulses we should be ashamed of. Control is highly valued – "get a hold of yourself", "be cool", "don't worry!", "don't look so miserable!" There is, of course, a counter-movement to this tendency based on the sensible notion that too much control is still less desirable than too little. The 'stiff upper lip' of the English occasionally gives way to the Freudian, floppy lower lip – blubbing it out can be healthier than holding it in.

Fortunately, we don't have to opt for one alternative over the other; sometimes to control and manage our emotions seems the sensible thing to do, and at other times spontaneous expression is the only way to attain peak experiences. It is only by looking at specific examples that we come to a considered opinion. Bobby was interested, as she says, in the DBT technique called 'acting opposite to the emotion'. It is designed to help people who find themselves expressing extreme emotion under relatively minor provocation. The emotion seems, and often is, out of proportion to the situation, and can be bewildering to the afflicted person and to people on the receiving end. The origin of these emotions can often be found in childhood and, though useful or understandable at the time, they cease to be adaptive later in life. The client receiving therapy is encouraged 'to act opposite to their emotion'. Instead of letting out the emotion, the person cultivates the opposite tendency. *This is always with the proviso that the extreme emotion is no longer appropriate and serves no useful purpose in its present form.* For example, the person who by reason of an overzealous religious education feels guilty at the slightest self-indulgence is encouraged to act 'selfishly'. The purpose of this exercise is not catharsis (i.e. to induce a cathartic release of guilt), but a genuine transformation of perception – that there really is no need to see the situation as guilt-inducing, that others will not necessarily condemn you for being 'selfish', and that it can be quite harmless to act in this way.

Bobby Baker What fascinated me about 'acting opposite to the emotion' was that I'd found it to be totally transformative when applied, with due consideration, to difficult situations and emotions. I've experienced analysis and think that, although it's helpful sometimes to reflect on past and present experiences, it's extremely frustrating not to know how to change seemingly embedded feelings and patterns of thought. I've observed, in myself and others, how acting in the opposite way can almost miraculously resolve anger, misery or fear so that situations blossom into new and unexpected events rather than stagnate or endlessly repeat themselves. I sometimes feel when observing political events that the same thing could apply.

Fig. 4
How To Shop, 1993.

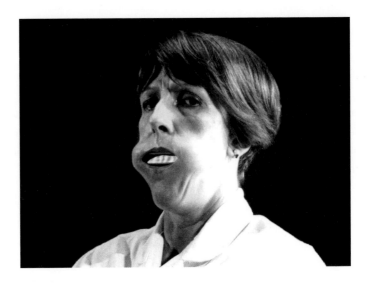

Richard Hallam Bobby and I decided to look at a training video that is sold as a tool for instructing clients in the technique of 'acting opposite' (AO). Having been involved in a minor way with making training materials myself, I know how difficult it is to hit the right note. There is a danger that the expert sounds pompous and over-technical, or the client is treated like an unreflective simpleton. The video was not as bad as this but we thought we could improve on it by drawing on Bobby's intimate knowledge of DBT and her skills as a performance artist. Bobby, of course, knew what it was like to be on the receiving end of instruction and what would appeal to her as a 'user'. My role was to advise on theoretical and practical content.

Bobby Baker My view of DBT training material is less equable than Richard's hav-ing been, as he says, on the receiving end of it. It strikes me that the makers of this stuff could benefit from a few more creative 'skills' themselves. Who's the expert at what? Even though the rational part of my brain knows that it's done with the best of intentions to try and help, the occasional clumsiness and lack of sophistication, at least in terms of imagery and presentation, can make it appear bland and crude. I also think that despite the fact that those preparing and presenting the material are clearly straining not to patronize their clients, the very nature of the relationship in terms of their being the psychologists – the 'experts' – is in itself a problem.

I've noticed that images and stories used in the teaching of these so-called 'skills' are traded amongst psychologists like gold dust. As an artist I think in

Fig. 5
Acting opposite to the emotion, training video, 2002.

images a great deal of the time and use them and stories as part of my work. I know how difficult it is to find the appropriate visual metaphor for each concept. It also occurred to me that I might find it difficult to work alongside Richard in making this material, as many of my own images and ideas are surreal, or try to subvert and explode accepted practice. An example is a metaphor that I used in a show called *How To Shop* (1993). I was trying to convey a complex and ambivalent attitude towards the Christian notion of unquestioning obedience, of being compelled to do something for reasons that are not necessarily clear at the time. The idea I came up with was to explain to the audience that my 'inner voice' told me to put a whole unopened tin of anchovies in my mouth. → Fig. 4 For me, the action and image was an extreme and absurd reflection of our need to obey rules and conform to strange rituals of behaviour in order to be an accepted member of society. I've done this action as part of the show and on television in many countries and it never fails to induce near hysteria amongst the onlookers, perhaps because it touches on a universal ambivalence towards the nature of obedience as a human value. However, 'acting opposite to the emotion', as taught in DBT, is a very subtle concept and I felt daunted and concerned as to whether I could come up with appropriate, and perhaps, less abrasive imagery.

I had very clear ideas about the 'look' of the training videos. I wanted them to be shot in stark black and white interspersed with brightly coloured, still images to illustrate the points that I was making. → Figs 5–7 I chose to wear my white

HOW TO LIVE

Fig. 6
*Acting opposite to the
emotion*, training video,
2002.

Fig. 7
*Acting opposite to the
emotion*, training video,
2002.

overall, which I wear in all my shows. I find that wearing it subtly alters my image
in relation to the subject matter that I'm dealing with and has many associations.
In this instance it was a perfect spoof on the concept of the white-coated expert.
In the training material we'd researched, there were homely flickering fires and
vases of flowers in the background, hoping, I assume, to convey an atmosphere
of comfort and welcome. → **Fig. 8** The starkly contrasting black and white imagery
that we used was more subtle and had further overtones of 'the scientific expert'
I was so intent on subverting. I wanted the colour images to stand out in an iconic
way, to impress themselves on the watcher's mind.

Richard Hallam Our first step was to plan an event that would introduce the training video to an audience, give them an opportunity to put their AO skills into effect,
and provide us with feedback on the way the ideas had been received and applied.
The technique of AO has a very wide application and can be useful even when
the unwanted emotion is as common as an unreasonable fear of spiders. We were
restricted to inducing emotions in the audience in a safe and ethical way but
decided that a taste of unreasonable guilt, embarrassment or anger might not be
too objectionable provided we proceeded with caution. Bobby turned to a
favourite theme of hers – daily life – and in particular, all the rituals around buying,
cooking and eating food. The idea we came up with is described in the introduction to this piece and in the report of our 'experiment' (see later).

Fig. 8
Dr Marsha Linehan in
*Opposite Action: changing
emotions you want
to change*, Dialectical
Behaviour Therapy Skills
Training Video, 2000.

Bobby Baker When planning the test scenario for our experiment, we needed to find a way of provoking strong feelings in the participants while staying within ethical and time boundaries. I recalled a show (*Packed Supper*), which I did at the Institute of Contemporary Arts in 1990, where I served the audience of 200 with hand-prepared fish suppers in foil cartons. The suppers were made according to the distribution of wealth in Britain and ranged from a few exotic caviar meals down to a lot of rather unappealing fish paste sandwiches. I was astonished by the strength of feelings provoked amongst the audience members receiving the cheap meals. Squabbles broke out and it was difficult to regain their full attention! It seemed worth exploring whether unequal treatment would work again in our experiment.

Richard Hallam I was not especially surprised that Bobby's show had aroused so much emotion. After all, what are the usual triggers for emotion but circum-stances that violate our expectations? We experience joy at unexpected windfalls and anger when we fail to get our 'just deserts'. Bobby's show may have violated an expectation of fair and equal treatment (they had all paid the same price for their tickets!). I thought we should take our cue from Bobby's experience and design a tea party at which half the participants were clearly treated unfavourably. We speculated that this might provoke generosity, envy, anger or embarrassment. We tested the scenario out with a group of family and friends who were, of course,

iv Oscar Hills forms part of the Camden and Islington Healthcare Trust.

unaware of what to expect. Half received the tasty items they had chosen and half did not receive their choices; instead they were given two dry biscuits. Prior to the tea party we explained the concept of 'acting opposite to the emotion'.

We observed that the initial reaction was a studied (but apparently uncontrived) politeness and mutual concern. Food was shared. On reflection, our party-goers seemed to realize that this was not how they wanted to feel at all and began to act opposite! From our perspective, they seemed to reject their initial emotion as too conventional and began to indulge in the opposite of polite tea party behaviour, becoming more uninhibited and spontaneous. The AO instructions may have given them licence to act more playfully. In view of these reactions, we decided to make a video for our future experiment that reinforced the pilot group's initial response (i.e. general good manners) and to compare this with one that conveyed the essence of AO. We were hopeful that the comparison would tell us whether the message of the AO video had been understood and was considered to be relevant.

Bobby Baker We decided to adopt the method I use in some of my shows of telling true stories from my life relating to difficult situations I have found myself in. When I do this, people seem to reflect on their own similar experiences and see them from a new perspective. Since I was clearly fallible, and because of the humour employed, we hoped the experience would be engaging rather than patronizing.

The video for 'good manners' (GM) was much easier to write and shoot. I told a variety of stories illustrated by simple colour images that gave advice about true good manners being more to do with consideration of other people's feelings than of sticking rigidly to codes of etiquette.

The real problem arose with the AO video. We had meticulously prepared the script with advice from DBT trainers from the Oscar Hills Service[iv] as to the essence of when and how it is useful and appropriate to act opposite to the emotion. We had selected the stories carefully and I had come up with a series of images to illustrate the points I was making. One of my favourites was an image to show what can go wrong when a person attempts to 'bottle up feelings'.

The image seems to me somewhat ambiguous as, though it's 'bad form' to explode emotions like erupting ketchup, there is a certain beauty to the result! One of the key points we were trying to make was that it is essential to be able to observe a situation and decide whether the skill of AO is the one you want to apply. For this I came up with the image of a fish slice, explaining that finding the most effective skill was similar to using the correct kitchen implement when cooking. As an example of failing to find the appropriate skill I tell the story of a car swerving towards me on the road and my making a V sign in anger at the driver, only to recognize him as the vicar. Had I 'acted opposite', I would have been able appear in church without embarrassment!

We were working with a number of my long-term collaborators, including film-maker Deborah May, performance director Polona Baloh Brown, and photographer Andrew Whittuck. We had decided, due to restrictions of time and budget, that the videos should each be approximately ten minutes long. Deborah and Polona also felt strongly that we should avoid too much theory and scientific jargon in the AO script. In the end we had to compromise, but from the response of the participants it was clear that we could make a video twice as long that would still be entertaining and weave in the theory seamlessly. This we plan to do using the experience we've gained from this research period along with training videos on other CBT/DBT techniques.

Early on in our collaboration I told Richard that, when making a new piece of work, I always consider in what frame of mind I want the audience to leave. In this instance we hoped to encourage self-reflection and a reappraisal of personal behaviour. Judging by the lively feedback discussion we held with participants at the end of the experiment day, this is just what we achieved.

The debate focused on the minutiae of interpersonal relationships, and participants appeared stimulated and intrigued by the notion of being able to alter scenarios by the skilful application of CBT and DBT techniques. The experiment had clearly enabled participants to observe their behaviour in a more analytical way.

In this respect, the research we undertook was successful. However, with hindsight we realized that the AO video, although entertaining and informative,

Fig. 9
Tea party experiment –
observers group.

v Our training videos have
been shown and discussed
by patients at The Oscar
Hills Service.

should have been twice as long in order to convey the subtlety of the ideas in an appealing manner. I felt I hadn't completely 'caught' metaphors and images that communicated the concepts we were dealing with, but recognized that this process is merely a step on the road to a finished artwork. It has been my experience that CBT/DBT involves teaching skills that require time and thought on the part of the user to absorb and incorporate into daily life. Judging from the response of our participants through the ratings and feedback session, we have succeeded in initiating this process.

I have found this meeting between science and art, working, in a sense, as an 'applied' artist, provocative and exhilarating. As well as making more training videos with Richard, I look forward to using this experience to develop my own idiosyncratic artwork, *How To Live*.'

References

Beck AT (1976) *Cognitive therapy and the emotional disorders*. New York: International Universities Press

Eysenck HJ (1975) *The future of psychiatry*. London: Methuen. In Rose, N. *Governing the soul: technologies of human subjectivity*. London: Routledge & Kegan Paul. 229

Kelly GA (1955) *The psychology of personal constructs*. New York: Norton.

Rose N (1989) *Governing the soul: technologies of human subjectivity*. London: Routledge & Kegan Paul

Salter A (1952) *Conditioned reflex therapy: the direct approach to the reconstruction of personality*. London: George Allen and Unwin

Fig. 10
Cream cakes for the
experiment.

Tea party experiment: method and analysis

The topic of expressing emotion has recently been reviewed by Kennedy-Moore and Watson (1999). Amongst other things, these authors examine the contradictory cultural traditions of valuing self-control (stoicism) and celebrating authentic emotional expression (romanticism). Our study reflects this tension but does so in the context of a therapeutic technique that aims to give people control over excessive and unwanted emotional reactions, and replace them with a style of expression that feels authentic but is better adapted to their circumstances. There is a family of techniques of this type associated with (CBT), but we addressed ourselves to the technique of 'acting opposite to the emotion' as described by Linehan (1993)– an offshoot of CBT called dialectical behaviour therapy (DBT). We wished to explore whether the ideas behind this technique could be conveyed in a brief instructional video and then successfully put into practice in a test situation in which emotion was deliberately provoked. The method was to mimic real-life but to do so in a way that was entertaining to the participants. The study was both a serious social psychological experiment and a performance art event.

Method

Design

The design was a comparison between two instructional videos: an 'acting oppo-site' (AO) video, and a comparison video – 'good manners'(GM). We had discov-ered in a dry run of our 'test' situation that polite consideration of others was the usual response and we assumed this would be maintained in the absence of instructions to the contrary. Our hypothesis was that, by contrast, the viewers of the (AO) video would demonstrate evidence of assimilating the technique and apply it in the test situation as they had done in the dry run. The programme of events was identical for both videos. To evaluate the impact of the videos, we assessed participants' moods before and after the tea party and collected their comments, including thoughts and feelings about the videos and whether they had felt influenced by them. This was to provide guidance on making more effective training materials in future. Given the limited resources available for making the videos and mounting the event, we regarded the study as a pilot.

Procedures

The organization of the event (the programme) is shown on page 93. Following some introductory remarks and completion of questionnaires measuring mood states (see later), participants viewed their respective videos in small groups. Two AO and two GM groups were planned, together with a separate group whose members took part in the AO trial as observers. After watching the video, each group entered separately the 'tea party' situation (see later), which was filmed by static and roving cameras. They were then escorted to a different room for a repeat of the mood scale exercise, and a further, more extensive questionnaire on their response to the event as a whole. Later in the day, all participants were invited to discuss their experiences in an informal setting.

Instructional videos

Two videos, each of 10 minutes' duration, were constructed from material taken from manuals, training videos, books and Bobby Baker's personal experiences. The videos combined general principles, and anecdotes and vivid visual imagery.

Tea party

On the grounds that emotion is provoked by the interruption of established habits and expectations (Mandler, 1975), and consistent with Bobby's own experience of audience reactions, a formal and elaborate tea party was devised at which partici-pants were warmly welcomed by her and an actor, given tea, and asked to make a choice from a selection of delicious sandwiches and cakes. On a random basis, half of the participants were given their selection and half were given, without explanation, two dry biscuits. Bobby and her assistant then left the room with the food trolley and the tea party was allowed to continue for 20 minutes. → **Figs 9–11**

Measures

Before the video and after the tea party, participants completed a checklist mea-suring seven mood states (depression, vigour, fatigue, anger, tension, confusion and friendliness) adapted from Boyle (1987). In a more extensive questionnaire completed after the tea party, they were asked to write down their thoughts and feelings about: the video, completing the questionnaires, the effect on their behaviour (if any), and any other comments of their choosing. The comments were transcribed and coded into themes.

Participants

These were selected from three sources: postgraduate students in the arts and psychology aged 18–40 years, personal contacts in this age group (but ignorant of the study) and invited observers who had an interest in performance art and Bobby Baker's work in particular. We recruited sufficient numbers for four of the five groups and so decided to omit one GM group. Final sample sizes (complete data) were: GM – 8, AO1– 8, AO2 – 9, AO observers – 6.

Results

Mood checklist

The mean scores for each mood before and after the event are shown in the table on page 95. Initial scores were compared with normative data (289 Australian college students). This revealed that our participants scored as significantly more 'vigorous' and 'friendly', and less 'depressed', 'fatigued', 'angry', 'tense' and 'confused', perhaps reflecting both sample and context differences. None of the individual groups differed significantly on any of the mood scales at first testing.

The AO groups were combined (23 participants in total) and compared with the GM group to examine mood change following the tea party. The data were analysed by 'repeated measures analysis of variance', which compares the amount of variation between individuals, with the variation in scores attributable to the experimental manipulation (in this case, exposure to the videos). The resulting F ratio yields a probability that the experimental effect has occurred by chance. If the probability is low (conventionally less than one in 20 or 0.05), the effect is assumed to be a genuine one and not attributable to chance. The analyses revealed a significant experimental effect for depression (F, $1/29 = 8.71$, $P < 0.006$), vigour (F, $1/29 = 5.93$, $P < 0.02$), fatigue (F, $1/29 = P < 0.002$), and anger (F, $1/29 = 4.89$, $P < 0.05$). All mood effects were in the direction of a lessening of negative emotion after the tea party. There was only one significant difference between the AO group and GM video groups: this showed up in the Confusion scale and indicated that the GM group became less confused and the AO group slightly more so (F, $1/29 = 4.81$, $P < 0.05$).

Written comments on the event

Participants wrote down their replies to several open-ended questions after the tea party. The text was broken down into two major themes:

1. The instructional videos (presentational techniques, messages received, their personal relevance and feelings engendered).
2. The tea party experience (how people behaved, personal reactions, reflections and influence of the videos).

The response to the presentational techniques used in the videos was almost entirely positive. People said that the content was clearly articulated, informative, interesting, enjoyable and humorous, and they particularly liked Bobby's use of frank, personal stories that resonated with their own experiences. Amongst a small number of negative comments were the following: "too directive", "simplistic", "patronizing" and "nothing new". Some participants wondered whether they would be able to apply the AO idea in practice.

The comments on the tea party were more evenly balanced but, on the whole, positive. People experienced it as friendly, amusing, and enjoyable even though they sometimes wondered what would happen and what they were supposed to be doing. Some thought it was weird. They mostly shared their food, cracked jokes, started conversations, flirted or concealed any discomfort they might have. Some participants acknowledged that they felt embarrassed, tense, cheated, self-conscious or scrutinized. Often though, both positive and negative reactions were engendered together. The majority of participants, however, did not feel that their behaviour had been influenced by the videos. Some explained that the opportunity to apply the ideas did not arise or they did not think it appropriate; others remarked that the tea party was over too quickly.

Discussion

The data we collected on participants' moods show that, overall, the tea party was an emotionally invigorating experience for the viewers of both instructional videos. This was also reflected in the animated nature of the informal group discussion held later in the evening. The only difference we found between reactions to the two instructional videos was that AO led to slightly more confusion, and GM to somewhat less. According to written comments, this confusion seemed to relate to how to apply the idea to the tea party rather than to a lack of understanding of the concepts. Of course, AO is a technique that might be applied when, on reflection, a person wants to change the way they are acting emotionally. Participants were often content with their behaviour at the tea party and so the desire to change it did not arise. We thought that the provocation of being denied one's choice of food

Fig. 11
Two dry bisquits for
the experiment.

vi A symposium relating
to *How To Live* and to the
ideas discussed in this
chapter will take place at
the Barbican Centre,
London, in autumn 2004.

might elicit unwanted reactions, but for many people this did not appear to be the case. Our own interpretation is that participants did not have sufficient time to move beyond their initial reactions to a strange situation and to instigate an alternative to being polite, sociable and considerate; or, that they did not feel a different reaction would have been appropriate.

Finally, where does this combination of performance art and psychological experiment lead? Events like this are not therapy, but they are certainly involving. The audience has to be willing to participate, but if the event is well thought out and deals with issues of common concern, the result has the potential to be transformative; at worst it will be irrelevant and uninformative. Unlike a true experiment where theoretical hypotheses about the outcome are being tested, events of this nature are justified by their potential to generate new perceptions and to open up debate. This does not preclude an evaluation by methods that are sound from a scientific point of view. What people take away from an event will depend on the state of mind in which they approach it and their current preoccupations.

From our perspectives as performance artist and psychologist, working together on this project has been exciting and has already opened up new possibilities. One of these is to mount an entertaining and educational programme of events that combines performance art with lectures and discussions on CBT/DBT.[vi]

Tea party programme

Arrival of groups at spaced intervals
Welcome and brief explanation of event
Completion of mood questionnaire
Video screening
Tea party
Completion of open-ended questionnaire
Discussion (all groups together)

Tea party questionnaires

Mood scale instruction

Below is a list of words that describe feelings. Please read each one carefully.
Then circle *one* of the answers on the right that best describes how you are
feeling *right now*.
(0 = Not at all, 1 = A little, 2 = Moderately, 3 = Quite a bit, 4 = Extremely)

Mood scale adjectives

Depression scale	unhappy, lonely, sad, blue, helpless
Vigour scale	lively, active, alert, energetic, vigorous
Fatigue scale	fatigued, worn out, exhausted, weary, sluggish
Tension scale	tense, nervous, shaky, on edge, panicky
Friendliness scale	friendly, helpful, good natured, considerate, sympathetic
Anger scale	angry, annoyed, rebellious, furious, bad-tempered
Confusion scale	confused, bewildered, unable to concentrate, restless, sorry for things done

Open-ended questions

Please write down any thoughts or feelings you had about:

The video you watched

_____

_____

_____

The tea party

_____

_____

_____

Do you think your reactions to the tea party or your experience of it
were influenced by watching the video?

If *yes*, please say in what way

If *no*, please say more to explain why not

_____

_____

_____

Please add any other comments you would like to make about this
afternoon's event:

_____

_____

_____

_____

_____

_____

Mood scores before (1) and after (2) the 'event', and normative data. (Means and SDs)

Mood	GM	OA1	OA2	OA-ob	Norms
Depress-1	5.00 (6.0)	3.13 (2.8)	1.22 (1.0)	4.00 (2.7)	4.57 (2.5)
Depress-2	1.38 (2.2)	2.38 (1.9)	1.44 (1.5)	1.67 (2.6)	
Vigour-1	8.88 (5.1)	9.75 (4.6)	8.00 (4.0)	8.50 (5.1)	7.93 (2.6)
Vigour-2	10.75 (1.9)	10.88 (4.2)	9.78 (5.2)	10.17 (5.4)	
Fatigue-1	7.50 (6.5)	3.63 (1.5)	7.22 (3.7)	7.50 (5.2)	8.49 (3.0)
Fatigue-2	4.63 (3.6)	2.75 (2.7)	3.67 (3.0)	6.83 (5.7)	
Anger-1	4.13 (6.0)	2.13 (1.4)	2.11 (1.8)	3.67 (4.0)	3.42 (2.3)
Anger-2	1.63 (2.7)	2.25 (2.6)	1.89 (2.0)	1.17 (0.9)	
Tension-1	3.88 (4.8)	3.50 (3.1)	2.89 (1.6)	4.50 (2.8)	4.75 (2.5)
Tension-2	1.88 (1.7)	2.75 (3.5)	4.33 (4.7)	2.33 (2.0)	
Confus-1	6.00 (5.6)	4.63 (3.3)	3.11 (1.6)	4.83 (1.9)	6.27 (2.7)
Confus-2	3.38 (2.9)	4.88 (3.1)	4.56 (3.0)	3.50 (1.3)	
Friend-1	12.38 (3.5)	11.75 (3.5)	12.22 (2.7)	12.83 (3.5)	11.38 (2.3)
Friend-2	12.88 (2.8)	13.50 (2.3)	10.67 (3.9)	13.33 (3.2)	

(GM: good manners, AO: acting opposite, OA-ob: acting opposite observers group)

Acknowledgements

How To Live is an Artsadmin project. Daily Life Ltd. acknowledges funding from the sciart Consortium, London Arts, and the Calouste Gulbenkian Foundation. Performance Director: Polona Baloh Brown.
Film: Deborah May.
Photography: Andrew Whittuck.
Performer: Liz Kettle.
Technical Production: Steve Wald.
Writer: Jeni Walwin.
Administration: Judith Knight and Jessica Wiliamson for Artsadmin.

References

Boyle GJ (1987) A cross-validation of the factor structure of the profile of mood states: were the factors correctly identified in the first instance? *Psychological Reports* 60: 343–354

Kennedy-Moore E and Watson JC (1999) *Expressing Emotion.* New York: Guilford Press

Linehan MM (1993) *Skills training manual for treating personality disorder.* New York: Guilford Press

Mandler G (1975) *Mind and Emotion.* New York: Wiley

HOW TO LIVE

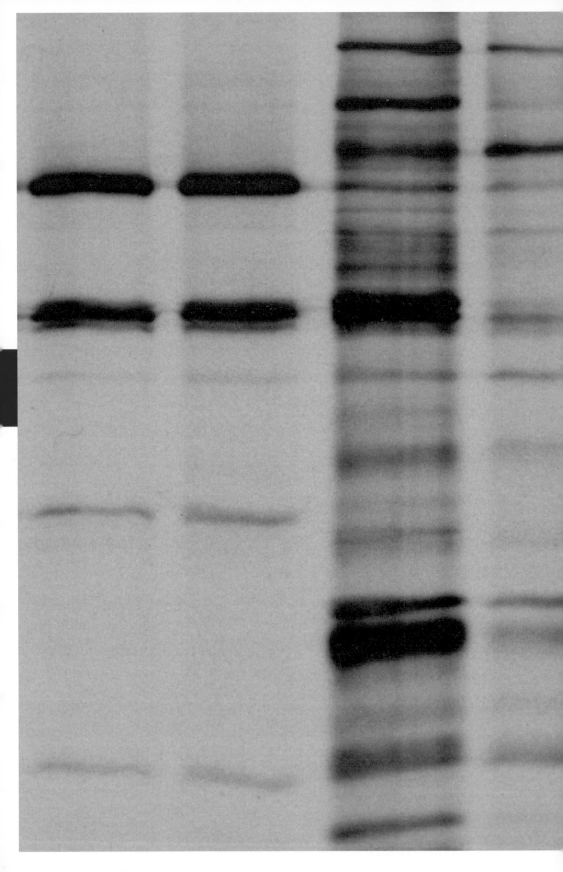

Red and Wet on the Iron Air

Computer image of a merozoite protein on the parasite surface, which is the basis of a malaria vaccine that is being developed.

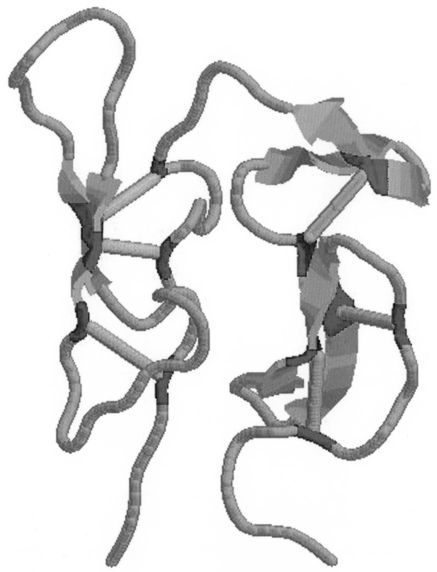

Red and Wet on the Iron Air focused on malaria. In December 2002 scientist Dr Tony Holder and artist Zarina Bhimji travelled to Uganda and Kenya to investigate the conditions surrounding the disease: the human and environmental factors that contribute to its transmission, and the search for methods of cure and prevention. Their journey put many issues into perspective and produced a significant body of photographs. At the time of publication, much of the research has yet to be distilled and Zarina's photographic work is still in progress. The documentary photographs illustrating this chapter were taken by Tony.

Introduction

Fertile red soil, automatic sequencing machines, bloody liquids in culture flasks, impregnated bed nets, the buzz of mosquitoes, the stale smell of water-filled holes.... These are some of the markers in the research of scientist Tony Holder and artist Zarina Bhimji. Together, they set out to investigate malaria, its parameters, and the debilitating effect of the disease on communities in Kenya and Uganda. Their research is topical. In 2002 the genome sequence of *Plasmodium falciparum*, the most deadly of the four known malaria parasites, was decoded. This scientific advance brought malaria, an endemic disease with profound implications for the African continent further into the political and ethical foreground.

The partnership was ambitious in terms of the range of material planned and covered. As the team progressed they came into contact with malaria's many faces: the history of clinical research, contemporary scientific advances, the social and political backdrop against which the disease proliferates and the images and the sounds in which it speaks. Frustrations over time and money, as well as occasional moments of friction, inevitably arose as the work was forced to contend with numerous personal, human and scientific challenges.

The early stages of the research took place at the Division of Parasitology at the National Institute for Medical Research, where Tony is based and Zarina once undertook a residency. Other scientific institutions – the Department of Biology at Imperial College, the London School of Hygiene and Tropical Medicine and the Wellcome Trust Sanger Institute, Hinxton, Cambridgeshire – all yielded further insights and connections. Finally, the field trip to Kenya and Uganda at the end of 2002 brought the research into focus. Here they visited district hospitals and laboratories, a malaria field-station in Apac Town (300 km north of Kampala) and the Wellcome-KEMRI Research Programme in Kilifi. The African landscape, especially the swamps that harbour the mosquito larvae, took on significant meanings. Equally, the 'shop programme' in Kenya, where village shopkeepers

are trained to sell the right drugs to combat malaria, became a point
of inspiration.

For the artist, who belongs to the Ugandan–Asian community evicted
from its country by Idi Amin in the 1970s, the journey back to Uganda awoke
many emotional resonances. The search for images and poetry amidst
the pressure of returning to Africa proved demanding and poignant. The
results of her investigations are still intensely fresh, and at this stage, she
prefers to hold the impressions and images retrieved close to her chest.
We publish here the scientist's visual and written account of their journey,
revealing his perspective of the research and the issues that, for him, are
the most compelling.

It is in the very nature of research that it may or may not produce conclusive outcomes; this is especially true for experimental collaborative work.
Discussions, thoughts and images will often find outlets far beyond a fixed
timeframe. Unfortunately, the timetable of this publication could not accom-
modate all the results that have yet to arise from this intense period of work.
Both Zarina and Tony are to be congratulated on their achievements so
far. Further directions and developments will undoubtedly emerge for us
to appreciate in the future.

Bergit Arends

Population Density:
Kilifi Epi-Dss, 2001.

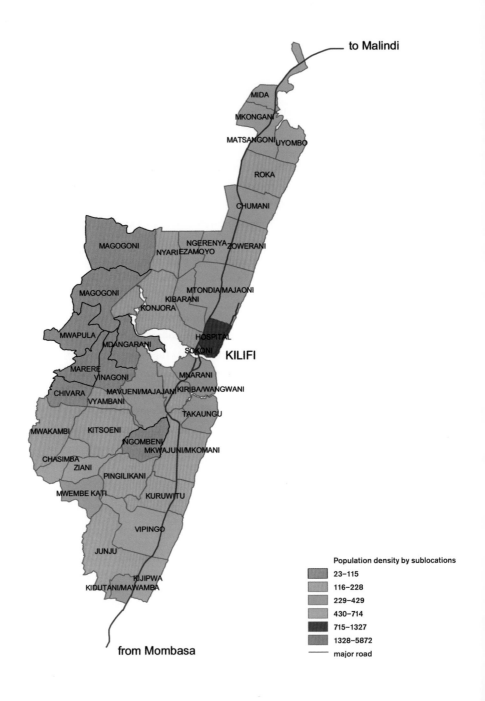

to Malindi

MIDA

MKONGANI

MATSANGONI UYOMBO

ROKA

CHUMANI

MAGOGONI
NGERENYA ZOWERANI
NYARIEZAMOYO

MAGOGONI
MTONDIA/MAJAONI
KIBARANI
KONJORA

MWAPULA
HOSPITAL
MDANGARANI
SOKONI **KILIFI**

MARERE
VINAGONI MNARANI

CHIVARA MAVUENI/MAJAJANI KIRIBA/WANGWANI
VYAMBANI
TAKAUNGU

MWAKAMBI KITSOENI
NGOMBENI
MKWAJUNI/MKOMANI

CHASIMBA
ZIANI
PINGILIKANI

MWEMBE KATI KURUWITU

VIPINGO

JUNJU

KIJIPWA
KIDUTANI/MAWAMBA

Population density by sublocations
23–115
116–228
229–429
430–714
715–1327
1328–5872
major road

from Mombasa

0   4.5   9   18   27   36 km

Red and Wet on the Iron Air

Tony Holder

The history of malaria is littered with symbols of humanity: *mal'aria*, the unwhole-some atmosphere of the marshes and swamps; fever, the body's primitive defence to unwelcome attack; the blood of family and race; the scientist's restless obses-sion with understanding.

One solution to malaria is clear: scientific and clinical research with the poten-tial to make an impact on a devastating disease. But what can science offer? How relevant is pure science to ordinary lives and what are the social, cultural and political factors that shape the translation and application of knowledge? Vaccine development and other forms of prevention need to be seen in the historical context of malaria control. For whose benefit will they be and at what risk? Will they be for corporate imperialists, pleasure-seekers in the sun, or malnourished children offered the hope of a better life?

This collaboration aimed to challenge our idea of both art and science, to reach a deeper understanding of mutual territories. Exploration of the spaces between laboratory and fieldwork, science and humanity, rational and empirical approaches, offers an inspirational framework for interaction and the opportunity to explore diverse worlds: from test tubes and microscopes to the flight and sounds of mos-quitoes and the red earth of an African village.

Malaria landscapes

At the outpatient department of a district hospital in East Africa, the low benches start to fill with mothers and children. Many have travelled by foot and others have paid the few pence for the Matatu taxi ride. Some have spent the night outside under the trees in the hospital grounds. The heat of the morning builds relentlessly while the air fills with the sound of cicadas, cockerel crows and the crying of babies and children. Many children will have malaria. For some, a drug provides a rapid cure; for others admission to a ward, a blood transfusion and more powerful drugs are the only hope. For some there is no hope at all. What about those who do not get to hospital? Many do not attempt the long red road, and a charm is the only possible cure. The local grocery store or trading hut provides some basic medicines but at a price, and are they the right ones for the job? What determines whether a mother will take a sick child to hospital, use a traditional remedy, or give a tablet bought from the local store?

At the local primary school two miles down the road, children in bright pink shirts are chattering in the playground. Within each one the parasite lurks contained, but still malevolent. The obvious symptoms of malaria are not there, but the parasite can cause constant anaemia as it destroys red blood cells, as well as lasting damage to brain and other organs. A sixteen-year-old girl died the day we were there, cause unknown.

In the swamps that surround the town, in the pools of water standing in the mud pits excavated for brick materials, in the tyre tracks of the international

Apac is a small town in Northern Uganda and the site of malaria
work carried out by Dr Tom Egwang and his colleagues.
Apac is Tom's hometown. It lies five hours' drive north of Kampala
on the road to Lira and Gulu. The roads are pretty good for the first
200 km, then a dirt road provides a direct route that crosses the
Nile via a small ferry.

←
The Chigere Road out of Apac. Apac is surrounded by malaria-
intense swamps crossed by few roads.

agencies' four-wheel drives, and in the swimming pools of hotels and houses for
the rich, the mosquito larvae thrive. Mosquitoes make their way through open door-
ways and windows, under the eaves of the thatched or rusty corrugated-iron roofs.
Plant juices sustain a male mosquito, but for a female, blood is essential for life
and laying eggs. Some mosquitoes feed on birds, others on cattle or rodents; but
those that feed on humans can themselves be infected and pass on the malaria
parasite from one person to another. Yet nothing in this environment is straightforward. Apac Town in Uganda lies to the south of the Sudanese border, home to
the terrorist Lord's Resistance Army. By sustaining and nurturing mosquitoes, the
swamps that surround the town protect against terrorist incursions into the region.

In rural Cambridgeshire, meanwhile, landscaped grassland is home to a cluster
of glass and concrete buildings. Lines of identical machines, fed by robotic equipment, stand silent, yet busy, in air-conditioned rooms. There is no sign of human
or any other form of life, but the sequence of the malaria parasite genome is quietly
unfolding, as does the human genome in similar rooms alongside. In the pond
outside mosquito larvae thrive, but there are no traces of the parasite that once
inhabited the East Anglian fens. Further south, however, in a London laboratory,
in incubators holding flasks of human blood tended by scientists, it flourishes.
More of the parasite's secrets are being revealed. How does the parasite get into
red blood cells where it multiplies and causes disease? Patience, enthusiasm
and inspiration are all needed to pry into this world.

Background

Malaria has been thought to be caused by many factors, for example the noxious air of swamps (mal'aria), the drinking of foul water, or the influence of evil spells. However, at the end of the nineteenth century a revolution occurred in the study of malaria. The cause of the disease was found to be a tiny parasite that lives inside red blood cells, is passed from one person to another by mosquitoes, and can only be seen with a powerful microscope.

The parasite that causes malaria was first observed by the French army surgeon, Charles Louis Laveran, while working in Algeria in 1880. It was 17 years later in India that Ronald Ross identified the parasite in the blood meal of an *anopheline* mosquito. The single-celled parasite that causes malaria is called *Plasmodium*. There are four species of *Plasmodium* that infect humans, but *P. falciparum* is the most important because of the severity of the disease and the high incidence of mortality it causes. Only one group of mosquitoes – the *Anopheles* – can transmit malaria parasites from one infected person to another.

Throughout history malaria has profoundly influenced human life and existence in large parts of the world. Human biological evolution, social structure and the aspirations of empires have been moulded by its touch. As an invisible hand, the unseen harbinger of disease and death, it has silently shaped societies and mocked human ambition. It is a disease of which few living in Britain or the rest of western Europe have had experience because it is largely restricted to tropical

← Outpatients department at Apac District Hospital. In the morning the low wooden benches of the outpatients department are filled with mothers and children. About 100 cases of malaria are received everyday and a lot suffer from severe anaemia requiring blood transfusion. By 2 p.m. the outpatients department is closed and the room is empty.

↓ Paediatric ward, Apac District Hospital. Empty in the afternoon, except for very serious cases.

and subtropical areas of the world. Once it was much more widespread and indeed was rife in England 300 years ago in marshy areas; but climate change, human agricultural activities and control measures have now eliminated it from Europe. Long after many of the infectious diseases that ravaged the western world have been brought under control, malaria continues to have far-reaching consequences in other parts of the globe.

Although not headline news, the problem of malaria is massive. Over 40 per cent of the world's population is at risk from the disease, but it is most prevalent in tropical regions. Currently 90 per cent of acute disease and deaths due to malaria occur in Africa, representing at least 1 million deaths per year. The majority of these deaths are amongst young children south of the Sahara. On top of this there are several hundred million clinical cases reported each year, which drain precious resources from healthcare facilities. The impact of the disease on health, economic well-being and society is tremendous for the people of this continent. The interplay between the factors and forces that drive it are still as important now as when the disease was first defined. Human activity and behaviour, whether through their impact on the environment, wars and migrations, or through political and economic measures to reduce poverty and exercise control, have shaped the distribution of the disease today.

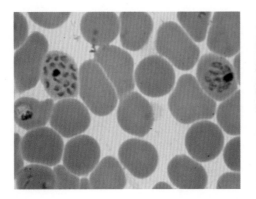 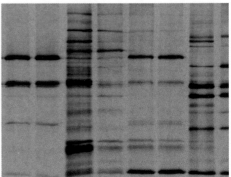

Early attempts to control malaria focused mainly on the mosquito. In the 1950s and 1960s there was hope that malaria could be eradicated by extensive spraying with DDT (dichlorodiphenyltrichloroethane – a residual insecticide), and by impregnating bednets with insecticides such as pyrethroids. Now, malaria is once more increasing as the disease moves back into areas from which it had once been eliminated. Why has control broken down? As the mosquitoes have become resistant to insecticides and DDT has gathered controversy on account of its environmental impact, insecticide sprays have been abandoned or become ineffective. Moreover, the parasite that causes the disease is becoming increasingly resistant to drugs. Chloroquine, a cheap and once effective drug, is now useless in large parts of the world. Even more worrying is the fact that there are few drugs to take the place of chloroquine.

New, radical approaches are needed at many levels, from basic research to better application of current knowledge and more effective implementation of existing methods of control. The failed global eradication campaign (which was not even attempted in Africa) dissipated enthusiasm and caused funding at all levels to haemorrhage, so that by the mid-1990s resources for malaria research worldwide were a tiny fraction of the amount needed. Now, after years of neglect, the international community is recognizing the size and consequences of the problem. At the beginning of the twenty-first century, governments, international agencies and national funders have increased their support. Politicians now talk of HIV (human immunodeficiency virus), TB (tuberculosis), malaria and poverty.

←←
Malaria parasites developing in human red blood cells. The parasites grow, enlarge and multiply before bursting open the cells and invading new ones.
←
Measuring merozoite proteins. Parasite proteins are separated and displayed as black bands according to their size.

Biology

The malaria parasite is a single cell, but both bigger and more complex than either bacteria or viruses. Despite its apparent simplicity it has a complex life, spent partly in a mosquito and partly in an animal such as a human. There are different sorts of malaria parasites that have adapted to life in a variety of animals including lizards, birds and small mammals such as rats, or large ones such as humans. The female *Anopheles* mosquito must feed on blood in order to lay eggs. When an infected female *Anopheles* takes blood, it may inject some parasites with the saliva. These parasites are carried to the liver and invade liver cells, hiding to avoid the body's defence system.

Once inside the liver, the parasite begins to change its form and to multiply many times, giving rise to several thousand new ones that burst out into the bloodstream and home in on the red cells that carry oxygen around the body. This is the next and most dangerous phase of the infection, when the parasite's lifecycle is responsible for the disease of malaria. Inside the red blood cell, each parasite multiplies again to produce further parasites called *merozoites* that invade new, undamaged, red blood cells, establishing a remorseless cycle. If not controlled by the immune system, or by treatment with anti-malarial drugs, one symptom will be a fever that recurs every time the cycle of red blood cell invasion takes place. However, the infection may have much more severe consequences. *P. falciparum* can multiply up to 20 times every two days and infected red blood cells can become lodged in organs, leading to dysfunction and clinical syndromes such as cerebral malaria and severe anaemia.

 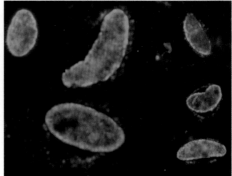

For the parasites to continue to survive, they must be transmitted from one human to another and so have to get back into a mosquito. To do this, some of the parasites in the infected red blood cells change into yet another form: the sexual stages that are necessary to complete the lifecycle. If swallowed by a mosquito when it feeds, these parasites will result in the mosquito becoming infected. Infection will ensure that the parasites can get back into the saliva of the mosquito, ready to invade other individuals and continue the cycle.

←←

The Wellcome Trust Sanger Institute. No sign of life? Lines of identical DNA sequencing machines in an air-conditioned room relentlessly unfolding the parasite's genetic secrets. The secrets are being decoded, but we need to be able to interpret the instructions.

←

Malaria gametocytes develop in the blood before infecting mosquitoes in a sexual cycle. Coloured fluorescent stains are used to identify DNA (in blue) and specific proteins (in green and red).

Malaria universe

The malaria universe is a complex interaction of overlapping biological worlds – of parasite, human host and mosquito vector. Superimposed on top of this is the effect of the environment, human activity, and human and mosquito behaviour. Each world is multi-layered and in fine equilibrium. What does science and research have to offer?

Laboratory and field research go hand in hand, studies of human behaviour complement the work of entomologists and clinical research informs community care. To attack the parasite, we need to understand how it gets into red blood cells, how it survives there and how it causes disease. What is it that determines levels of malaria in a community and the number of people who will die? There are also numerous critical issues, such as the importance of primary health care, clinical diagnosis and hospital management. By understanding how the parasite lives, we should be able to discover how to kill it, either by developing drugs poisonous to the parasite (but not to humans), or by developing a vaccine that will stimulate the body's immune system. The scope of malaria research is broad, from molecules to mosquitoes and parasites to people.

Science and research

Malaria has shaped humanity, imposing strong selective forces on the human genome. The best known of these lead to defects in the function of the human red blood cells that provide some protection against the disease. One hundred years after the incrimination of mosquitoes, science offers evidence to shift the delicate balance between parasite and people.

Malaria research received a considerable boost in the 1970s, when for the first time *P. falciparum* was grown in suspensions of red blood cells in the laboratory. The twenty-first century has begun with another revolution in malaria – the revelation of the structure of the genomes of the parasite, its mosquito vector and human host. An international consortium has revealed the genetic blueprint for the malaria parasite – the complete library of all 5000 genes that define the malaria parasite.

The information contained in the genomes of *P. falciparum* and *A. gambiae*, the principal mosquito vector in Africa, is now available to all. But building and stocking the library with the books of genes, being able to use the information they contain and understanding the complex relationships between the genes and the proteins they code, is just the beginning. This new knowledge must lead to the application of new control methods that complement or improve current approaches. In addition, there must be the resources and commitment at all levels to ensure that molecular knowledge is exploited for the benefit of those that need it most.

Insectary

←

Insectary. A field insectary on the banks of the Jaribuni river provides all that is needed to rear and maintain mosquitoes and their larvae. One half of the roof is palm thatch to provide shade, the other is polythene sheet to allow in the light.

The malaria parasite genome contains the genes that code for the proteins making up the organism. These include the enzymes that carry out the biochemical transformations essential for life, the molecules that define how the parasite recognizes and invades host cells and the mediators that evade the immune responses of its host and vector. Knowing the metabolic pathways (for example, the processes of getting energy, of growing, multiplying, and dividing) enables potential targets for drug therapy to be defined. Establishing which genes are present (and how similar or different they are to the equivalent genes in humans) and which are absent, is essential for planning new strategies for drug development. Enzymes that digest the haemoglobin in the host red blood cell, or make fatty acids within the plastid of the parasite, have already been selected for further development. Some of the proteins are made in the mosquito vector and some are made in the human host. Many proteins have characteristics to suggest that they might be important components of future malaria vaccines, and the human genome project will also help to identify which components of the immune system are switched on or off during infection. However, for about 60 per cent of the parasite genes there is scant knowledge to go on since they have little similarity with known genes in other organisms; the big challenge is to discover what they do.

The mosquito genome is much larger than that of the parasite, containing approximately 14 000 genes. Fortunately, the genome of a fruit fly has already

been studied, and the two flies have approximately 50 per cent of their genes in common, facilitating analysis of the mosquito genome. Interestingly, the mosquito seems to have many more genes involved in its immune defence against pathogens, perhaps because its diet makes it more susceptible to invaders. What will the new molecular information on the mosquito provide? There are three areas where it is important to obtain more information: how can the numbers and life expectancy of infectious mosquitoes be reduced, what attracts some mosquitoes to humans rather than animals, and can the ability of the parasite to develop within the mosquito be reduced?

Mechanisms for resistance to insecticides, and how these can be overcome, can now be examined; this will facilitate the development of new insecticides. The molecular basis of attraction to a variety of odours, which may determine who mosquitoes bite, is currently being investigated and could lead to the development of more effective repellents. The basis of mosquito resistance to infection is also being explored. Many believe it will soon be possible to introduce genes for resistance into wild mosquito populations so that they can no longer transmit malaria. To achieve this, suitable genes and mechanisms for driving them into the population will need to be identified, and the absence of damaging effects associated with genetically manipulated mosquitoes will have to be ensured.

In terms of application (the translation of basic knowledge into useful products), the genome information is likely to have its biggest impact on the

←←

Jaribuni, indoor mosquito collection. In the darkness inside the houses, mosquitoes resting on the walls are spotted using a torch and collected by sucking them into a tube.

←

Jaribuni, bedroom, mosquitoes resting in a box.

development of new drugs and an effective vaccine. In future, drugs will need to be harmless to patients and prevent development of resistance by the parasite, perhaps by use in combination therapy. For many people, vaccination offers the more promising long-term solution.

Following extensive exposure to malaria, people do develop immunity, but in areas where malaria transmission is high, young children and visitors are among the most vulnerable. The basis of vaccination against disease is to prime the defences so that they are prepared and can be called upon more quickly to deal with an attack. To pursue this strategy, we need to identify the less well-defended stages of the parasite and use these weak points as a means of combating the disease. As the parasite hides inside cells and changes its appearance at different stages to avoid the immune system, defences that might be effective against one form will not be effective against another. The ideal would therefore be to prepare the body to defend against all the different stages of the parasite lifecycle.

Proteins cover the surfaces of all cells and those on the surface of the malaria parasite are potential targets for the body's immune system. If the body can be exposed to these proteins by immunization before the parasite attacks, the immune system will be primed to destroy the parasite. How are the important proteins for inclusion in a vaccine to be identified? Since the parasite has several thousand genes, each coding for a distinct protein, finding the small number that are responsible for the proteins of interest can be a daunting task. However, the search

can be focused. For example, identification of the proteins that are recognized by the immune system of people who have had malaria and developed immunity can narrow down the search even further. Despite all of these advances, progress towards developing a malaria vaccine will not be straightforward and there have been many disappointing results. It is still too early to say whether or not a malaria vaccine is a real possibility.

Malaria research is not, however, just about drugs, vaccines and bed nets. One successful programme in Kenya is examining how local shopkeepers dispense anti-malaria tablets and whether their effectiveness in the web of malaria control can be enhanced through education. Another approach is to motivate local community groups in controlling mosquitoes. Burning leaves and flowers from both the Neem and the Baobab trees can be used to help keep mosquitoes away. Cultural strategies can also be a vital tool. In languages such as Swahili, there is very little scientific vocabulary, and concepts such as research, clinical investigation and intervention are extremely hard to convey, often creating obstacles to obtaining consent and explaining procedures. Community field workers need to act as cultural brokers, to find ways of translating messages from scientific research through songs, pictures and dramatization. Every aspect of the malaria universe is open to exploration.

Shopkeeper project. Shop owned by Johnson and Eunice Piri,
Roka Maweni. Training the local shopkeepers to provide the
appropriate medicines and in the right amount is an excellent
and cost-effective way to ensure that a first line of treatment
for malaria is available to the community.

←

Shopkeeper project. Shop owned by Harrison Koi in Roka Mjini.

Politics

Malaria is very much, but not exclusively, a disease of the poor and is exacerbated
by war and unrest. To control malaria, a range of economic, social, political and
scientific hurdles will need to be overcome. In the first part of the twentieth century,
malaria control was an integral part of the pursuit of economic and commercial
interests. DDT was not effective in eradicating malaria but was highly effective at
inhibiting research. This 'solution' for malaria led many to believe that no further
investigations were necessary. The current campaigns must not stifle the on-going
research that is the foundation for the future. For example, the World Health
Organization's Roll Back Malaria campaign must not only provide tools to prevent
infection and provide rapid access to treatment; it must also build the political will
to maintain momentum. Whether or not the ambitious goal of malaria control in
Africa will be achieved, none of the research being carried out in laboratories today
is likely to have a major impact on current campaigns. This is because of the long
time delay in translating fundamental knowledge into products.

The history of malaria research is littered with rivalries between entomologists
and parasitologists, vaccine and drug developers, and promoters of low-tech
or high-tech approaches. In reality, there is a need for a much more integrated
approach that binds existing and new knowledge to local solutions, well-funded
research and an informed African public. The countries and the communities
that malaria affects must lead control of the problem. In ten years' time the best
laboratory research will be carried out globally, not just in the labs of North

America, Europe or Australia. As one of the first steps in this direction – to create, restore and build the necessary infrastructure and train the next generation of researchers – the Multilateral Initiative on Malaria, established after a landmark meeting in Dakar in 1997, is attempting to fulfil these needs. Perhaps malaria will only be taken seriously when it threatens the rich and powerful.

←←

The Arocha swamp around Apac. The swamps provide plentiful breeding sites for the mosquitoes that transmit malaria (Scout camp site).

←

Kitabi (by Malago Hospital) and Maribu storks. This site is just beside the large Malago Hospital in Kampala and is close to densely crowded areas of human habitation. The storks are scavengers that keep the streets clean. The area is flooded intermittently and provides a good breeding site for mosquitoes that transmit malaria in this urban setting.

Epilogue

As a scientist, how did I benefit from collaborating with an artist? Fascination with the beauty of the natural world and its secrets revealed by science has been with me since I was a child. Microscopes, mechanisms for multiplying molecules and colourful stains all reveal the beautiful structure of parasites, the elegant simplicity of DNA and the 'living' form of a protein. The laboratory benches and shelves are littered with boxes, bottles and balances, centrifuges, electrophoresis gel apparatus and chromatography columns; computers line up across the room, and culture flasks with red blood cells are stacked neatly in incubators at 37°C. How accessible is the laboratory to others, and how does it relate to the world outside? How do molecules and merozoites, disease and death, people and places overlap? Can art and science communicate in a creative way?

Perhaps making connections between different realities causes us to question our assumptions, examine with fresh eyes what we take for granted and encourage us to see things more inventively. Perhaps by stopping and paying attention, new ways of looking at the process will emerge and different perspectives result. At the end of the project I have a deeper, more holistic view of this complex subject, even if my excitement over merozoites and the perfection of molecules could not always be fully conveyed or appreciated.

Acknowledgements

I would like to thank the following people for their help and encouragement and for making the project possible in Uganda and Kenya: Zarina Bhimji; in Uganda: Tom Egwang, Godfrey Mujuzi, Tom Ogwal, Mary Atyang and Gabriel Matwale; in Kenya: Kevin Marsh and Norbert Peshu, Vicki Marsh and Baya Karisa, Mtawali Chai, Brett and Pauline Lowe, Charles Mbogo, Nelly Njeru and Samuel Kahindi, Janet Midega and Gabriel Nzai, Francis Ndungu and Sam Kinyanjui, James Berkley and Kathryn Maitland, Moses Mosobo and Evasius Bauni.

Further sources

Some of the text in this article is based on three earlier essays written for a series produced by the National Institute for Medical Research. Other articles of general interest may be found on The Wellcome Trust website by typing 'malaria' into the search function.

Holder A (1995) Malaria vaccines
    www.nimr.mrc.ac.uk/millhillessays/1995/malaria.htm
    (2000) The red road
    www.nimr.mrc.ac.uk/millhillessays/2000/malaria.htm
    (2002) The malaria revolution: from mosquitoes
    to molecules
    www.nimr.mrc.ac.uk/millhillessays/2002/malaria.htm

Swamp at Majajani – a mosquito breeding site.

←
Malindi – a neglected pool. The swimming pools and ornamental ponds of the tourist hotels and beach houses can provide an excellent habitat for mosquitoes to breed, especially if they become neglected. Mosquito larvae are scooped up from the water and examined to see whether or not they are the type to transmit malaria.

Soundless Music

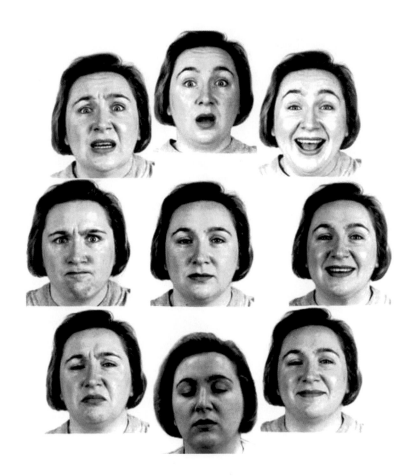

Soundless Music is a live experiment, staged as a series of public concerts, which aims to investigate the psychological effects of infra-sound. Each concert features new works by Sarah Angliss and Roddy Skeaping as well as compositions by Glass, Pärt, Parsey, Skempton and Tanaka. Live music performed by the pianist GéNIA is mixed with electronic sounds, a film piece by Ravi Deepres and occasional deep, bass frequencies. The latter are supplied by an infrasonic generator designed for the event by the National Physical Laboratory. While they experience the concert, audience members take part in a series of subjective tests conducted by psychologists Ciarán O'Keeffe and Professor Richard Wiseman. The first *Soundless Music* concert (titled *Infrasonic*) took place at the Purcell Room, London, on 31 May 2003.

Introduction

Music is a very powerful medium. It can have a profound influence on our emotions, moods and behaviour. This has been recognized through the ages. Historically, it has been used for such varied purposes as bolstering courage before battles, singing babies to sleep, enhancing the courtship process and accompanying rites of passage through life. It has been used to incite rebellion and it can challenge the status quo. It has powerful therapeutic effects: it can promote relaxation, alleviate anxiety and pain, improve the quality of life of those who are beyond medical help and play an important part in enhancing human development in the early years. It is also used commercially to manipulate behaviour and create environments appropriate for particular tasks. These effects occur largely without our conscious awareness.

Music is experienced physiologically (through changes such as heart rate) and cognitively (through knowledge and memories, which may be personal, or related to the music itself, such as its style or period), as well as through mood and emotion. Current thinking suggests that when we hear music or other sounds our responses to them are controlled by the amygdala. The amygdala receives input about sensory information directly and quickly from the thalamus, a relay station for incoming information, before it has been processed by the conscious thinking part of the brain, the cortex. Information is received from the cortex but more slowly. The amygdala also has close connections with the hypothalamus, the part of the brain that instigates emotional behaviour. This ensures that we can respond quickly to incoming stimuli, particularly when such reactions are important for our survival. In the same way that we might respond to a loud noise, we can respond immediately to the sound of music without conscious thought.

The evidence to date regarding our responses to infrasound suggest that they operate in a similar way to those for music. Infrasound is largely unavailable to our conscious thought processes; our responses to it appear to occur at a primitive emotional level. Those responses are then rationalized leading to references to psychic phenomena and the development of an aura of mystery and fear.

Soundless Music offers an exciting opportunity to add to our understanding of infrasound and human response to it, and to dispel many of the myths surrounding it. This tightly controlled, ingenious experiment will enable careful scientific study of the effects of infrasound, and offer further insights into the mechanisms that underpin our responses to music.

Susan Hallam

Soundless Music

Sarah Angliss*

Fig. 1
Our infrasound generator comes from a fine tradition of scaling up acoustic generators, championed by instrument makers such as the late Arthur K Ferris (pictured here with his bass harp, c. 1930). Ferris used his eccentric collection of outsized and pocket-sized string instruments to play sacred music.

Fringe music

…the universe is probably full of music that we cannot perceive …

Sir John Lubbock, considering the limits of the audible spectrum, 1879

At first glance, *Soundless Music* seems absurd: a concert of inaudible sound; an exercise in engineering emotions; a scientific study of the paranormal. These apparent contradictions are not lost on the project team – nor on the friends, work associates and journalists who have asked the inevitable question: is this group really planning to stage a silent concert? The answer is no.

Rather than silence, the focus of this project is extreme bass sound – to be more precise, a low-pitched vibration known as infrasound. The scientific study of infrasound has a long and interesting history, some of which is summarized in this chapter. This project investigates infrasound's psychological effects, putting to the test some fascinating claims about infrasound and mood.

Independently, musicians and psychologists have discovered infrasound may be linked to our mood in two strikingly different contexts: one is sacred organ music; the other is at sites of ostensible hauntings. → Fig. 1 Could infrasound have similar effects in these two settings? This is a question we are exploring in a series of live concerts. Featuring electroacoustic piano music laced with infrasound, the *Soundless Music* concert series (aka *Infrasonic*) is the largest public experiment of its kind.

* with scientific analysis from Ciarán O'Keeffe

To put this effect in context, it is worth considering some prevailing theories about infrasound. No end of claims has been made about infrasound's unusual effects. Type 'infrasound' into any Internet browser and you'll see this mysterious phenomenon has been associated with just about everything, from beam weapons to bad driving, with varying degrees of authority. It has been woven into our sacred music, implicated in apparent hauntings and blamed for 'the fatigue of modern living' in our cities. Sadly, few of the more flamboyant claims about infrasound are backed up by a hefty dossier of evidence or by a study of its emotional effects. Psychologists and musicologists share a fascination with infrasound but generally, in their research profiles, have let it fall between the cracks (leaving conspiracy theorists populating the Internet, free to sweep up – and reassemble – the bits). So the psychological effect of infrasound has become the stuff of junk science – a topic to file in the same box as dog telepathy and faked moon landings. Couple that with tremendous (largely erroneous) hype over infrasound's toxic effects and cautious researchers may opt to avoid the subject altogether.

This heady mix of disapproval has strengthened our resolve to put certain claims about infrasound to the test. As much a recital as an experiment, this is a project that uses science to create an engaging contemporary concert, and music to engage people in the process of science.

Infrasound – a primer

Sound is, quite simply, a vibration that the human ear can detect. One note will sound higher than another if it vibrates the air at a faster rate (in other words, at a higher frequency). We are used to talking about the visible light spectrum – the range of colours that the human eye can see. Acousticians also think of sound in spectral terms. As sound rises in pitch, from bass to treble, it moves across the audible spectrum. Just as there is infrared and ultraviolet at the cusps of the visible spectrum, there is infrasound and ultrasound at the fringes of the spectrum of audible sound.

Infrasound lies at the extreme bass end of our hearing range. It is usually defined as a vibration that occurs fewer than 20 times/second. Humans (unlike some other animals) do not communicate with infrasound and are not very good at detecting it. But infrasound is not always inaudible. To understand why, it is worth knowing more about human sensitivity to sound.

Physicists measure frequency in units called hertz (Hz) and call 1000 Hz 1 'kilohertz' (kHz). Most physics textbooks say we can hear airborne vibrations that occur between 20 and 20 000 times/second (20 Hz–20 kHz). But in truth, this is a gross simplification. Hearing varies from person to person, with countless factors influencing the range of frequencies that any one of us can detect. Your age and genetic make-up play a part – so do many other variables, such as the time you have punished your ears in foundries or heavy metal concerts and the amount of wax in your ears.

Rather than cutting off sharply at 20 Hz and 20 kHz, our hearing ability fades gradually as we approach these frequency limits. A piano's bottom note C, for example, vibrates at roughly 33 Hz, a frequency near the edge of our hearing range. Top C on the piano vibrates at around 4190 Hz, a mid-range frequency at which human hearing is extremely acute. To seem as loud as top C, bottom C needs to make a sound that is roughly 1000 times more powerful (in acoustic terms, 30 dB louder). In general, extreme bass and treble sounds need more power than mid-range sounds in order to cross the 'threshold of hearing' – the minimum loudness that can be heard. With enough volume, even sounds that lie outside the often-quoted '20–20 k' frequency range can be heard. This is true of infrasound.

Infrasound should not be confused with the more familiar term 'ultrasound', which refers to sound above 20 kHz, the upper limit of human hearing. Today, ultrasound is most often associated with clinical scanners. These make sound-waves with a frequency of several million Hz. A scanner detects these waves as they bounce off the tissues of the human body, analysing them to draw an image of the structures inside.

Infrasound clearly lies on the cusp of our perception, rather than outside it. But our experience of infrasound is still a mysterious issue. When we sense these vibrations, what do we actually hear? Researchers at the University of Salford asked this when they tested our ability to hear low frequencies in 1967. Subjects described the sensation of infrasound as 'rough', a 'popping effect'. Infrasound below 5 Hz was described as a 'chugging' or 'whooshing', a sensation they could 'feel'. (Yeowart et al., 1967).

The chance to hear infrasound in a large auditorium seems very enticing. But it is the hypothesis that infrasound can affect people's mood that intrigues us even more. The existence of infrasound, in both sacred music and reputedly haunted sites, makes exploration of infrasound and mood all the more fascinating.

Infrasonic zoo

Far from being an exotic phenomenon, infrasound is with us all the time. We continually bathe in a sea of barely perceptible, ambient infrasonic noise. Sometimes described as the 'infrasonic zoo', most of this is generated by natural processes and events: thunderstorms, earth tremors, ocean waves, volcano eruptions and curious phenomena such as meteor impacts, aurora and 'sprites' (sudden electrical discharges in the upper atmosphere).

Human activity also contributes to background infrasound. Deep below the rumble of city traffic, there is a cacophony of very low frequency noise from factories, lorry engines, fireworks, passing aircraft, distant quarrying and many other human sources. In 1957, the French physicist Vladimir Gavreau highlighted this overlooked noise pollution, citing it as a possible cause of city dwellers' stress. (Gavreau et al., 1966).

Infrasound from any source can travel extremely long distances through the atmosphere as it is attenuated very little by air. In fact, geophysicists look for faint traces of infrasound to find evidence of approaching tornadoes and other distant events. A global array of 60 listening devices, set up for this purpose, constantly monitors background infrasound levels around the world. In April 2001, researchers at the Scripps Institute of Oceanography, San Diego, CA, USA, picked up the infrasonic signature of a meteor crashing into the earth's atmosphere.

The meteor, around 3 m in diameter, would have exploded on impact, high in the stratosphere, with as much power as the Hiroshima atomic bomb.

It is an altogether different explosive source that interests the geophysicists using this network. The sensors are used to check the enforcement of the world-wide Comprehensive Test Ban Treaty. Detonated in air, a nuclear bomb can make an infrasonic shock-wave that can be detected in another continent. Infrasound listening posts have been around since the 1950s, when physicists started monitoring enemy nuclear tests at the height of the cold war era. Interest in these sensors gradually declined as countries moved their tests underground. Today, airborne infrasound has a new importance as another raft of countries is on the brink of making their first nuclear bombs.

Trunk calls

It's quite incredible to see these high-level signals produced on a direct-writing oscillograph and yet be unable to hear them on an 18-inch ... loudspeaker.

Patterson and Hamilton, on the discovery of underwater infrasonic calls, 1964

Humans aren't infrasonic communicators (except, perhaps, during organ recitals), unlike countless other species. Zoologists have found some animals are sensitive to vibrations as low as 0.05 Hz. Infrasonic animal calls were discovered in the 1950s, when oceanographers first detected the sound of the North Atlantic fin whale (originally mistaking it for a Soviet submarine on manoeuvres). Interestingly, this came almost 70 years after the discovery of animal ultrasound. This was confirmed in 1883 by Victorian polymath Francis Galton. Galton took some ultra-sonic whistles to the zoo and observed the reactions of caged animals as he blew them 'as near as safe' to their ears.

Rhinos, cod, squid, pigeons, guineafowl, capercaillie and elephants are among the planet's many infrasonic species. All the infrasonic communicators discovered so far instinctively migrate, home, or call to one another over vast distances.

Infrasound can travel a long way, even through thick forest or scrubland, so it gives these animals a distinct evolutionary advantage. The female elephant, for example, is only in oestrus for four days or so, once every four years. When she is ready for mating, she emits a distinctive, infrasonic call that attracts males from up to 4 km away.

Organ pipes and haunted sites

64-foot pipes don't exist, except as an extremely rare, freak, obsession of someone with too much money and not much sense.

Organ builder's comments on infrasonic pipes, Canada 2002

Look at the organ pipes in any large cathedral and there is a high probability you will see some '32-footers'. The longest of these pipes are over 8.5 m long (approximately 28 ft), so will be producing infrasound. On a technical note, these are effectively open at both ends so are 'half-wavelength' pipes. Infrasonic organ pipes are surprisingly prevalent – they can be found in most cathedral cities in Britain. The pipe organ in St Alban's Cathedral, for example, can play a bottom C at 16.4Hz, four octaves below middle C. These are not a recent innovation. In *Syntagma Musicum*, Praetorius's ancient catalogue of musical instruments, there is evidence that 32 ft pipes have been in use since the late fifteenth century. → Fig. 2

Sydney Town Hall, Australia, and the Atlantic City Convention Hall, USA, both have extremely rare 64 ft pipes that produce notes as low as 8.2 Hz in frequency. The Atlantic City organ was built in 1926, an era when large theatre organs attracted great publicity and were a source of civic pride. → Fig. 3 Officially recognized as the biggest musical instrument ever built, the Atlantic City organ took the crown from another instrument, bought by store owner, John Wanamaker. He purchased his pipe organ to ornament the main court of his Philadelphia store. With great fanfare, the Wanamaker organ was inaugurated in 1911, at the exact moment George V was crowned. A Shetland pony was posed inside the largest pipe for publicity photos.

Fig. 2
Foot-pumping a pipe organ, 1619. This woodcut is from Michael Praetorius's catalogue of instruments *Syntagma Musicum*. In the twentieth century, electric blowers gave organ builders scope to make larger instruments. The Atlantic City Convention Hall organ is supplied with up to 17000 litres of air a second.

Using magnificent infrasonic pipes, organ builders can dress any grand, open space (although Wanamaker was not ultimately convinced his organ did his shop justice). But do these giant pipes also serve any musical purpose? In general, organists agree that sounds from the deepest pipes add support to choirs singing with the organ. In some way, they fatten the tone of the music, making it easier to sing in ensemble and keep in tune. But on the dramatic effect of infrasound, opinion is deeply divided. Some say the largest pipes add a sense of profundity and awe to the music; others dismiss their output as 'an expensive draught'.

As organs vary from venue to venue, a great deal of organ music leaves the performer free to choose the register of their performance (which pipes they will use). But some composers write music with particular registers in mind. This is true of the twentieth-century composer Olivier Messiaen. A synaesthete who directly related sound to colour, Messiaen used his sacred music to paint vivid scenes. In 'Apparition de l'Eglise Eternelle', Messiaen specifies the use of powerful, infrasonic pipes. Performance notes direct the organist to make the sounds of hammers hitting the anvils of the apocalypse.

Church organists are not the only musicians performing sacred music with infrasound. Infrasonic pipes and sounding boxes can be found in sacred music around the world. In fact, archaeologists have found tentative evidence of the sacred use of infrasound in the Neolithic Age. Much of this research is summarized by Paul Devereux in his book *Stone Age Soundtracks*, (Devereux, 2002).

Fig. 3
Installing diaphone and
bombarde pipes in Atlantic
City Hall, c. 1932. Many of
these produce bass notes
in the infrasonic region.
Listed in the Guinness
Book of Records, the
Atlantic City Convention
Hall organ has around
33 000 pipes, including
the world's only diaphone
profunda. Twice the length
of the pipes in this photo,
this has a fundamental
frequency of 8.2 Hz.

Reading University researchers, Aeron Watson and David Keating, measured the dimensions of Camster Round, a neolithic passage grave in Caithness, Scotland. Using their data, they were able to build a computer model of the site. From this they estimated the site had a resonant frequency of 4–6 Hz. According to their calculations, anyone striking a 30 cm drum inside the grave could use this resonance to produce infrasound over 120 dB in amplitude (well above the threshold of hearing). Similar findings were made about other passage graves, including the sandstone cave, Dwarfie Stane, in Orkney.

The evidence linking infrasound to reputed hauntings is still only tentative, but equally intriguing. Apparitions in peripheral vision, cold shivers and feelings of discomfort and fear have all been reported in places where infrasound is present. Notable research in this area was conducted by Vic Tandy, an engineer from Coventry University. Working in the laboratory, Tandy and his colleagues had strange experiences that led to suggestions that the place was haunted. When he investigated the lab building, Tandy found a ventilation fan was producing an infrasonic standing wave with a frequency of 19 Hz. As soon as he switched off the fan, the standing wave disappeared and the unusual sensations evaporated. This discovery – a possible connection between infrasound and his experiences – prompted Tandy to look for infrasound in other allegedly haunted sites. A second investigation took place at a fourteenth-century cellar in Coventry, where people had seen apparitions. At this site he also found a spike of infrasound at 19 Hz.

To establish whether infrasound is causing strange experiences, rather than simply correlating with them, we need to generate infrasound in a controlled way. We plan to do so using our own custom-made generator (see later). Rather than a sacred place or site of a reputed haunting, we will be playing infrasound in an ordinary concert hall. Here, we can use infrasound in an emotive context (a musical performance), stripped of any sacred or spooky connotations. By analysing listeners' responses to the sounds they hear, we hope to advance our understanding of infrasound and its effects in music. We also hope to learn more about the way physical phenomena, such as infrasound, can cause seemingly paranormal experiences.

Investigating unexplained phenomena

Infrasound is just one of the many physical variables that have been linked with unusual experiences. Scientists have studied these experiences in many different ways to try and understand their causes. Some collect and document anecdotal accounts; others, including Dr Richard Wiseman, run systematic quantitative investigations. This latter approach may be the most interesting. It enables researchers to look for the presence of physical phenomena, such as magnetic fields and changing temperatures, and correlate them with people's subjective experiences.

Participants are asked to walk around an ostensibly haunted site, and to give reports of any unusual experiences they have, such as apprehension, a sensed presence, or a sudden feeling of coldness. Participants mark the location of their experience on a floor plan and complete a questionnaire to indicate the nature and intensity of their experience. Physical measurements are also taken in the area under test – for instance, measurements of temperature and electromagnetic field. Statistics are used to see if there is any relation between variations in these measurements and the location of people's experiences.

In a study undertaken by Wiseman in the Haunted Gallery at Hampton Court Palace, participants' reports of unusual experiences were associated with the presence of local magnetic fields. Similar research carried out at the reputedly haunted Edinburgh Vaults found a significant correlation between local magnetic fields and lighting levels with the location of people's experiences. These findings suggest that, at least in some cases, alleged hauntings may be the result of people responding to 'normal' factors in their surroundings.

Dr Caroline Watt, experimental psychologist, Edinburgh University

Dangerous noises?

Infrasonic assaults on the body are the more lethal because they come with dreadful silence.

Borderland Science, fringe science website, writing on infrasonic weapons, 2002

People may not be very sensitive to infrasound – but is it safe for them to experience it? On the one hand, this seems like a simple question to answer. After all, infrasound is simply a deeper version of the bass notes we hear every day. Bass notes are not normally considered to be toxic (although too much of any sound can knock the edges off your hearing). So if infrasound is kept to reasonable levels, it must surely be safe to use.

Monitoring volume in an infrasonic concert is tricky if we have to rely on human hearing. We are very insensitive to infrasound, so there is a risk we could pump up the volume of our generator too far, oblivious to any hearing damage we may be causing. Furthermore, the range of levels, between just-audible infrasound and infrasound that can damage hearing, is relatively small. Fortunately, the acousticians at the National Physical Laboratory (NPL) have a host of measuring equipment that can monitor infrasound with higher precision and sensitivity than the human ear. With a real-time digital frequency analyser, they can also monitor the spectrum of infrasound (and audible sound) during the infrasonic concert as the music progresses. Several microphones will be needed to get a true picture of the sound at various points in the hall.

Hearing loss is something to be avoided, but sensational reports about the danger of infrasound focus on even more alarming concerns. Visual blurring, nausea, organ rupture and death have all been associated with exposure to infrasound. But extremely high levels of infrasound would be needed to create such physical effects. In 1979, the acoustician Norman Broner calculated that you would need 1000 times the power of a 'Saturn V rocket' launch to make enough infrasound to rupture a human lung 250 m away (Broner, 1978).

Interest in the dangers of infrasound was fuelled in the cold war by the search for non-lethal weapons. In this respect, one of the strangest and most memorable research programmes was carried out by the physicist, Gavreau. After experiencing an infrasonic wave that made him feel uncomfortable, Gavreau embarked on a research programme to make an infrasonic 'beam weapon'. His prototype, a scaled-up version of a Parisian police whistle, could supposedly immobilize anyone who heard it. Gavreau claimed his whistle was most toxic when played in a room that resonated at the so-called 'death frequency' of 7 Hz. Later researchers have tried to replicate Gavreau's work, with little success. But this hasn't stopped his death whistle becoming the stuff of legend – a favourite among the Internet's fringe science community.

Gavreau's story has been followed by other claims about infrasonic weapons designed to immobilize troops and control unruly crowds (Altmann, 2001). Accounts include a cannon, built in Moscow that could generate deadly 10 Hz pulses and a box, called the Curdler or People Repeller, bought by the British Government for riot control in Northern Ireland (but never used). Appearing occasionally in the national papers and the general science press, few of these stories have been substantiated.

Infrasound's reputation as a silent danger is a persistent one, even though it cannot be supported by research. It has led to resistance to our own project from the most unlikely quarters. One physicist has suggested we may need our audience to evacuate their bowels before the concert. Assistants in a top London electronic music store have also warned us off 'dabbling with brown noise'.

On the other hand, scientists and engineers working with infrasound have no first-hand reports of any deadly effects. In fact, behavioural ecologist Karen McComb pointed out that extreme bass sound has been found to stimulate the sacculus (McComb, 2000). This part of the ear helps maintain our balance. It is also linked to the hypothalamus, a region of the brain that drives our need for food, sex and other gratification. So perhaps a little infrasound can enhance our sense of pleasure!

Of course, church organists have been dabbling with the stuff for around six centuries. As far as we can tell, their frequent, long exposure to infrasound has not had any lethal effects – anyone who has driven in a car with poor suspension has had their internal organs vibrated at infrasonic frequencies. It may have made them somewhat car sick, but they probably lived to tell the tale.

Making infrasound

The secret of making good infrasound is a simple matter of scaling up: double the length of a music pipe and you halve its resonant frequency, making it sing an octave lower. Our infrasonic pipe relies on this principle. It is based on a plastic drain pipe that is around 7 m long. We use a loudspeaker, rather than an organ blower, to move the air through this pipe and get it to sing. This is to minimize harmonics – the extra notes that sing with the bass note of a pipe (its 'fundamental') and give the pipe its characteristic timbre. Organ pipes are rich in harmonics. These make the pipes sound beautiful but can be problematic in infrasound studies. A 15 Hz pipe, for example, will have harmonics at 30 Hz, 45 Hz, 60 Hz and so on. As our ears are far more sensitive to these higher frequencies, the harmonics may swamp the infrasound under test.

Placed one-third of the way along the pipe, the loudspeaker can vibrate a column of air around 4.7 m long. In theory, this gives it a resonant frequency of roughly 18 Hz (the loudspeaker effectively stoppers one end of the air column, making it act as a 'quarter-wavelength' pipe). This is a useful resonant frequency to aim for as 18.35 Hz is the musical note D and 19 Hz is the frequency detected by Vic Tandy at his 'haunted' sites.

To create an audible, low-frequency wave, our loudspeaker needs to move a huge volume of air as it vibrates to and fro. A typical, domestic speaker does not have a long enough 'stroke' to do this so we are using a servo-driven speaker instead. This uses a motor to drive the speaker back and forth. The signal we send to the speaker is a sine wave – a pure note with no harmonics. It is likely the speaker will distort this wave slightly, so our generator will not be completely harmonic-free.

Given the length of our pipe, we knew it would be tricky to build and move from venue to venue. We decided to commission exhibit makers, Tim Hunkin and

Fig. 4
Testing the infrasound
generator, September
2002. Richard Lord
monitors sound levels
with a spectral analyser
while Sarah (middle)
adjusts the volume of the
power amp. GéNIA (right)
is listening attentively
for unusual sonic effects.

Graham Norgate, to put a portable version together for us. An experienced exhibit maker, Tim has the added advantage of owning a very big shed. Tim and Graham built the pipe in three sections, supported on a metal stand and held together with flight-case catches. The suspension wire was added to stop the pipe drooping rather pathetically under its own weight. → Fig. 4

Richard Lord from the NPL, GéNIA and Sarah were present for the inaugural switch-on of the pipe. As they pumped up the volume of the signal generator, they felt a certain trepidation. To their relief, the pipe resonated strongly at 17.5 Hz and the generator could produce infrasound above the threshold of hearing. But it did have one unexpected design fault: the suspension wire, holding up the pipe, was vibrating, making an ugly, high-pitched buzz. Rubber mounts under the wire soon alleviated this problem, leaving everyone able to hear the chug of the pipe at infrasonic frequencies.

In the close quarters of the shed, the pipe began to resonate strip lights, furniture and other loose odds and ends. As the pipe made very little audible noise, this was an odd experience. Seeing these objects vibrate for no apparent reason, it is easy to imagine how infrasonic energy could be mistaken for a ghostly sighting.

Fig. 5
GéNIA practising in
Liverpool Metropolitan
Cathedral, a few hours
before the preview
concert. This photograph
was taken through a
section of the infrasound
generator.

Infrasonic performance

Infrasonic is the debut concert for two new pieces. Sarah's piece, 'She Goes
Back Underwater', for piano and electronics, has been joined by an up-tempo work
for prepared piano by Roddy Skeaping, a London composer. Hayden Parsey has
also adapted his existing work, 'Lo but Hi', specially for this event.

As they step inside the concert hall, the audience of the *Infrasonic* recital will
see the usual paraphernalia of an electroacoustic piano concert as well as our
giant generator. → Fig. 5 This will be switched on at certain points in the concert
to lace the auditorium with infrasound. → Fig. 6 Every member of the audience
will be given a questionnaire. This will be used to take a snapshot of their emotions
at allotted points in the show.

In this recital, infrasound is the accompaniment to GéNIA's piano playing and
the audible electronic track. Like any other performance, GéNIA's is likely to have
an effect on our emotions; so is the accompanying film piece created by Ravi
Deepres. How can we possibly measure the influence of infrasound in this setting?
The answer is to run back-to-back concerts and make them identical in every
respect (venue, performer, programme, visuals) except for the use of infrasound.
If we invite a different audience to each event and leave them 'blind' to the infrasound condition, we may be able to make some meaningful comparisons between
music with and without infrasound. As a performer, GéNIA will also need to be
unaware of the placement of the infrasound. This is possible if we switch on our

Fig. 6

A spectral plot of 'Maelstrom' (Steve Watson, 1992), for electronics and piano, providing useful information to acoustic engineers. This plot was recorded during GéNIA's performance at Liverpool Metropolitan Cathedral. It shows the relative amplitude of high- and low-pitched sounds during her performance. Higher-pitched sounds are on the right of the plot. You can clearly see a peak at around 20 Hz, created by the infrasound generator, which was switched on during the piece.

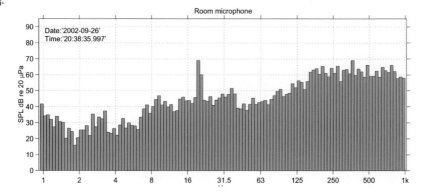

pipe during louder sections of the music where other notes mask the infrasound. Of course the variables we can't control are the differences in GéNIA's playing from concert to concert. With this in mind, we plan to film one of our concerts. This will give us a performance we can use repeatedly for experiments in the lab.

Composing for *Soundless Music*

I think I'm a curator at heart as I often collect sounds that I think I can use one day in a composition. Our house is littered with musical saws, old electronic toys, salvaged organ pipes, communications equipment, a dead harmonium and other tat I've acquired when I've been on the lookout for sonic raw material. When I'm creating a new piece, I often layer vocal fragments with highly processed recordings of these objects.

Over the last few years, I've been composing exclusively for sound installations like the *Booth of Truth* and *Instant Eclipse* (with Tim Hunkin, both now on Southwold Pier). I use sounds to turn small spaces, inside and around exhibits, into bizarre, imaginary worlds. This work never takes itself too seriously, so the prospect of writing something for a formal concert left me feeling rather daunted.

My first instinct, faced with writing for *Soundless Music*, was to create something haunting. With this in mind, I recorded an ancient English song,

'The Wife of Usher's Well', and mixed it with a recording of my niece, Flora. A few weeks earlier, I'd felt compelled to record Flora's voice when she started to tell me, in vivid detail, how she thought she'd seen a mermaid. Usher's Well is a song I've known since I was a child. It's a very dark song, concerning a mother who is visited by her dead children on the feast of Martinmas. This song has always captivated me, partly because I'm unsure if the visitation is real or imagined. I thought it had interesting resonances with Flora's account of a mermaid – another convincing apparition. Flora told me about her mermaid in an undertone, as though she was imparting a secret. Under compression to bring out her breaths and so on, her voice had an unsettling edge, especially when she said her apparition "goes back underwater when mummy comes near the window, or anyone else".

I'm glad I went through the process of setting Usher's Well although I wasn't entirely happy with the result. Verbal clues hammered home its emotional content, rather than letting the music take the lead. Some time later, I decided to abandon it in favour of a more suitable follow-up. 'She Goes Back Underwater', uses the same raw material but abstracts it further. Voices are processed using Praat, a speech analysis program introduced to me by psychologist Chris Darwin. Praat can be used to extract 'formants', characteristic tones in the voice, and use them to modulate other sounds. I was really struck by its effect – especially when the software was misbehaving and making some surprisingly beautiful, digital 'artefacts'. The resulting piece has an arresting, voice-like quality, without too many intelligible utterances to labour the theme. On a practical level, this new piece also has long sections of heavy bass. These will enable us to mask infrasound if we opt to use it in the work. → Figs 7, 8

Sarah Angliss, composer and engineer

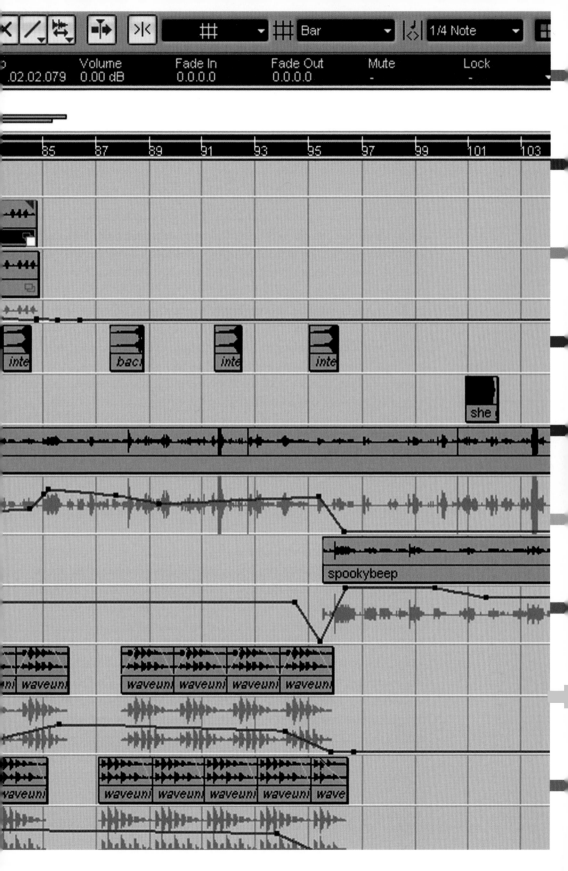

Fig. 7 ↑
Composing the electronic
elements of 'She Goes
Back Underwater' (Sarah
Angliss, 2003) in a
sequencer program.
Rather than musical notes,
a sequencer places frag-
ments of sound-waves
in time. The blue lines
modulate the volume of
the sounds being played.
Sounds played together
are stacked vertically
on the screen, like notes
in a musical chord.

Infrasound – a performer's view

I was already working on a multimedia project for live piano, electronics and visuals when the possibility of creating a mass experiment with infrasound came up. Since the aim of music is partly to produce an emotional impact on the audience, I felt that harnessing the special properties of infrasound could enrich the listening experience.

This really is a unique, experimental opportunity and I don't know exactly how it will turn out. I myself will be part of the experiment and won't know when the infrasound waves are turned on. I just have to perform as usual and hope that I won't get distracted. Could infrasound produce negative emotions and sensations? Obviously the last thing I want is for the audience to feel sick or leave with a headache!

I believe the artist should be open to risk. Traditional classical concerts are losing their audiences. Contemporary music should adapt to the society in which we live. I hope it will encourage people to open their minds and reflect on some of the paradoxes in our universe.

GéNIA, pianist

Where psychology meets music

From the outset, this project tapped into all my areas of interest. My original liberal arts education fuelled a taste for interdisciplinary research whenever and wherever possible. This has included collaboration with computer scientists, geographers and religious scholars. Additionally, an early fascination with parapsychology and spontaneous case research (i.e. spontaneous paranormal phenomena such as hauntings and poltergeists) constantly weaved its way through my psychology studies, culminating in a doctorate in parapsychology. I am also an amateur musician, and have made efforts to continue active involvement in musical trios and duos while carving out a career in psychology. But in coupling the two, I have mainly succeeded in keeping up with progress in music therapy. When I was approached by

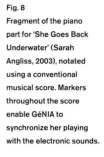

Fig. 8
Fragment of the piano part for 'She Goes Back Underwater' (Sarah Angliss, 2003), notated using a conventional musical score. Markers throughout the score enable GéNIA to synchronize her playing with the electronic sounds.

Professor Richard Wiseman to take a role in "this new project that Sarah is setting up", I jumped at the chance.

The team's staging of a music psychology experiment of this magnitude in a concert setting is unprecedented, and the opportunity to innovate rather than replicate (as is frequently the case in psychology) is also significant. In particular, the development of a standard emotional response questionnaire for audience members, whilst recognizing the importance of free-response descriptions of their experiences, is a valuable opportunity to collect unique data. The most exciting moment, however, is when the team – a sound engineer, a pianist, a physicist and a psychologist – comes together for the concert. Everyone contributes their own expertise and gives their own, individual performance while bringing a fresh perspective to other areas.

Ciarán O'Keeffe, psychologist, Liverpool Hope University

Measuring emotion

There is plenty of scientific literature claiming that infrasound can be perceived – through the ears and body. But while there has been some very interesting work done on infrasound and the hypothalamus (see earlier), the bulk of research comes from environmental noise experts who consider infrasound an annoyance. Annoyance is a possible factor, but we are not convinced that it fully describes the effects of infrasonic music. It seems unlikely that organ builders would devote such huge resources to a sound that simply annoys. Our intention is to broaden the scope of existing infrasound studies and see which other emotions come into play.

Emotions are tricky to define and quantify but psychologists do have some practical methods of assessing our emotional state. In 1993, Klaus Scherer pointed to three attributes that are useful to examine: subjective feelings (e.g. boredom, happiness), expressive behaviour (e.g. laughter, crying) and physiological responses (e.g. heart rate, blood pressure). He called these the 'reaction triad' (Juslin and Sloboda, 2001).

The reaction triad has been used extensively to assess emotions in everyday situations. Juslin and Sloboda also suggest using it to study our emotional response to music. Ultimately, researchers hope to develop a theoretical framework that can explain why we have certain emotions, rather than simply measure them. Leonard Meyer's 1956 book *Emotion and Meaning in Music* attempted to do this. (Meyer, 1956). The longevity of this book is a testament to the strength of Meyer's theoretical approach.

The simplest emotion studies use spoken or written words to assess only one part of the reaction triad: subjective feelings. Word-based studies require subjects to report their emotions using adjective checklists, rating scales or open-response forms. This approach is open to criticism as it can be intrusive, interrupting the experience under examination. But it has been successfully used to measure emotional responses to music, and to compare the emotions of listeners and performers at the same event.

It is difficult to design adjective checklists that accurately describe emotions. Researchers have suggested many different schemes. One of the most significant

Figs 9, 10
This circumplex is a
descriptive model of
emotion developed
by James Russell.
The two axes of the
circle are the dimensions
of affect and arousal.

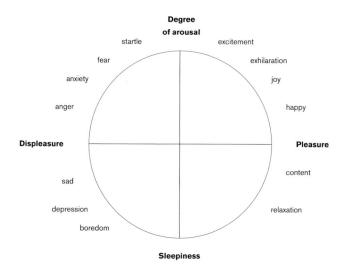

**Degree
of arousal**

startle   excitement

fear   exhilaration

anxiety   joy

anger   happy

Displeasure   **Pleasure**

content

sad

depression   relaxation

boredom

Sleepiness

Fig. 11
Example of the
questionnaire.

To be completed after the sound test
Your present mood

The following four scales contain words that describe different feelings and emotions. Please place a mark on the line between each pair of words to reflect how you feel right now.

For example, the end points of the first scale contain the words *happy* and *sad*. If you are feeling quite happy at this moment then you should place a mark nearer to the left (i.e. closer to the word *happy*) like this...

happy   —|—————————————   sad

... but if you are feeling rather sad at this moment then you should place a mark nearer to the right (i.e. closer to the word *sad*) like this...

happy   —————————————|—   sad

Here are the four scales for you to complete...

happy	———————————————	sad
aroused	———————————————	sleepy
excited	———————————————	bored
angry	———————————————	calm

---

is the 'circumplex', developed by James Russell. → **Fig. 9** Emotions with no features in common (e.g. happy and sad) are diametrically opposite each other on the circle. The circumplex graphically organizes emotions in terms of their pleasantness – with pleasure on the right semicircle – and level of arousal – with high arousal in the top. → **Fig. 10** is a version of the circumplex that uses photos to show each emotion.

The *Soundless Music* questionnaire uses opposite pairs of adjectives from the circumplex, presenting them at either end of response scales. → **Fig. 11** This is to be complemented by a 'free response questionnaire' given out to around ten per cent of the audience. The alternative questionnaire invites listeners to supply their own written descriptions of their experiences during the show but does not supply a ready-made list of adjectives.

One of the most interesting aspects of the *Infrasonic* concert is its natural setting: a real concert hall. A recording of the concert will give us an unrivalled opportunity to compare responses in this location and responses in the lab. Environment and social context may influence the way we respond to both music and subjective tests.

Next steps

At the time of writing this chapter, we are preparing for our first London concert. A dry run, which took place in Liverpool Metropolitan Cathedral in September 2002, gave us a chance to check the logistics of the performance and the usability of our questionnaires. GéNIA's programme featured works by a number of twentieth-century composers, from Debussy and Satoh to Glass, Pärt and Tanaka, as well as Sarah's and Hayden's pieces. This single, open rehearsal in Liverpool did not enable us to say anything definitive about infrasound, but it did reveal a few interesting facts about our audience. Based on results from over 100 question-naires, we know most audience members were professionally connected to the science–art field. Around two-thirds of the over-30s considered themselves to be artists, while 85 per cent of the under-30s were students. Over one-quarter of everyone present said they believed in the paranormal and the existence of ghosts. This percentage is in keeping with the national average. (Daily Mail/ICM poll, 1998).

The open rehearsal in Liverpool has left us with a long list of new things to try. Our first discovery was that our infrasound generator could not produce enough low-frequency sound to fill a cathedral. In short, the effects we were noticing in our rehearsals were not matched in the cathedral setting. Infrasound produced by a generator can be boosted by turning up the amplifier, but when levels approach 105 dB, the pipe is vibrating at such high amplitude that it produces noticeable, unwanted harmonics, rattles and other extraneous noise that swamp infrasonic frequencies. Although energy can also be increased in certain, smaller spaces by directing the generator at a reflecting corner (such as the corner of a stone room), this is not always a practicable solution. Sarah, Richard and Dan have decided to experiment with more generator designs. As a back up, Sarah is also planning a 'junk track'. This will be a recording of extraneous noise, minus infrasound that can be thrown into any concert to put people off the scent.

Although we are confident our infrasonic concert is engaging, we realize a concert introduces many confounding variables that make it tricky to pinpoint the cause of interesting subjective responses. In fact, this is why many music psychologists have shied away from concert-based experiments, preferring to work in the lab. We are planning to record our concert and run further subjective tests, with and without infrasound, in laboratory settings to add some rigour to our experiments. We may also use our generator in a new mass experiment, exposing people to infrasound in the absence of music.

In our open rehearsal, questionnaires only were used to gauge subjective responses. But there is scope for us to consider other parts of the reaction triad during the show, for example by filming members of the audience to assess expressive behaviour. Ciarán is also hoping to record and study GéNIA's reactions in each concert, particularly the moods she is trying to create during certain musical passages. He would like to compare her intentions with the audience's response.

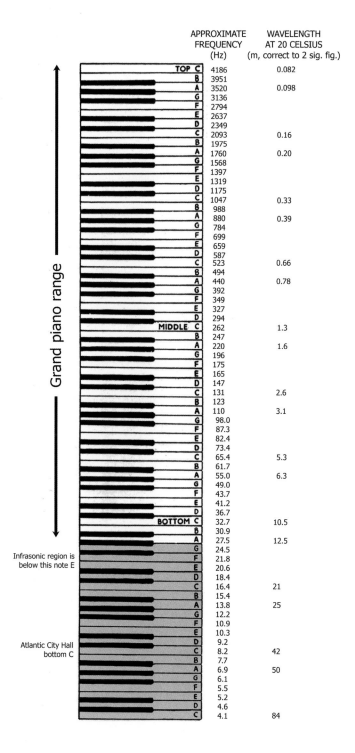

	APPROXIMATE FREQUENCY (Hz)	WAVELENGTH AT 20 CELSIUS (m, correct to 2 sig. fig.)
TOP C	4186	0.082
B	3951	
A	3520	0.098
G	3136	
F	2794	
E	2637	
D	2349	
C	2093	0.16
B	1975	
A	1760	0.20
G	1568	
F	1397	
E	1319	
D	1175	
C	1047	0.33
B	988	
A	880	0.39
G	784	
F	699	
E	659	
D	587	
C	523	0.66
B	494	
A	440	0.78
G	392	
F	349	
E	327	
D	294	
MIDDLE C	262	1.3
B	247	
A	220	1.6
G	196	
F	175	
E	165	
D	147	
C	131	2.6
B	123	
A	110	3.1
G	98.0	
F	87.3	
E	82.4	
D	73.4	
C	65.4	5.3
B	61.7	
A	55.0	6.3
G	49.0	
F	43.7	
E	41.2	
D	36.7	
BOTTOM C	32.7	10.5
B	30.9	
A	27.5	12.5
G	24.5	
F	21.8	
E	20.6	
D	18.4	
C	16.4	21
B	15.4	
A	13.8	25
G	12.2	
F	10.9	
E	10.3	
D	9.2	
C	8.2	42
B	7.7	
A	6.9	50
G	6.1	
F	5.5	
E	5.2	
D	4.6	
C	4.1	84

Grand piano range

Infrasonic region is below this note E

Atlantic City Hall bottom C

Fig. 12
An extended piano keyboard, showing the fundamental frequency of each note. Middle C is at approximately 262 Hz. This chart is for a piano tuned to an equally tempered scale at modern pitch (A=440 Hz).

Our event in Liverpool prompted a very interesting inquiry from biophysicist Dr Mark Lythgoe, who offered to complement our work with some physiological measurements in the lab. These would expose subjects to infrasound while looking for evidence of its effects on the emotional centres of the brain. We have already sketched out some tentative plans to mix MRI scans, observing the limbic system, with measurements of metabolites in the blood and urine. Our next test is to find a reliable way to produce high levels of infrasound in a cramped laboratory. Earphones are one solution, but we also want to study infrasound detected through the body, for instance using subjects who are deaf.

In recent concerts in the UK and USA, GéNIA has been talking to many other composers about our work with infrasound. Hopefully, she can interest a community of electroacoustic composers to incorporate infrasound, extending the frequency range of their work. If we are able to confirm a connection between infrasound and emotion, our pipe could become a very interesting element in future live performances.

64-foot pipes

This list of the world's biggest organ pipes has been compiled by David Willey, London, UK.

Only two venues in the world have true 64-foot pipes: Sydney Town Hall, Australia, and the Convention Hall, Atlantic City, NJ, USA. Others on this list use the physical principle of 'sum and difference tones' to produce very low pitches. Rather than a single 64-foot pipe, they consist of two smaller pipes that play together. Their tones combine to produce a ghostly, 'resultant' note at a lower pitch. Its pitch is the difference between the pitches of the original notes (List gives venue then name of pipe).

Auditorio Nacional, Mexico City – **Acustico 64**

Broadway Baptist Church, Fort Worth, TX – **Bourdon Grave 64**

Cadet Chapel, West Point, NY – **Bourdon 64; Dulzian 64**

Central Reformed Church, Grand Rapids, MI – **Gravissima 64**

Chatanooga Auditorium, TN – **Gravissima 64**

Cleveland Auditorium, Cleveland, OH – **Gravissima 64**

Convention Hall, Atlantic City, NJ – **Diaphone Profundo 64**

Davies Hall, San Francisco, CA – **Basse Acoustique 64**

Eger Cathedral, Budapest – **Rezultant 64**

Holy Trinity Lutheran Church, Buffalo, NY – **La Force 64**

Houston Second Baptist Church, Houston, TX – **Gravissima 64**

Hull City Hall – **Gravissima 64**

Irvine Auditorium, University of Pennsylvania – **Resultant Bass 64**

Lawrence First UMC, Lawrence, KS – **Gravissima 64**

LDS Conference Centre, Salt Lake City, UT – **Gamba 64; Trombone 64**

Legion of Honor Palace, San Francisco, CA – **Gravissima 64**

Liverpool Cathedral – **Resultant Bass 64**

Longwood Gardens, PA – **Gravissima 64**

Lorenzkirche Nürnburg – **Tromba 64**

Los Angeles First Congregational Church, Los Angeles, CA – **Gravissima 64**

Mariahilfekirche, München-Au – **Akustikbaß 64**

Messina Duomo – **Gravissima 64**

Milano Duomo, Milan – **Acustico 64**

Minneapolis Convention Center, Minneapolis, MN – **Gravissima 64**

Old South Church, Boston, MA – **Gravissima 64**

Orlando First Baptist Church, Orlando, FL – **Resultant 64**

Radio City Music Hall, New York, NY – **Gravissima 64**

Roosevelt Memorial Park, Gardenia, CA – **Diaphone 64 (resultant)**

Royal Albert Hall, London – **Acoustic Bass 64**

St Fridolin's Münster, Bad Säckingen – **Vox Balenae 64**

St George's Hall, Liverpool – **Resultant Bass 64 (bass C only)**

St Ignatius, San Francisco, CA – **Grand Bass 64**

St Mary, Massilon, OH – **Resultant 64**

St Patrick's Cathedral, New York, NY – **Gravissima 64**

San Francisco Municipal Auditorium, San Fransisco, CA – **Gravissima 64**

Sydney Town Hall – **Contra Trombone 64**

Wanamaker Store, Philadelphia, PA – **Gravissima 64**

Washington Cathedral, Washington, DC – **Bombarde Basse 64**

Woolsey Hall, Yale University, Conneticut, CT – **Gravissima 64**

Worcester United Congregational Church, Worcester, MA –
Grave Acoustique 64

Why not ask an elephant?
We asked organ builders around the world for their thoughts on infrasonic pipes. Here is a selection of their replies:

On 32-foot pipes
In the right musical context, it can set the hairs on the back of your neck on end!

Only large organs have real 32-foot pipes (although smaller organs have electronic versions) and their use is sometimes specified by the composer but always considered optional as a 'luxury' effect that is not really essential to the music.

There are a couple of different ways that 32-foot sounds are used. Sometimes there will be a soft 32-foot stop – this produces what amounts to a purr which can be used underneath a soft string or flute. The tone is felt, as much as heard, and can be very lush, especially in a room with good bass response, i.e., stone or concrete walls. The other major usage is 32-foot reed tone, which amounts to a throbbing to rattling sound, depending on the pipe construction. This produces a very grand sound during full organ passages, and because the tone is harmonically rich, it can really be heard.

The use of 32-foot stops by organists is generally regarded as something kept on a short leash. A full hymn accompaniment or a piece of organ music played with 32-foot registers on for the entire time is something that grows tiresome quickly.

…Perception is everything. Non-musicians may be left wondering if the low rumble is even part of the music. I once pointed out the low sounds while listening with a friend and expecting him to be suitably impressed, and he said he thought the sound was a truck rumbling by outside.

On the extremely rare 64-foot pipes

I have no doubt that pipes of [16 Hz] pitch have a profound effect on the music one hears, but to go to a sound which might be an octave lower...seems to me like a very expensive draught — i.e. breeze — because the sound no longer affects the human body as a tuned sound.

These low notes are a satisfying part of the organ's musical spectrum, but I think pure inaudible infrasound is irrelevant, as it does not exist in the organ (other than in the extremely rare curiosity area).

If there is any real use for these very low frequency sounds, this might finally be the place where electronic synthesis might be useful.

64-foot organ pipes are really only a curiosity. I know only one, in the organ of Sydney Town Hall, Australia. This is a reed pipe, and one side of the boot provides a glass window, so that one can see the tongue opening and closing, which it does, producing an effect like regular taps on a side-drum. Musical utility is, I feel, nil.

Why not ask an elephant?

Acknowledgements

This text was written and compiled by Sarah Angliss, with contributions from Ciarán O'Keeffe, GéNIA, Dr Caroline Watt and Professor Richard Wiseman.

The team are grateful to the sciart Consortium for funding this project and to the NPL for supporting us with their invaluable donation of time, equipment and expertise. This includes the significant contributions of NPL acoustician Mark Jiggins, Dr Richard Lord and Dan Simmons. We would also like to thank the following people for the support, guidance and expertise that made this project possible: Bergit Arends, The Atlantic City Convention Hall Organ Society, Dr Karen McComb, Ravi Deepres, Claire Griffiths, Tim Hunkin, Isabelle Clarke, Colin Fallows, Chauntelle Ingarfield, Dr Mark Lythgoe, National Pipe Organs Register, Graham Norgate, Hayden Parsey, Roddy Skeaping, Verity Slater, Davina Thackara, Clare Thornton, Vic Tandy, Stephen Watkins, Colin Uttley.

References

Altmann J (2001) Acoustic weapons: a prospective assessment. *Science and Global Security* 9(3): 165–234

Broner N (1978) The effects of low frequency noise on people: a review. *Journal of Sound and Vibration* 58(4): 483–500

Daily Mail/ICM poll (1998) http://www.icmresearch.co.uk

Devereux P (2002) *Stone Age Soundtracks: the acoustic archeology of ancient sites.* London: Vega Books

Gavreau V, Condat R, Saul H (1966) Infrasons: generateurs, detecteurs, proprietes physiques, effects biologiques. *Acustica* 17: 1–10

Juslin PN, Sloboda JA (2001) *Music and Emotion: theory and research.* Oxford: OUP

McComb K (2000) University of Sussex, conversation referring to the work of Neil Todd *et al.*, University of Manchester

Meyer LB (1956) *Emotion and Meaning in Music.* Chicago: The University of Chicago Press

Yeowart NS, Bryan ME, Tempest W (1967) The monaural MAP threshold of hearing at frequencies from 1.5 to 100 c/s. *Journal of Sound and Vibration* 6(3): 335–342

Navigating Memories

Psychologist Nigel Foreman, anthropologist Dr Laura Camfield, and artist Jennie Pedley, worked with a group of young people with physical disabilities to create drawings and stories illustrating events in their life histories. These were assembled in chronological order into three-dimensional (3D) virtual environments (VEs), enabling each participant to travel through and navigate their autobiography. The aim was to assess and improve chronological and spatial thinking. An exhibition featuring the work of Jennie Pedley and an interactive virtual reality projection of the group's stories will be held at Camden Arts Centre, London, April–June 2004.

Introduction

Storytelling humanizes time by transforming it from an impersonal passing of fragmented moments into a pattern, a plot, a mythos. [i]

i Kearney R (2002) *On Stories.* London: Routledge, p. 4.

The meeting of art and science has deep resonance for disabled people. Disability and scientific discourse are tightly entwined. Sometimes it has seemed that disabled people exist in society only so long as their differences can be measured or explored, or as long as they can be made the object of scientific study. The relative absence of disabled people as producers of art and culture has suggested that they have only one story to tell – that of their different bodies. Artworks by people with disabilities over the last few decades have shown that this is not so. Disabled people have become active tellers of stories and producers of discourse. Today we can see great cultural achievement in the stories that derive from the vivid personal histories of disabled people themselves.

This project puts science into the service of stories. Its subject is memory, not bodies, and it demonstrates connections between the fragmentation of experience, perceptions of self, processes of representation and the construction of histories. By using memories of young, disabled people to build virtual autobiographies in 3D space, the project offers a glimpse of the complexity of these relationships. More tantalizingly, it also proposes methods for helping disabled people conceptualize time and space. Exploring different forms of navigation through their own past to produce accessible, visual narratives can enable individuals to form a better understanding of historical and chronological events.

The stories and drawings contained in these narratives are themselves highly compelling. Stories are important because they provide a profound and multi-layered account of individuals' experiences that cannot be simply reduced to brief descriptions. It is easy to label any individual; young people, particularly if they are disabled, are sometimes seen as embodiments of labels. Artworks and personal histories confound this simplification. They open our understanding of the individual to doubts, questions and humour.

The links between the different forms of rich and varied data presented in this chapter cause us to understand perhaps a little more of the creative potential that emerges from such bewildering complexity. The spatial representations of personal narratives remind us that our stories and identities are never really linear or simple. To engage in processes of representing, ordering and manipulating memories is to seek to take control of our own stories. When we tell stories and create artworks about ourselves we start to take control of our place in the world.

Colette Conroy

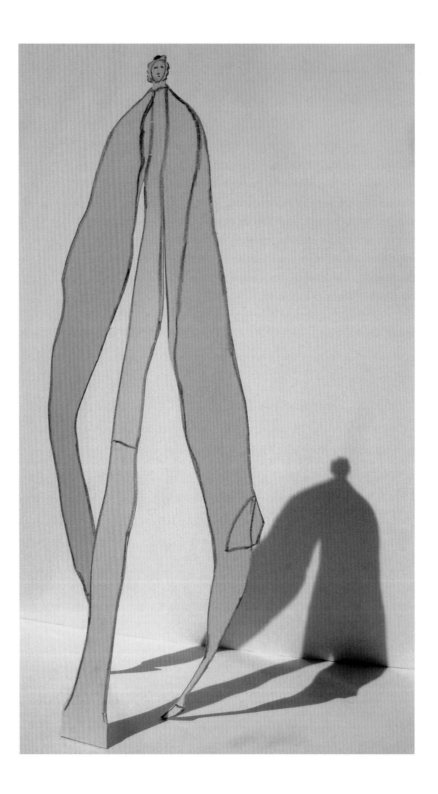

Navigating Memories

Jennie Pedley, Laura Camfield and Nigel Foreman

Spatial perception and chronology

For many people who experience brain damage, or experience physical disabilities, visual and spatial perception is altered. The way in which they interpret the visual world, perceive or navigate the space around them, and even experience their own bodies, may be radically changed. In some cases, problems of spatial aware- ness may result from inability to explore space independently since we develop our understanding of the world through childhood activities such as rolling over, crawling, and later walking around (Foreman et al., 1989).

The same may apply to our understanding of time. Time is also 'spatial', the past lying behind us and the future in front. How does this chronological thinking develop in someone who cannot move their body or twist around, and so may have no concept of 'behind'? Difficulty in understanding time, successive life events and sequencing, limits the ability to plan, understand and carry out many daily activities.

In the classroom, a poor time concept must make the learning of history very difficult. How to teach history in a vivid and memorable way is a universal challenge for educators; but perhaps, due to their unconventional understanding of time–space relationships, it becomes particularly acute when working with young people with learning difficulties (Wilson, 1988). Various strategies have been developed to help students with disabilities to understand chronological events. These include the 'washing line' (pictures of events pegged sequentially along a line as a metaphor for ordering those events in time), handling artefacts like tools and domestic equipment, or dressing up in period costume and making field trips to castles. Video and other media are sometimes used to reinforce these experiences.

Before learning about historical periods, students are often introduced to historical and chronological concepts by being asked to think about events in their own lives. They may represent these by drawing a 'road of life' prior to mapping historical events in the same way (Sebba, 1994), or be encouraged to concentrate on the emotional aspects of situations (e.g. 'What would it have felt like to go into battle on a rigged sailing ship?') (Turner, 1998). One of the aims of the current project was to use virtual reality (VR) technology to allow time-related events to be experienced continuously and sequentially. Since the understanding of sequences is essential to many life skills, improvement in this aspect of cognition would stimulate intellectual development and, therefore, might also improve employment opportunities.

VEs and drawing

VEs have the benefit that an individual with limited movement skills can navigate under their own control through a virtual space, using a mouse, keyboard keys or joystick. He or she can thus experience a novel freedom of movement, taking control of their own activities and planning ahead. The value of VEs amongst children and adults with disabilities to promote understanding of environmental layouts has already been widely demonstrated (Brooks et al., 2000; Wilson et al., 1999).

VEs have been used in many ways in special-needs education (Foreman, 2000), but extension to the time–space domain represents an entirely new application. An important feature of the present project was that participants generated their own materials for the VE through drawing, rather than navigating in an environment built by someone else. To use drawings in this context creates an intriguing contrast between participants' own handmade images and the slick atmosphere of 3D programs. The drawings they created were affected by their

motor control and ability to plan the design, but also revealed difficulties with spatial–visual perception. Creating a 3D digital environment using these drawings perhaps allows others to glimpse how these young people 'see' the world.

Recruitment and assessment

Potential participants recruited by Action for Kids were invited to attend a drop-in day held at their centre in Hornsey, north London, during which the project was explained to them and they were given various assessment tasks. The project created particular difficulties vis-à-vis confidentiality since some of the material produced by the participants was personal in nature and could potentially be used for public display. This was carefully explained to the group members who were made aware that they could withdraw their material at any stage of the project, including the final exhibition, and from any publications that might arise.

The purpose of the assessment tasks was two-fold: firstly, to assess skills, including abilities to perceive, communicate and draw, and to ensure that the individual was able to participate and benefit from participation in the project; and secondly, to measure skills prior to the programme so that comparison with post-participation scores would indicate whether these had improved.

Despite their enthusiasm for the project, several participants were initially reluctant to draw. To provide motivation, Jennie helped them experiment with a variety of techniques including frottage (rubbing textures with crayons) and reaching into bags to feel objects inside which they then drew.

Fourteen people with disabilities volunteered to take part, of whom 11 were recruited. Three could not be included due to severe communication difficulties. In the course of the ten weekly workshops, five participants dropped out giving health or non-availability as reasons. The final six participants who finished the programme were aged 15, 16, 18, 21, 23 and 30 years, and all had different forms of cerebral palsy.

Cerebral palsy is a disorder of posture and movement caused by various types of damage to the brain around the time of birth. It is an extremely broad term, covering a wide range of conditions. The condition is frequently associated with perceptual and/or cognitive difficulties and is classified according to the parts of the body in which motor control is most affected. In the current group, two people had hemiplegia (affecting mainly the left side of their bodies), two had quadriplegia (affecting their whole body) and one had diplegia (affecting mainly their lower limbs). Another group member had ataxic cerebral palsy, which affects control and co-ordination of movement across the whole body.

Prior to taking part in the workshops, testing was carried out on participants using pencil, paper and a standard laptop computer. Five sets of tests were applied: the Benton line orientation test (adapted from Benton, 1955); the Gollin incomplete figures test (adapted from Gollin, 1960); the Beery-Butenika test of visual motor integration; VR navigation tests and sequencing tests (see pp 229–235 for details and diagrams).

The pictures on the left show the group members' freehand style and on the right the self-portraits they made by tracing photographs.

Another exercise involved making large-scale drawings on the wall using a long bamboo stick with charcoal or oil pastels attached. Some group members commented that they particularly enjoyed this way of working, enabling them to make larger gestures and more expressive, confident drawings.

Procedure and workshops

i Statistical test results are provided at the end of the chapter (pp 232–235).

During the ten weekly sessions, each participant worked on two separate tasks. They first related their life histories and stories to Laura Camfield on a one-to-one basis in a quiet room. Subsequently, working with the other team members and staff from Camden Arts Centre led by Jennie Pedley, they produced drawings illustrating important events in their lives. After each session Jennie would scan the drawings in 3D Studio Max and begin to build scenes based on their stories. Following further consultation with the group, Nigel Foreman, assisted by staff at Middlesex University, constructed the 3D autobiographies.

A month after the final workshop session all participants returned to the centre to take part in a follow-up day, when they were able to view their fly-through environments. Screens begin blank but are successively revealed via a mouse click. They also repeated the tests used in the initial drop-in day to check for any changes in their cognitive function.

Results[i]

We were cautious about drawing conclusions about development in specific cognitive functions on the basis of a small pilot group, although some general changes were clear. While participants had initially found it difficult to think of just three significant events for inclusion in a chronological series, they could now

As a way of helping members of the group who found planning creative 3D constructions difficult, Jennie suggested building stage sets and acting out life events with plasticine props and figures made of pipe cleaners.

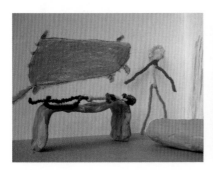

easily remember, describe, and chronologically situate a number of events. Four out of six participants stated that they now felt more confident about being able to remember significant life events in their proper order. All participants said that, had they been embarking on the project at that point, they would have included additional or alternative materials. Three participants had spontaneously included 'future' events in their autobiographies, suggesting that producing the work had encouraged them to think about their futures as well as their pasts. The fact that, on completing the programme, all participants said they were now able to think of more sequential events in their lives suggests that more preparation, and opportunities to think through life events, might make the process more productive in the future.

With the exception of one group member, all were able to identify their draw-ings associated with events and place them in chronological order. One participant also identified a frame in their 3D autobiography that was placed incorrectly. So drawings appeared to be meaningful to them, perhaps reflecting their active role and effort in producing the images. Two participants, however, said that they had had difficulty thinking of events to draw and found drawing difficult. Overall, lack of enthusiasm for drawing was the main reason for withdrawing from the project. As we had asked them to think back over childhood, the materials they produced were related to earlier periods in their lives (the youngest was 15 years

A chronological sequence illustrating loaves baked on an island where the participant spent a memorable holiday; a self-portrait with his new wheelchair; an Action for Kids day out; and (in the distance) the participant supported in a standing position by his father at the most recent event in the sequence.

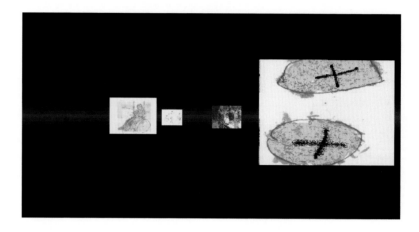

old, the oldest 30). This might have contributed to the feeling that some images seemed juvenile. Training in drawing skills was not felt to be a solution to this since the quality of the experiences recorded was the main objective and outcome of the project. Laura found family photographs a particularly useful way of sharing and discussing memories. Jennie felt that difficulties with drawing revealed perceptual and motor problems as indicated by the visual motor tests.

Some members of the group were keen to talk about their experiences of discrimination, as well as hospitalization, treatments and the prognosis of their condition. At the same time, the fact that they had many interests in common with ordinary teenagers emphasizes the degree to which the lives and preoccupations of people with disabilities differ little from those of the able-bodied.

Creating VEs allowed the group to explore their own life histories in new ways. The VEs are not realistic documentary descriptions of life experiences, but digital spaces presenting stylized illustrations of young people's lives. As an educational approach, the project demonstrates the possibility of using VEs to enhance time–space awareness, and as a tool for discussing personal histories and planning for the future. It remains to be seen whether they also have benefits in teaching history, to those with or without special needs.

References and further sources

Akhutina T, Foreman N, Krichevets A, Matikka L, Narhi V, Pylaeva N, Vahakuopus J (2002) Improving spatial functioning in children with cerebral palsy using computerised and traditional game tasks. A. R. Luriya Conference, Moscow, September

Benton AL, Van Allen MW, Fogel ML (1964) Temporal orientation in cerebral disease. *Journal of Nervous and Mental Disease* 139: 110–119

Brooks BM, McNeil JE, Rose FD, Greenwood RJ, Attree EA, Leadbetter AG (2000) Route learning in a case of amnesia: the efficacy of training in a virtual environment. *Neuropsychological Rehabilitation* 9: 63–76

Foreman N (2000) Finding a place for virtual reality in special needs education: a review. *Themes in Education* 1: 391–408

Foreman N, Orencas C, Nicholas E, Morton P, Gell M (1989) Spatial awareness in seven to eleven year-old physically handicapped children in mainstream schools. *European Journal of Special Needs Education* 4: 171–179

Foreman N, Stirk J, Pohl J, Mandelkow L, Lehnung M, Herzog A, Leplow B (2000) Spatial information transfer from virtual to real versions of the Kiel locomotor maze. *Behavioural Brain Research* 112: 53–61

Rose FD, Brooks BM, Attree EA *et al* (1999) A preliminary investigation into the use of virtual environments in memory retraining after vascular brain injury: indications for future strategy? *Disability and Rehabilitation* 21: 548–554

Sebba J (1994) *History For All.* London: David Fulton Publishers

Turner A (1998) "It would have been bad": the development of historical imagination and empathy in a group of secondary age pupils with severe learning difficulties. *British Journal of Special Education* 25: 164–166

Wilson MD (1988) *History for pupils with learning difficulties.* London: Hodder and Stoughton.

Wilson P, Foreman N, Stanton D (1999) Improving spatial awareness in physically disabled children using virtual environments. *Engineering Science and Education Journal* 8: 196–200

One member of the group wanted to make posters about an issue she felt strongly about and an event she was organizing. She created the text and the images that Jennie assembled.

Do not discriminate against people who have a disability.
People like me for example.

Participants' life stories

Marcus

Age 6 months I remember being in an incubator with a tube full of red liquid coming out of my nose – that's why I'm so dark now. Everything was dark. I think my memories come from my mother telling me about it. Now I dream about the incubator closing in on me.

2 years I went to Center Parcs with my play scheme.

3 years I remember getting a toy police car with red and blue lights and sirens that were really good in the dark. I went to a play scheme where I was the only kid with disabilities and I got attention from the girls. I remember sitting in a circle of bushes with a girl on a bench and kissing her on the cheek – it felt nice. I also remember snuggling up to a girl on a cinema trip. Girls are fascinating because they think differently and are easy to have good conversations with. I remember the care and mothering I had at the play scheme, where I had lots of female friends – somehow I always end up talking to girls.

4 years I learnt how to sing with a girl-charming whistle (I come from a very talented family).

5 years I started school but still went to the play scheme in the evenings. Initially I was scared because I would be interacting with able-bodied people and people from new cultures like Turkey. They were all black at the play scheme, except one Indian and one Pakistani girl. People asked me why I can't walk but I didn't know. I still don't know – why me? I always wanted to do things and other people were always stopping me. I started martial arts after watching a Bruce Lee film and I used to play wheelchair basketball until I had problems with my right hand. It really is a 'bad tale of a boy'.

6 years I was begged to sing at a public event. My Mum was so shocked by how beautiful I sounded that she dropped her glass. Women were so moved they were crying. My mum was really proud and told everyone about it so I had to sing for every new visitor.

I first had sarsparilla, which I love, because my Mum bought it to try and didn't like it.

7 years I didn't get to go anywhere much. I'd heard about Pen Darren in Wales and they told me I could go there in 3 years, when I was older. I worked hard and well, and made friends and waited. When I was ten the Head told me that I wouldn't even be considered as Pen Darren doesn't have facilities for people with disabilities. I knew it was bum fluff as I saw people with disabilities go there when I was in year 3. I was very angry; I was screaming, swearing and crying.

8 years My little sister was born and I was really happy about it. She was like a new play toy. She was sitting, sleeping, making little groany noises, and was the spitting image of me when I was younger. Of course, now she's a right brat, screaming the place down if she doesn't get her own way.

10–11 years I remember getting a bit scared about secondary school and being worried about losing my friends. Before I got there, everyone at my new school seemed so tall – they actually all seemed the same size once I'd been there a while. I soon became a recognized character – people I didn't know were saying hello to me.

I won the 'Shield of Endeavour' in year 6; I was actually the first to get it. I had just received five different certificates in assembly and this big shield was brought out. At first I wondered who or what it was for. I was so excited that I ran over someone's toe on my way to get it, but although the real trophy was chest-sized, my award to keep was hand-sized!

I miss having girls around now. The curvy girls I fancy don't think I'm cute. All I get are little waves – no hugs and kisses. It all changed when I was 13 and my voice broke and my face matured. From being 'cute little Marcus', I was thinking, "Damn, I'm ugly". I don't get noticed anymore and now I get "no" when I ask people out. I can't get used to it.

13 years My little sister was screaming the place down because she wanted a dress on my birthday. My physios baked me a birthday cake. But my new voice meant I couldn't sing. I try to imagine singing again, but in a manly, sexy voice. But practising is frustrating because I'm not getting any results. I couldn't walk with my new walking frame, which really upset me because I tried so hard with my physio to stretch out my leg, but my body still worsened. My parents were calling me lazy but I tried so hard. My mum was blaming me but the doctor explained that you can get worse, however hard you try. Maybe I'll never be able to walk, though I thought I would when I was a kid, like everyone else. Able-bodied people see me as a boy in a wheelchair. To them, that's what matters, even though I'm just as brainy and good at making friends as they are.

Future I want to sing, and to travel, even though I've never been outside the UK. I also want to drink milk fresh from the cow! I'd also like to publish more of my poetry. I never thought of writing poetry because I couldn't write songs when I was younger, but I've developed my own style with lots of swear words in it. My first poem was about my incubator experience and my frustration at trying so hard and still falling behind. I called it *My fucked-up life*. My friend tried to protect me by throwing it in the bin, but the supply teacher really liked it because he said it was hard-hitting. Before I thought my class didn't like me, but now I realize I'm actually an important part of the class. My class encouraged me to write more and more. My next poem was called *I wonder*, then *Clouds of red*, then the poem I got published, which was called *Strawberries*.

Five Finger mountain
in Nicosia, Cyprus, with
the Turkish flag flying.
Drawing produced using
the bamboo stick and
crayons as shown on
p. 184.

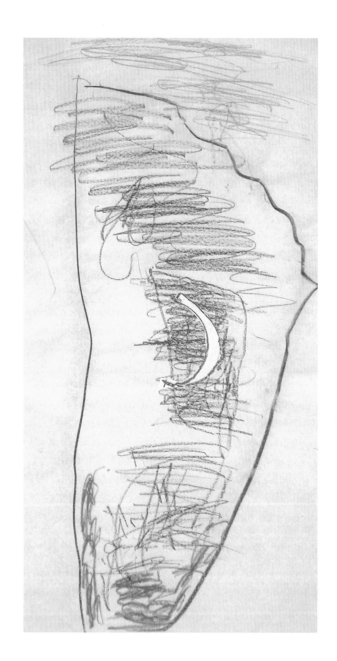

Victor

I was born in Limassol in Cyprus, like my dad. My mum was born in a village in Cyprus and brought up very strictly.

I remember leaving Cyprus after the invasion, when the war started. We weren't forced to leave but my parents also wanted treatment for me. It was sad because we were leaving the 'home country' to go to the UK. At first it was only for a month or so and we were supposed to return, but once I started treatment we were stuck. I was fairly young, which made it worse as more things stick in your mind. I find listening to Greek pop music very evocative.

We were living in Turnpike Road, on top of the hill between Crouch End and Finsbury Park. I don't have any brothers and sisters (it would have been nice), but I have eight cousins, two in Greece and two in the UK, who are as close as brothers and sisters. Funnily enough, I see more of the ones in Cyprus than I do of the ones here. Greek Cypriot families don't need to live together as we're very closely knit; you know they're only a phone call away. That's true of Greek Cypriots over here, but not of the British. They see their grandparents once or twice a year; where we come from Grandad's always there. Every afternoon he's offering to help out at home, or in the shop, or with any building, while Mum and Grandma are making cakes and tea. Aunts, uncles and cousins are all dropping in. They can drop in and out in Cyprus, but in Britain you have

to go up north to see this. Because Cyprus is a small island, everyone knows each other. Villages are very close-knit communities – they may not know a person personally but they would know their granddad or great-granddad. You've got to be careful about the way you act, especially in the villages. Be very aware who's around. It's the way you're brought up.

I was kept on the straight and narrow by my parents, who set me firm boundaries. Because of the treatment I had, all my relatives in Cyprus wanted me to do well so there was a great weight of expectation put on my shoulders and on my mum's and dad's. It accompanied me everywhere; it became too much. The worse thing was I knew that if I couldn't get results (although they'd never accuse me of anything – "you went over there and did nothing"); personally it would have been a nightmare.

I go back home now and everybody's waiting to see an improvement. Yes, I'm 50 per cent improved, but they would want to see me free from the chair, even if I were walking with an aid. They want total freedom for me. They don't blame me, but I can tell I've let them down. As an athlete and a person it hurts more than anything to know I've let them down by not fulfilling their hopes. That's pressure! The last thing Grandad said before he died 2 years ago was, "Try to come back walking so I can see you before I die". I said, "I'm going to try to do it for him to make everybody happy". With everything I've done, something's gone wrong. One step forward, two steps back – it's like snakes and ladders.

Without my parents I couldn't have done anything. I'm angry that I can't give them what they want. My dad always carries an icon next to my baby picture so it's there when he needs it (it's like wearing a cross or carrying a little bible). When he needs strength or inspiration he prays to the icon, or he might talk to a priest or elder. My mum does the same. The pressure is unbearable but I also love it as it pushes me on, makes me want to bring back what they want. No matter how long it takes, I'm going to go home walking. I define myself as an athlete because I've spent all my life training and doing physical activity (I even tried to go to the USA). I've spent nearly all my life looking for a different method of training – swimming, physio, acupuncture – it's like a job. Unless you're involved, you can't understand how difficult it is. Now I've slowed down a little to allow my body to recuperate. My condition is seen as a family responsibility – I remember a great aunt, who my dad grew up with, had a wooden leg. Cyprus needs to improve a few things, like the National Health Service, but basically they have everything.

I went abseiling in my wheelchair and helped other people in wheelchairs by holding the ropes.

I want to go home and get married. That would be really nice and whatever comes after – that is more than welcome. I need to have my hip replaced first though, as I broke it after an accident when I was having physio for a pulled hamstring. The hospital tried to cover the accident up but my dad chased it

Victor's dad's wallet
containing an icon and
a photo of Victor.

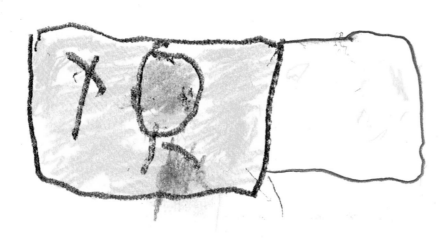

all over the place. They would have given me free surgery for my hip in the end.
A Hungarian orthopaedic surgeon offered to operate. I had to do 4 months'
physio first but I thought, "This is it, I'm going to walk". Before the operation
I had surgery on both my Achilles tendons and my abductor muscles to make
them longer. I also had an operation on my back as I used to lean away from
my dislocated hip. Knowing about my friends' and family's support when I was
recovering brought me through. I was fighting the system in eastern Europe
to get proper treatment – you really needed to know people.

I'm most proud of never smoking or taking drugs. I've kept myself clean
because once you get involved, you're lost. Parents play a role in this because
if they can give you anything you need and share your life, it shouldn't be
a problem. Young people are getting more involved in gangs now, but it's
important to keep on a straight line.

I'm grateful to be here, happy to be alive. I do cry but I don't allow myself
to break down easily. As I tell you my story, I'm visualizing painful experiences
from the past. The important things for me now are training (in a normal gym)
– all the different sorts of physio I've done in England and the rest of Europe –
looking after myself, keeping healthy, and putting the past behind me.

Ducks coming into
our house.

My legs in plaster
with a 'broom handle'
between them.

Nicola

Age 3 years I remember seeing ducks coming into our house but my mother didn't
believe me!

4–5 years When I had to do diaries at primary school, I would make up stories,
like poking my brother in the eye with a knitting needle. When I wrote about
my brother breaking his arm, the school wrote to Mum to sympathize.

7 years I had my first trip to the cinema to see *The Little Mermaid*. It was lovely;
I had a Little Mermaid bag with sweets in it.

11 years I went to secondary school without any of my friends from my class
(because of my disability I didn't have a big choice of schools), but I was
surprised at how fast I made friends.

13–14 years I had an operation to reduce the tightness in my legs. They cut my
abductors at the hips and down the legs and my legs were put in plaster with
a broom handle between them.

I couldn't get into the house and they had to turn me sideways! I couldn't
sleep in my room as I couldn't get up the stairs. I had to sleep at the other
end of the front room and I could hear everything people watched (on TV)
during the night.

My bed was too small (because of the splints) so I kept falling out.
I also got stuck in Dad's armchair for 20 minutes! My classmates were very

After surgery she had a hospital bed in the living room.

A model made by Jennie.

supportive. The whole class stayed together during lunch breaks – we just clicked. Even though I went to mainstream schools my class included me, although some classes didn't. They wouldn't talk to one girl for 2 weeks because she accidentally tipped me out of my chair when she was pushing me!

16 years I had a holiday on my own (without my family) for the first time. It was organized by PHAB[ii] and I went again this year. We stayed in a boarding school in Watford: 18 campers and two helpers each from universities and local sixth forms. You get to be a normal teenager, to make the holiday what you want. We went to the theatre to see *Grease* and watched videos at my helper's house. I was scared at first but the theatre trip convinced me it was a good idea.

18 years I had a great holiday in Portugal. I was very scared the day before as I'm frightened of flying. It was hot and the food was different. It was also hilly so I had my dad pushing me everywhere. I met my best friends, Leah, Niki and Abby, for the first time – I can remember the exact date. I met them all on the Internet, from the Capital FM chat room. I don't go to the chat room now as I have a messenger that tells me my friends are online. I don't really like chat rooms. When people hear I met my best friend through a chat room they don't approve and assume she's an axe-murderer. I've lost contact with my best friend from school now because she tended to mother me and stop me doing what I wanted.

ii **PHAB** is a charity that creates opportunities for people with and without disabilities to share their social lives on an equal basis.

19 years I met Atomic Kitten. I met them again a year later and they remembered
me because I had a photo with them in the local newspaper.

20 years I left college and joined AFK (Action for Kids). I had done work experience with them in the past. For 2 years I wanted to join Chicken Shed to
perform (after doing my admin. courses). At interview they said I had great
potential and got my hopes up, but then they turned me down as there weren't
any places. I didn't want to be put on a waiting list. Now I want to do drama
as a hobby as it's a good way to get my feelings across. I do role-play with
friends on the Internet so I can tell secrets that I wouldn't tell in my own voice.

21 years I had a big birthday party with lots of pop music. My friends were at
one end of the room and my family were at the other! I also went to a Westlife
concert with some new friends – some I'd met on the Internet and the others
at Chessington World of Adventure.

Future Sharing a house with my best friend, Leah, and being near her.

A poster for a concert
that Ilana would like to
organize to raise money
for charity.

Please may you come to a charity concert
to raise money for

CLIMB

Children Living with Inherited Metabolic Diseases.

> To ensure the best possible quality of life for children, young people and families affected by metabolic disease and alleviate their suffering with the ultimate aim of prevention and cure.

The money is going towards the research into the ingredient in the enzyme.

Ilana

Baby I remember being sick all the time. I was fed through a tube and I nearly
starved to death. They were trying to give me a blood transfusion to find
out what caused my condition.

   The transfusion just made it worse. It caused my legs to turn inwards and
go all wrong; I couldn't straighten them. I fell over a lot and banged my knees
on the ground; my dad used to help me get up.

   I was in hospital for 12 weeks and had several operations. They splinted
my legs so it was hard to go to the loo – painful. I was on a ventilator for my
breathing problems. My condition is common all over the world but they have
different ideas about how to treat it.

9–10 years It was the same problem of being sick all the time, like on a school
bus on my birthday. I remember one time I had flu as well and was lying on the
sofa drinking pineapple juice and being sick at the same time. My legs were
too weak to get up and I had to crawl on the floor; it was embarrassing. My dad
took me into hospital and I was given anti-emetic medicine. Once I had a fit
on a plane when I was going to Israel because I didn't have any medication.
My liver doesn't work, it's missing one enzyme; that's why I'm sick so much.
Once I was so sick of being sick I refused to eat food; I nearly starved myself.
I was gasping for breath every 5 minutes.

Ilana in a special care baby unit having a blood transfusion.

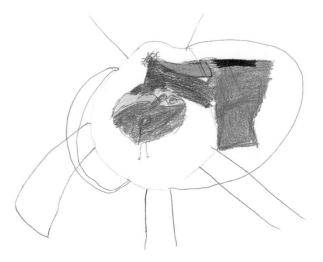

11–12 years I had a hip operation to insert a plate to turn my hip around (the one before, to straighten my legs, hadn't worked). My leg was bleeding internally and it made me collapse on the floor.

18 years My legs were weak and I couldn't move them; they were spasming.

20 years Being sick again, all the time. It takes your life away.

23 years I'm having attacks all the time. I wet my bed 2 weeks ago; it was so embarrassing when my mother found out. My brother was there and he tried to calm her down.

All my friends are able-bodied but they understand how I feel. People copy me when I clap and walk and so on; it happened at my last college. One girl did it many times and got me angry; I had to see a counsellor. My tutor didn't give a damn; the girl got more support than I did. I live with it every day and night. Nothing goes right for me. I often feel so weak I can't stand up; it's painful. I don't want to say, "this will be okay" if it won't. People don't understand; they discriminate against you when you have cerebral palsy. At the swimming pool they won't let you play with other kids; they exclude you from a group. I've been discriminated against twice, at school and college. I want to make a poster about the need to be nice to people and ignore their colour, religion, etc. People are horrible across the world but it will come back on them, like karma. The way people walk, talk and mock people out of hand, the way they make fun – that's why I want to do a poster.

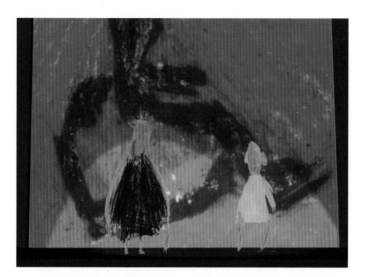

I'm doing a charity concert for people with liver and digestive problems who need to feel like normal people because they had no chance to make their bodies work properly. People have died from this – I want to help them stay alive. Many other countries don't have money for equipment. I will need medication for the whole of my life, even though I get fed up taking medicine with me everyday. I'm going to go on a high-protein diet so I can eat carbo-hydrates without my mother having to weigh them. Then I'll be glad to eat cake and everything and be like other people.

I used to have physio twice a week at school with a Swiss woman, then at home with a German woman to reduce the stiffness in my legs. I used to play on an electric bed.

I still fall on the pavement sometimes. I have a wheelchair at home with a cushion and a sheepskin but I don't need to use it that often. I have a scooter to go to the shops and back but it's too big to use at home. People look at you as if you're doolally if you're in a wheelchair. I get on with my dad but I argue with my mum. I've got two brothers (one's a pain in the neck, the other in the backside) and a sister, all younger. I like college; I'm doing Business in September, with learning support.

Food that I can't eat.

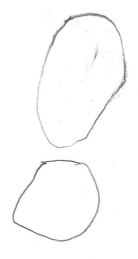

Future There's a high-protein medicine that could be tested on me when I'm 30. But I could die from it. At the moment I'm not allowed to eat eggs, cheese, etc. and I can't take any tablets as my stomach can't take it. I'm scared now. I want to get rid of my medicine and everything I have to have at the moment, like daily blood tests. I used to ruin my fingers doing it everyday, even though I've been terrified of needles since I was a baby.

I would like to sing as a hobby. I'm too embarrassed to sing in front of others. I like computers; I order CDs on the Internet so I don't have to go back and forth to the shops. I phone up friends and I go out when I have the time, usually to Brent Cross. I also go to my grandma on Sundays.

I had a make-over in a
Nigerian national costume.

Edna

Baby I remember being in a cot and having to lie down. I don't remember having any toys or games.

2 years I went to school for the first time. I remember being nervous but it got better. I used to go out on trips – trips to museums like the Science Museum, which had paintings of artists at work. I also went to the resource centre to cook, garden, and have mobility training. I like making cakes, especially chocolate ones; I find them beautiful.

4–5 years It was strange when my brother was born, when he came out of my mum. I wasn't worried beforehand but I was expecting a girl. I wanted a girl because girls are pretty.

6–7 years I went to Paris with my school. We went swimming and I remember having lunch outside. I don't remember any other holidays, or going to see relatives. Actually, I've never met them because they live in Africa, in Ghana. I might go and see them in the future. My parents have lots of friends so I don't miss them. I have dinner with my parents' friends instead.

13 years My sister was born. I liked cuddling her. She looked just like me when I was young. I've got three younger brothers and one sister. They're 13, 11, 12 and 4. The oldest is okay; he's not too annoying.

Edna visits Center Parcs.

Edna in the expensive
shop that she would like
to work in.

14 years I went to Blue Peter to see how the programme was made. I met
S Club 7. I went on my own!

15 years I had a makeover when a woman came to school to show us Nigerian
national costume.

16 years I went camping and sailing with a school group from Bounds Green.
I go to Scout meetings every week and last year I did a fête to raise money
for AFK. I went to a restaurant – it was fun. I also went to a fair. My school
moved to a new site I don't remember anything else about school. I had
my 16th birthday party. It was a celebration with loads of people, including
friends from school. We danced – it was so special.

I went on holiday with my helpers.

I did work experience with AFK. It was all right. I was inputting data and
using databases and there were lots of others from my school.

17 years I started my sixth form. There was a football tournament with a group
of schools. There were people coming to the school to do pop music and soul
the week before the end of term and the singers got people to join in. In the
last week of term there was a music concert with staff performing S Club 7
for a joke. I like performing and going to discos – it's especially interesting
because it's a mixed school. Sports day is very interesting. I don't go out with
friends from school; I go to the cinema with a club organized by the respite
centre but I don't remember the last film I saw. It's called the 'sleep-over club'

and I go every 6 weeks from Friday to Sunday. We don't just to go to films;
we also go to the park.

I remember Christmases because at Christmas we have a special dinner
with potatoes and chicken, but no Christmas pudding because nobody likes it.
I remember getting a painting set one year, with lots of tubes of paint; I use
it a lot. I like to paint people. I don't have a favourite artist though.

In our house we have a living room, three bedrooms (I have my own), a
bathroom, and a garden, which is okay. We live in Muswell Hill, which is a nice
area because you can play in the Field (that's a big park). I play football with
my sister; I also like running around with her. We moved last year but I don't
remember it. We have more space compared with the old house in Tottenham
but it's a longer journey to school by special bus.

Future I want to go to college to study computers and then go to university to see
if I like it or not. I would like to do more painting. I don't think I want to travel.
I would also like to work in a shop, selling expensive things like mobile phones
and CDs.

Charlotte

I used to go to the USA every year when I was a kid as my grandad had a
house out there. I would get in the pool with him when he returned from work
and we'd swim at night too. When my grandad died, I remember my mum
crying a lot and going out to the USA for the funeral. He was buried near the
RAF base. My stepgrandmother and her son then moved to St Louis (my
grandma divorced Granddad when my mum was young and they both remar-
ried). Mum would visit her dad in the USA on her own every summer holiday.
She would like to live out there but Dad doesn't want us to have American
accents! I was born in Westminster, then we moved to Chardmore Road in
Stoke Newington and I went to Tyson School. I remember the man who bought
our old house fell down the stairs and died. Then we moved to Watermint Quay
(I remember the houses really clearly from now on) and I went to Stormont
School until year 10. Then we moved to Barnet and I went to Whitevilles, which
integrated children from Hackney, Barnet and other places. I was there for
years 10 and 11 but when we moved to New Barnet I went to Barnet College
for my sixth form. I didn't like Whitevilles because there was a rude boy who
picked on me in my Textiles, English, Art, and Business classes. I was going to
stay on for my sixth form but he stayed on so I couldn't. My helper left, but then
I had another and I spent most of my time in her office. I had to write down

when he picked on me. He was white but he thinks he's black; he thinks he knows everything. I couldn't change my lessons to avoid him because I was halfway through the year.

I remember when my mum had Hannah because Dad was looking after me and Lucy. Mum asked him to bring us to see her and he put my dress on back to front. We brought teddies for her; I think she still has them.

9 years This was the last time we went to the USA. I fell down the polished wood stairs in my granddad's house and there was blood everywhere. They took me to hospital and I had a private room and a telly. It wasn't as noisy as hospitals in Britain – in Barnet Hospital they only had BBC1, so I missed Pop Idol.

10 years I remember a funny thing that happened on holiday in Spain that year, when I accidentally locked myself in the bathroom. My dad had to kick the door down while I stood in the bath!

16 years My nan died of cancer; I knew she was in hospital but I didn't know how bad it was. I woke up at 2.00 a.m. or 2.30 a.m. and my mum had gone. When I woke up again at 9.00 a.m. my mum said she'd died. We were both crying. We had a party as Nan didn't want a funeral and we scattered her ashes at Selfridges because she shopped there all the time. I also went to AFK for the first time. I was recommended by my teacher at Whitevilles because my mum said I was bored all the time and I didn't do anything. I do data inputting, filing, and writing letters there. My friend comes as well.

17 years (Easter 2001) I spent 2 weeks in Thailand with my mum, my dad,
and my two sisters. It was really nice; we stayed in Koh Samui in bungalows.
I remember when my sister got trapped in the bathroom after seeing a cock-
roach and my other sister kicked the door down. It was only a bamboo panel
so we saw her foot coming through the door. I remember going to get some
cash before going to Brent Cross with a friend. When I cut through Waitrose
car park, I tripped over a grey stone and bruised my lip and hurt my head.
My mum took me to hospital because I was concussed and I had to stay
overnight. I was slipping off the bed because the mattress was so slippery
and I couldn't sleep because the woman who'd broken her collarbone was
screaming. The doctors checked my blood pressure every hour. My friend told
everyone in college so they all asked if I was okay. I did my BTEC (Business
and Technology Education Council) entry for Leisure and Tourism with a
friend after the teacher swapped me from Business.

18 years My dad's organizing an event in Marbella for Madness. It was meant
to be a surprise that Dad was doing it as he's been friends with the saxophone
player since before Mum and Dad met, but Mum told the guy about it by
mistake. My parents actually met at a Madness concert because Mum was
cooking the food and Dad was doing the lighting. Dad did the Party in the
Park on Saturday but there wasn't a very good line-up. My mum used to work
in a school but she does freelance typing now.

It was my birthday in October and I saw *American Pie 2* with a friend
from college who had left because she found it too difficult. The people at the
cinema wouldn't let my friend in because she's only 4 ft tall and they didn't
think she was 18, but they phoned my mum and she got us in.

I've got a boyfriend, Nathan, who I met 4 months ago on the Internet (he
lives in Kent). He's got a hoop in his ear. My friend at college, Jamie, also met
his girlfriend on the Internet. I met her on the Internet too and I was surprised
because I thought Jamie had imagined her. I talk to lots of people on the
Internet; I spend about 2 hours on it a week. Once I was sent stuff I didn't order
from a dating website called www.chainsofheart.com. It's a service where you
pay to meet people. I want to have my eyebrow pierced but my mum won't
let me. She said I've got two piercings already and she doesn't want me to
have loads of tattoos and piercings. I only wanted to have my eyebrow pierced
though; I didn't want my tongue done because you have to clean it every
time you eat and it can chip the enamel off your teeth.

I'm not very happy that I'm not going away this year. My sister's going to
Felleracci for 2 weeks with friends (the place where they did that programme
about club reps). My mum's worried she'll follow what they do on telly and
doesn't want her to go because of the news reports. My sister has to be
'sensible' while she's out there – no alcohol or drugs and she must stay in
a group. She's only 17 but looks old for her age.

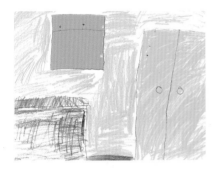 

Future We're moving next Wednesday and Mum's panicking because it's not
all packed.

My parents plan to get a little house abroad when the kids leave home.
My two sisters are at the same school now and one of them is in the sixth form.
I've applied for an IT course in September with my best friend and 30 other
friends because I don't want to be bored. I would like to do my dad's job but
I can't because it involves climbing up high to fix the lights.

Learning to walk
with a walking frame.

David

Ages 2–3 years My brother was born but I don't remember much about it, though I remember going to see him with my dad and Aunty Sandra. My mum chose Vale school for me after looking at all sorts of schools. It made me more academic and I had really good fun.

5–7 years I remember learning to walk without holding onto anything. I had special boots until my mother found me some Caterpillar boots that support my feet. They're quite expensive but it means I can wear 'proper' shoes. I went to St Anne's for physio and speech therapy. I used to have long socks up to my knee underneath AFOs (Ankle Foot Orthoses), which support my ankles, but now I have short socks because I don't need AFOs anymore.

6 years I was having dinner with my younger brother one night while my mum was pregnant and we were thinking about whether the baby would be a girl or a boy. I wanted a girl and my brother wanted a boy. That night my mum went into hospital and the baby was born. I only realized this when I called out in the morning to ask my dad to help me out of bed and my Aunty Sandra came instead. I started to cry when I knew she'd had the baby. I went to school in the morning and my dad picked me up and took me to the hospital in Crouch End in the evening (via the flower shop). My mum was in hospital for a few days. My parents then decided they didn't have enough room in our house so

we moved from south to north Tottenham in colourful old-fashioned removal
lorries (they were a mixture of dark and light colours, even purple). After
the lorry went off my dad drove us to the new house in his car. The previous
owners had gnomes around their pond. Tim and I kept falling in so my parents
got rid of the pond and replaced it with grass. I remember my dad with large
ear-muffs over his ears because the sound of the drill was so loud when he
was digging up the pond. This was the only time I've moved, but my parents
want to move to the country when we leave school. I share a room with my
brother; my sister has her own room.

8 years I went into year 4. I remember my head teacher leaving the school. A fake
policeman cuffed her to the PE bars in the hall in the leaving assembly! She
now works with my mum. We got a new head teacher, who was the best one
Belmont has ever had. She could play the piano and taught us African songs.
Her daughter used to make special badges for us if we achieved things and
we had special assemblies and music concerts. Mr Wood would get us
to do murals and, most recently, we did a beach with beach huts. I liked our
teaching assistant at Belmont. She was called Bernadette and she was quite
small. Now I'm taller than her, which I hate because I don't like being taller
than adults, even my parents! I like to go back to Belmont whenever I can.

8–10 years We went to the Isle of Wight every year on holiday.

10 years I joined Chicken Shed theatre but then missed the next year because of my SATs (Standard Assessment Tests).

    I was lucky they accepted me back but I would have found it too pressurized to do both things – in year 6 it was all 'go, go, go'. I also had my first bike ride without stabilizers.

9 years When I was coming back from my granddad's house, the person in front of us on the escalator collapsed, knocking me and my granddad over. The fall was really frightening for my granddad – now he won't take me anywhere on the train on his own. My granddad lives in south London and I see him with my brother and sister. Sometimes we go down for the day and go to the park together to let him nap.

11 years I rejoined most of my friends at the Vale after some time at Belmont. It was strange at first but nice. I was bullied in year 7 but this was a tough year for everyone as we were all trying to fit into a new school. In year 8 I was moved to another class. I would have done better in PE at the Vale than NPCS (Northumberland Park Community School) as they teach to age, not ability, in NPCS. The teachers are now trained to work with people with disabilities but they occasionally make mistakes; for example, one told me to do eight laps around the Astroturf! The Vale teacher told me I should have done half that, especially as it's one of the biggest Astroturf's in London. I did a cycling proficiency test and got my certificate, even though I found signalling difficult.

My hearing aid mould.

Granddad and me falling
on the Tube escalator.

Bicycle proficiency test.

My brother wanted to do it as well but he left it too late so I trained him anyway.
I went to North Wales (I remember having long hair then). I cycled down the
Lea canal from Tottenham Hale to Enfield to Broxbourne (where the path gets
bad) and then to Hertford. Now I want to cycle the Regent's Park canal. I get
a bit scared when I go through the lock gates (I think "one wobble and I might
go in") and I won't go along the canal on my own. I gave up PE in year 8 but
I still do school sports days at the end of the year.

I have problems with my hearing aid so I have special fax sheets to (use to)
fax my hearing advisor so they can sort the problem out quickly. Last year
there was a boy just like me at the Vale, which was good as before I was the
only deaf person. He has slight hearing problems and has been bullied about
his hearing aid so doesn't want to wear it anymore. I have tried to persuade
him as it could be a problem when he goes into mainstream education. I know
I hated wearing a hearing aid when I was younger as I didn't want to be
different from everyone else. Now I have a plain hearing aid mould, but I had
red and blue ones before (the first made my ears look like they were bleeding,
and with the second everyone kept asking if they were cold!) I wanted a
Tottenham Hotspur one with a shield but it wasn't possible for my type of ear
mould. I'm going to get a new 'digital' one in January, which filters out background noise. They say it's quieter but more efficient.

NAVIGATING MEMORIES   225

15 years I got good results in my exams in June, did work experience and had a
really nice end of term. I remember watching *Cats and Dogs*, and watching the
Vale students perform in the end of term concert which they'd been rehearsing
for half the term. I see my friends in the holidays but I do get very bored, especially when I'm staying at home all day or it's too hot to go out and do anything.
I went to the USA in March 2002 and I also go to see my grandparents in
Shaftesbury and to Yorkshire, where we stay in a holiday cottage. My dad had
the last week of his holidays off and we went for days out around London, like
to the Science Museum and the Sherlock Holmes Museum. My brother Tim
likes going on trains, so last year we went on a big train trip around London.
I also want to go on the Millennium Bridge before it closes again. Last year we
went to Suffolk and the year before that to Yorkshire, where I had the accident
on my bike. We're going walking in the Lake District this year but it'll probably
be more like climbing than walking! Then we'll go to see my great-aunt
Margaret in Carlisle, whom I've never met, though she sends me money and
letters every year.

During the week I don't cycle as I do my homework, eat, have a bath,
and go to bed. This holiday I did 90 miles in the first 2 weeks, but then it was
too hot to cycle. My dad cycles 16 miles every day to his job in a library in
Limehouse. It's tiring for him because the route is so full of traffic, though he
does take the canals. My mum is a special needs assistant and a dinner lady.

She's worked at Belmont since I left.

Last Thursday I went to a show at Chicken Shed. There's usually one workshop per week, unless there's a special performance. This year we're doing *The Nutcracker*, which brings together adults and children; it's really good because there's a mix of different ages. It gets very intense in October and November because we have rehearsals, then the dress rehearsal (the last one was 4 hours but I remember when they used to be nearly 7!), then 14 shows from early December to late January. I'm worried I won't be able to revise for my mock GCSEs and do rehearsals. I hate pulling out at the last minute but if it's necessary, I suppose I'll have to. I also have to decide which subjects I like best at school (which is difficult because they all have good and bad bits) because I have to decide which college courses to do. I did 80 pages of coursework on my PC last year for just one subject!

My computer.

Perception and sequencing tests used in the workshop programme

1. **Benton line orientation test** (adapted from Benton, 1955)

   Five angled lines were shown, one at a time, which had to be matched against a series of 17 radiating lines, the participant indicating which of the radiating lines matched the angle of the sample. Since we were interested in perception rather than visual memory, the sample and radiating comparison lines were shown simultaneously. Radiating lines were numbered 1–17, and the error score for each sample was the number of lines between the correct angle and that indicated by the participant. The five error scores were summed for each participant.

2. **Incomplete figures test**

   This was an adaptation of the Gollin incomplete figures test (Gollin, 1960) but used stimuli (familiar prototypical figures) sometimes rotated through angles in both x and y axes, thus requiring mental rotations for identification. The percentage of figures on screen at recognition was recorded for each of the eight figures and then averaged. The Gollin test measures higher visual function (incomplete figure perception), which was felt to be important if participants were to perceive and interpret images in 3D autobiographies.

Above diagram shows a complete image in prototypical orientation (left),
a version of the same image at threshold for recognition (middle), and a more
complete representation of a rotated version of the image (right).

3. Beery–Butenika test of Visual Motor Integration

Participants were asked to look at a series of line drawings shown in the upper
half of an A4 page in landscape orientation (three per page), and copy them
in corresponding spaces below. The examples began with lines and simple
figures but became progressively more complex within the sequence of normal
development of drawing skills. Later figures consisted of intersecting and
overlapping shapes. Scoring was conducted according to a standard protocol.
This test further explored whether participants could reproduce shapes,
integrating visual and motor abilities. Scores were allocated to the quality of
drawings according to a standard protocol. Diagram above right shows some
of the easier shapes (upper) along with some participant's reproductions
(lower).

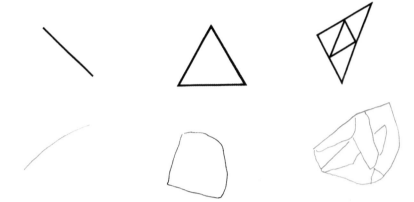

4. Navigation in VR

A complex virtual shopping mall environment (Foreman *et al.*, submitted) was used to allow the participant to navigate using keyboard keys (forward, back, and left and right rotation). Their ability to steer between obstacles and select routes in the virtual environment was noted.

5. Sequencing tests

Participants were presented with a random selection of cards, which they had to place in order of ascending size. Numbers (1, 2, 3, 4, 5 and also 3, 8, 12, 18, 27) were used, and shapes of different sizes. Sequences of daily events (get up, have breakfast, and so on) were also used, and sequences of events occurring throughout the calendar year. Finally, a series of cards with recent historical events had to be placed in order. The error score on each test was the number of cards placed out of correct sequence. Test scores were summed for each participant.

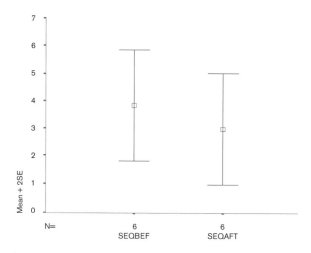

Sequencing errors (SUM)

Results

Sequencing errors

All participants scored zero errors on four simple numerical and size-sequencing tasks, but errors occurred in the four more difficult event-sequencing tasks. Above diagram shows the number of errors (mean and SE) for the six participants before (SEQBEF) and after (SEQAFT) participation. There was no significant reduction in scores, $t(5) = 1.54$, $p = 0.09$ (one-tailed), although the trend was in a downward direction, suggesting that with a larger sample, a significant improvement might have been achieved.

Sequencing errors before and after the training programme were highly correlated, Spearman's $rho(6) = 0.794$, $p = 0.03$ (one-tailed). Those who made most sequencing errors before training also made most errors afterwards.

Gollin score (%)

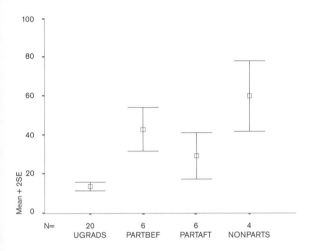

N=	20	6	6	4
	UGRADS	PARTBEF	PARTAFT	NONPARTS

Gollin test

Above diagram (left-hand side) shows the mean and standard error (SE) of scores on the Gollin test (the lower the score, the better the performance) for a group of 20 under-graduate students (10 male, 10 female) who were tested with the same figures as the participant group. The mean scores of undergraduates were signifi-cantly better than those of the participant group at the start of the programme (PARTBEF), $t(24) = 8.12$, $p < 0.001$. The participant group all showed an improve-ment between initial (PARTBEF) and final (PARTAFT) testing, $t(5) = 4.84$; $p < 0.01$; for five-sixths the reduction in percentage was between 24 per cent and 60 per cent, though one participant clearly exhibited a poor perceptual memory only showing a drop of 1.8 per cent. When retested at the end of the programme, the participants were still making more errors than the undergraduate sample (UGRADS) had scored at first exposure to the stimuli, $t(24) = 4.23$, $p < 0.001$. In above diagram (NONPARTS) the mean Gollin score is shown for the initial test session for those participants who were recruited but who did not complete the programme. The latter's scores were particularly high, suggesting that some form of perceptual disability may have discouraged participation.

Unfortunately, it was not possible to retest the non-participant group for control data. Our results are indicative, rather than definitive, pending the collec-tion of equivalent data for a control sample of individuals with similar disabilities.

Gollin v. Benton test scores

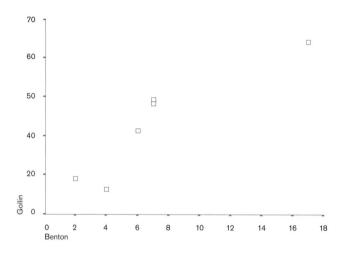

Benton test

There was a significant difference between the Benton error scores of the six participants and those of the four people who were recruited but did not participate, $t(8) = -3.46$, $p = 0.009$, two-tailed, participants making an average of 7.17 errors (+/− SD 5.2), summed across the five judgements, while non-participants scored 17.75 (+/− 3.86). This again indicates that participants having perceptual limitations were most likely to drop out of the programme.

Interestingly, within the participant group, there was a significant correlation between Benton scores and both Gollin scores at initial testing, $rho(6) = 0.93$, $p < 0.01$ (see above) and Gollin scores at the end of the programme, $rho(6) = 0.812$, $p < 0.05$ (two-tailed probabilities). This indicates that Gollin and Benton tests were measuring related perceptual skills, though this has not been shown previously. The strength of the relationship is indicated by its statistical significance in such a small sample. There was no significant correlation between sequencing errors and perceptual test performance, indicating that significant correlations between perceptual measures are unlikely to be explained by the degree to which participants understood or followed instructions.

Beery–Butenika test

Scores on this test, of visual-motor integration, showed no significant correlation with any of the other measures taken, including the perceptual measures. This is not surprising, since the Gollin and Benton tasks require only that the participant looks and matches or recognizes, no reproduction of figures being required. The Beery–Butenika test reflected, in large part, the motor skills of participants. Scores before (range: 11–26) and after participation (11–23) showed little change. Comparing the Beery–Butenika scores of the six participants with those of the four who dropped out of the programme, there was no significant difference, $t(8) = 0.58$; $p > 0.05$, suggesting that while perceptual skills predicted who would complete the programme (see earlier), visual-motor skill did not.

Acknowledgements

Navigating Memories is a Camden Arts Centre project.

The authors gratefully acknowledge the support of the sciart fund and the Calouste Gulbenkian Foundation, the participation of Action for Kids (Shaun French), programming assistance from David Newson (Psychology, Middlesex University) and the assistance of Peter Passmore (Computing, Middlesex University), who created the 3D Gollin test materials, using original models provided from www.3dcafe.com. We are also grateful to Oliver Sumner, Hayley Field and Hazel Northwood (Camden Arts Centre), and David Ingham (Head Teacher, Westbrook School, Derbyshire) who gave helpful advice in the early stages of the project. Adrian Senior provided advice to Jennie Pedley on 3D modelling. Finally, we are grateful to all the participants, who put so much energy into the project and made it so much fun for us, including Victor Antoniades, Ilana Blumenfeld, Charlotte Wynne, Nicola Yates, Leon Brown, Edna Obeng, David Slater, Hannah Wilkinson and Marcus Rowe.

References and further sources

Benton AL (1955) *The Visual Retention Test.* New York: The Psychological Corporation

Foreman, N, Wilson P, Stanton D, Duffy H, Parnell R (submitted) Transfer of spatial knowledge to a 2-level shopping mall in older people, following virtual exploration.

Gollin ES (1960) Developmental studies of visual recognition of incomplete objects. *Perceptual and Motor Skills* 11: 289–298

Viewing the Instruments

Viewing

L'aspect de l'apareil.

the
Instruments

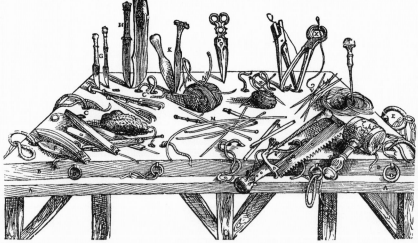

a medical and musical collaboration by
Dr Peter Isaacs, Philip Parr *&* Jane Wildgoose

Undertaken by consultant gastroenterologist, Dr Peter Isaacs, opera director and musician, Philip Parr, and artist and writer, Jane Wildgoose, *Viewing the Instruments* investigated the medical, musical and social history surrounding 'Le Tableau de l'Opération de la Taille' (The scene of the operation of the cut) – an eighteenth-century musical score by the composer Marin Marais. Using the unique nature of Marais's piece as a starting point, they commissioned three new pieces of music from contemporary composers, Eleanor Firman, Eddie McGuire and Rachel Stott, and explored the feelings of patients and medical practitioners provoked by a specific medical procedure. The project culminated in a work-in-progress performance at the Old Operating Theatre in London in November 2001, which presented the four musical scores together with the contemporary and historical findings relating to medicine and music uncovered by the research.

Introduction

The atmosphere in the Old Operating Theatre, Southwark, on 22 November 2001, was electric with anticipation. The room is a curiously splendid space in any case, but to visit it in the evening for a musical event was an intriguing experience for everyone who filed in to find a place on the curved wooden tiers of standings above the operating area.   → Fig. 1

In place of the old wooden operating table were a harpsichord and music stands. As the audience hushed, no one quite knew what to expect. Were these the instruments we had come to view? By the end of the performance, much of this mystery had been dispelled. What we had seen had been choreographed with precision: a trans-historical, aural and dramatic exegesis of a short piece of eighteenth-century music, imprinted with past and present healthcare experiences.

The performance began with a four-minute composition by Marin Marais, 'Le Tableau de l'Opération de la Taille', published in 1725 for bass viol and continuo. As the music was played, a presenter (opera director and musician, Philip Parr) declaimed accompanying passages of old French describing an eighteenth-century surgical operation. The words spread a sense of slight anxiety, since not everyone could understand them. Soon the intention became clear as we heard the recorded voices of people from the present – patients, a nurse, and a doctor – describing their own anxieties before embarking on a modern day-care procedure.

As the performance unfolded we were able to comprehend not only the Marais piece and its historical relationship with cutting for bladder stone, but courtly interest in and the experience of participants at public performances of the operation in eighteenth-century Europe ("there was not a Physician nor Surgeon who did not strive to get in ").[1] These thematic threads were interwoven with old and new images, accounts of an equivalent modern technique – endoscopy under sedation – and music written by contemporary composers performed on baroque instruments. The performance successfully conveyed the contrast between the danger and pain of surgery in the past with the routinization of surgical methods today, accompanied as they are by concerns over the alien aspect of healthcare settings and the pressures exerted on medical teams. The structure of this medical, musical, historical and modern drama seemed effortless, but reflection suggests it was underpinned by prodigious musical, historical and visual research and highly accomplished writing.

Viewing the Instruments is the outcome of an unusual collaboration of individuals and disciplines that breathes life into instrumental medical procedures, addressing matters of mind, spirit and body. The opportunity to hear Marais's original piece in four comparative interpretations, alongside three contemporary compositions and a wealth of historical material, revealed the social and surgical context of this unique work, and awoke reverberations for cutting for bladder stone to be felt today. The result was a performance of classical and new music, melded with modern perceptions and feelings, that reframed our understanding of surgical intervention.

The uniqueness of *Viewing the Instruments* makes it impossible to categorize: an outstandingly memorable experience for all present, which we hope will be seen by many more appreciative audiences before the collaborators who have so expertly created it put their instruments away.

— Brian Hurwitz —

↑   Fig. 2
Marin Marais, Pièce no.108,
Le Tableau de l'Opération
de la Taille

Le Tableau de l'Opération de la Taille
L'aspect de lapareil
Frémissement en le voyant
Résolution pour y monter
Parvenu jusqu'au hault
Descente dudit apareil
Réflexions sérieuses
Entrelassement des soyes entre les bras et les jambes
Icy se fait l'incision
Introduction de la tenette
Icy l'on tire la piere
Icy l'on perd quasi la voix
Écoulement du sang
Icy l'on oste les soyes
Icy l'on vous transporte dans le lit

The Scene of the Operation
Viewing the instruments
Shuddering at the sight
Resolution to get up there
Arriving at the top
Descent of the instruments
(they are brought to the operating table)
Serious thoughts
Tying the arms & legs with silk
Here the incision is made
Introduction of the 'tenette' gripping device
Here one pulls the stone
Here one has almost lost one's voice
Flowing of the blood
Here one unties the silk
Here one takes you to bed

Viewing the Instruments
Jane Wildgoose, Philip Parr, Peter Isaacs

In 1725, the renowned French composer and viol virtuoso, Marin Marais, published a composition for bass viol and continuo – 'Le Tableau de l'Opération de la Taille' ('The scene of the operation of the cut') – that describes, in music and accompanying text, an operation to remove bladder stone." The piece has a performance time of just under four minutes, reflecting the speed of the procedure practised by surgeons in the early eighteenth century.

Le Tableau de l'Opération de la Taille —
The Scene of the Operation

L'aspect de lapareil —
Viewing the instruments

PHILIP PARR I first heard 'Le Tableau de l'Opération de la Taille' over 20 years ago in my first week at university, when – as a first year music student, full of trepidation, self-importance, dates and great works and no real understanding of music – it was presented by members of the department in a welcome concert. The unique qualities of the piece were immediately apparent and the work remained with me on that single hearing.

JANE WILDGOOSE Philip and I had worked together on a number of projects and he suggested we might think of a way to present Le Tableau at the Old Operating Theatre in London (coincidentally, just prior to my first meeting with Peter Isaacs in October 2000). I mentioned Le Tableau to Peter and showed him a copy of the manuscript that Philip had looked up in the British Library, along with a translation of the text. I didn't expect Peter to see the piece as anything more than a curiosity that might amuse him, and it was therefore fascinating to discover that Marais's composition was as inspiring to him – as an historical model with a value in the present – as it was to Philip and me.

PETER ISAACS I wanted to develop parallels with modern practice and to use the historical material to stimulate discussion with medical students, particularly around issues of consent, anaesthesia, risk and good medical practice, then and now. Jane and Philip, and subsequently the composers, Rachel Stott and Eleanor Firman, saw some endoscopic work in BVH (Blackpool Victoria Hospital) and found aspects of it were strong stimuli for them. I was intrigued by how both Philip and Jane made immediate connections between the work in the Gastroenterology unit and theatrical performance: the need for discipline and well-rehearsed teams, with an ability to improvise when required, while the bustle of preparation and transporting patients was similar to activities on stage. This in turn prompted me and my team to re-examine (or see for the first time!) these aspects of our practice, and think about ways in which they might be improved.

Frémissement en le voyant —
Shuddering at the sight

PETER ISAACS Jane and I had discussed how the process of medical training in a young doctor inevitably encourages a degree of detachment from patients' emotions. Although Jane is deeply immersed in history and the social aspects of the body and death, the experience of seeing patients in a frail state undergoing endoscopy was a fascinating, yet shocking experience. Her reaction to this was a reminder of how necessary it is to lose this immediate reaction to painful or disgusting sights to work effectively. Though if the human connection is completely severed, worse disasters can result.

JANE WILDGOOSE The experience of visiting BVH to observe Peter at work was particularly enlightening. Having previously considered, at a theoretical level, the contrast between 'gut' responses to seeing the inside of the dissected human body and 'clinical objectivity', I was still unprepared for my reaction to the endoscopic image of a patient's body enlarged on a monitor during an ERCP (endoscopic retrograde cholangio pancreatogram) session.

Within moments, a patient – who had just walked into the X-ray room like the rest of those present – was anaesthetized, the endoscope inserted down his oesophagus, and its journey simultaneously relayed on a monitor. I was stunned – by my proximity to the patient and the monitor, and by the thought that the hidden, glistening, mobile world magnified on the screen also functioned inside me (without my knowledge), and inside everyone. The contrast between outer and inner, in all its gleaming red palpitation, though not distasteful, was so incomprehensibly different from the way we normally view other people, that I became (rapidly) very faint. Peter was remarkably patient and said that my response was a typical reaction for many students, and a refreshing reminder of the sense of awe commonly experienced when viewing the inner world of the body that had long since become routine for him and his colleagues. Observing subsequent sessions, I soon discovered how quickly the sight became 'normal'.

Résolution pour y monter —
Resolution to get up there

PHILIP PARR   My suspicions are that at the first performance I attended of Le Tableau, the musicians thought the piece was rather a joke – indeed most musicians I know who have come across the piece, and many of those who play it, consider it to be a comic turn or a party piece. What little musical research has been done on the piece has largely dismissed the work as an interesting trifle or curiosity – something quite separate from Marais's regular output – and not to be taken seriously.

   Marais's production for the viol was enormous – over 600 published pieces for solo viol, and a further 100 for two or more. On examining the whole oeuvre spread across the five books of viol music published between 1686 and 1725, a natural progression seems to arise. The earlier works are formal and the suites into which the pieces are arranged follow familiar dance forms, no doubt reflecting the importance of dance in the court of Louis XIV.

Fig. 4
Table in X-ray room used for
ERCP sessions at Blackpool
Victoria Hospital.

As Marais, the composer, gains in authority and experience, we see increasingly the introduction of *pièces de charactère* in which the composer seeks to explore colouration and sound, challenging both the player (presumably himself) and the instrument to come up with new expressive effects. In the early books, titles such as 'L'Inconstante' (a gigue), 'La Guitare' (a minuet) and 'Gavotte dans le gout du théorbe et que l'on peut pincer si l'on veut', show Marais pushing the conventional forms to new extremes. By the fourth and fifth books of *Pièces de Violes*, the dance structures, which were the backbone of viol music, are almost sidelined in favour of pieces with a narrative and descriptive quality. Most important is the 'Suitte d'un Gout Étranger' from the fourth book published just after the death of Louis XIV. Of 36 pieces, ten are dance based and the rest are highly programmatic and exploratory in musical inventiveness and technical development.

Looking then at Marais's output over time, 'Le Tableau de l'Opération de la Taille' falls more normally into a pattern of compositional development. If we remove the spoken text – which perhaps has its origins in the considerable amount of theatre and opera that Marais would have seen, and been involved in, at court – then musically, the piece explores a recitative-like style with each section having a rhythmic freedom that would be impossible to dance to. In this piece he also pushes the range of the instrument to its extreme, introducing the highest possible note playable on the viol – a top C – not previously used by any composer. The note, which extends the player's finger to the furthest reach of the fingerboard, coincides with the point just after the stone has been pulled (Ici l'on perd quasi la voix, *here one has almost lost one's voice*), providing a vivid metaphor for the stretching of the patient's endurance of pain.

It is easy to see that when considered outside its musical and medical contexts, Le Tableau could well appear a 'comic turn'. However, it seems to me that Marais was simply using an extreme situation to push his already well-developed ideas on programmatic music even further. That said, it has long been the convention of musicologists to attribute the peculiarity of the work to Marais undergoing the operation himself, but with that assumption it has been quickly passed by. Even Marais's only biographer, Sylvette Milliot, contents herself with a brief description of the text and images and repeats the conventional explanation that the composition was provoked by an operation carried out on the composer: *la tradition voit ici le récit d'une intervention subie réellement par Marais vers 1720.*[iii]

A number of commentators suggest Marais underwent lithotomy, and give c. 1720 as a likely date. However, none substantiates their theory, and the story seems to have become a case of academic rumour, starting (as far as we can tell) in 1952 in an article by Richard Newton.[iv] This conclusion was not restricted to musicologists. Urologists who have written about the piece – such as Joseph Kiefer, who repeats the suggestion made by musicologist Clyde H. Thompson in 1960 that Marais underwent the operation in c. 1720[v] – have perpetuated the story. Kiefer adds that, although he has been unable to find any "other more definite statement about this" (the operation and its date), "it is very likely true, since it was about this time that he [Marais] withdrew from active participation in the musical world of the royal court".[vi] However, according to our research, Marais did not retire until five years later in 1725, at the age of 69. To date we have found no contemporary documentary evidence that Marais was ever cut for the stone.

JANE WILDGOOSE While Philip investigated the musical history of Marais's piece, I was researching the medical archives. A colleague of Peter's with an interest in the history of surgery recommended Erich Riches's and Harold Ellis's papers on the history of lithotomy.[vii] These drew my attention to the way in which lithotomy – one of the most commonly practised surgical procedures at the beginning of the eighteenth century – became a hotly disputed topic in written material of the period, published largely in Paris and London.

PETER ISAACS Because Marais's music and text referred to the emotions of the patient, we started to record some conversations with patients who had undergone ERCP. Open-ended responses to simple prompts (derived from adaptation of Marais's original text: "How did you feel when you saw the equipment?") brought some unexpected replies. One man was greatly impressed by all the gleaming equipment: "All high tech"; but another reported being alarmed by the lead apron suspended around his neck (to protect the nurse from the X-rays).

Fig. 5

"Nature … governs all bodies … she is like a viol player whose music leads and rules the dancers: we doctors and surgeons are the dancers, and we must dance to time when natur plays the viol." Henri de Modeville, surgeon, (d.c. 1320), quoted in Pouchelle, M–C (1990) *The Body and Surgery in the Middle Ages*. New Brunswick, New Jersey: Ruttgers University Press, p. 38.

NATURE GOVERNS ALL BODIES
LIKE A VIOL-PLAYER
WHOSE MUSIC LEADS AND
RULES THE DANCERS

The presence of the visiting artists and musicians – neither medical inspectors, nor students in need of instruction – stimulated the medical team to review their work with a new curiosity. Rather than a defensive story, 'Questions for Medics' – our questionnaire compiled for the medical teams – provoked an anonymous reflection on their experiences of conducting a medical procedure. For the nurses, it was empowering that their narratives of a procedure normally dominated by a doctor were seen to be of value and interest.

Parvenu jusqu'au hault —
Arriving at the top

PHILIP PARR As well as looking back to the history and birth of Marais's music, we commissioned three new pieces that take inspiration from the theme and structure of the original and reflect contemporary medical procedures undertaken by Peter and his team at BVH.

From the outset, I wanted to keep the commissions of new music as unrestricted as possible, while allowing a strong sense of individual identity. It is always tremendously exciting when you ring up a composer to commission a new work. The entire process, from initial collaboration to nervous anticipation at first rehearsal, and then ultimately the first performance, is a series of thrilling stages in a great journey.

To achieve a separation of identity, we decided to give each composer a different stimulus. All three composers were provided with the Marais recording, our translation of the text, and a book of visual and textual material. I then paired a composer with each one of us: Rachel Stott with Peter, Eleanor Firman with Jane, and Eddie McGuire with me. It was our role to guide the composer through the generation of their piece, giving each one as much material as we chose, as well as acting, if necessary, as librettists. The only limitations placed on the composers were that they should use the same instrumentation as Le Tableau, and that their composition should not exceed the four minutes' playing time of Marais's original work.

Questions for patients

Viewing the instruments   When you came into the X-ray room,
did you notice the equipment?

Shuddering at the sight   If so, what did you think about the way
it looked?

Resolution to get up there   Do you remember getting up on the bed,
and if so, how were you feeling?

Arriving at the top   Were you feeling anxious about the
endoscopy?
a) while you were waiting to go in?
b) when you went into the X-ray room
and got up on to the bed?
scale of 0 – 10 (0 – not at all,
10 – overwhelmingly anxious)

Submitting to the equipment/   Do you remember anything after the
the restraints   sedative was given?

Can you describe waking up and being
taken back to the ward?

Any other comments?

If you had a stone surgically removed from your body,
would you object to it being displayed in an artwork?

If yes, would you prefer to remain anonymous,
or to have your contribution credited with your name?

If no, please tell us about your objections.

Questions for medics

Serious thoughts

Were you worried about the procedure
you had to perform, and if so, what were
your worries?

Tying the arms and legs with silk

Please describe the sedative given.

Here the incision is made

Please describe the use of the endoscope
and

Introduction of the 'tenette' gripping
device

(if appropriate) the treatment of the
stone.

Here one pulls the stone
Here one has almost lost one's voice

Flowing of the blood

How did you respond to the sight of blood
in this situation?

Here one unties the silk

Please describe the patient being
'brought round'.

Here one takes you to bed

Please describe the patient being taken
back to the ward.

Any other comments?

If you had a stone surgically removed from your body,
would you object to it being displayed in an artwork?

If yes, would you prefer to remain anonymous,
or to have your contribution credited with your name?

If no, please tell us about your objections.

Fig. 6
Figure pour le haut appareil
(Dionis [1708] Cours
d'Opérations de Chirurgie,
Brussels) Plate opposite
p. 160.

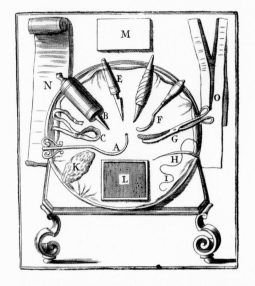

My choice of composers was governed by a number of factors. Firstly, they must be interested in the whole project. Secondly, I wanted composers with very different styles; as the instrumentation was to be the same, this would ensure variety. Thirdly, I wanted composers who would collaborate with the team. I knew all three composers' work and had commissioned music from Eddie (whose opera I had directed) and Rachel, and knew they would fit in with our tight schedule. Given, too, that we were constrained by rehearsal time and by the need to use an electric keyboard at the first performance, their tolerance was a vital characteristic.[viii]

Each composer responded differently to the brief. Although I had ideas about the direction in which I thought the collaborating teams might travel, in the end they all took very different journeys. Marais's preoccupation with the speed of the operation and the patient's distress caused by cutting without anaesthetic was reflected in Eleanor's and Jane's piece that layers text and character to show the urgency of modern surgical procedure and the thoughts of the patient. Eddie eschewed text to create a parallel with the word 'cut' – which in Scottish music is a type of ornament that gives articulation to bagpipes – and the concept of musical sedation. He also used the different instruments to express contrasting experiences of the operation: the bass viol signalling tension and fear, the flute signifying hope, and the mechanical aspects of the keyboard referring to the dextrous precision of the surgeon. Rachel, too, focused on the instruments and their particular roles, dissecting the performance of the baroque flute in an evocation of the endoscopic process as it affects both body and mind, and echoing Marais's own

Fig. 7
Clockwise from top left:
syringe – contains contrast;
sphincterotome; canula;
sphincterotome handle: for
opening and closing, with
thumb loop connection for
diathermy current.

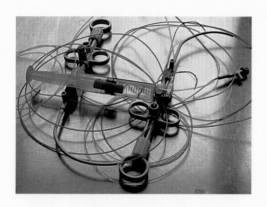

experimentation with technical possibilities. Similarly, the viol player is asked to make percussive use of the instrument and to explore unconventional uses for the bow.

Descente dudit apareil —

Descent of the instruments (they are brought to the operating table)

PETER ISAACS As a musician, Philip was particularly intrigued by the endoscopic instruments. The controls on the handle of the endoscope require the use of all the digits in much the same position as when playing an instrument such as the bass viol. The right hand performs side-to-side movements when inserting the instruments, and finger-on-thumb movements, which are similar to those used during bowing. → Figs 6, 7

JANE WILDGOOSE During the selection of composers, Philip invited me to the premiere of Rachel Stott's 'Ophelia in Transit' by Da Camera at the Purcell Room. A reproduction harpsichord (1995) was featured, decorated with elaborate scroll work and a written text on the lid clearly inspired by period originals. It occurred to me that period instruments continue to be made with decorative elements belonging to rich historical traditions, but that the motifs copy originals rather than developing new forms and content. This subsequently led me to draw some of the viols in the historical instrument collection at the V&A (Victoria and Albert) Museum as well as the instruments

Fig. 8

A French surgeon and his
helpers performing *l'opération
de la taille* on a patient tied
to the operating table, in
the early eighteenth century.
Traité de la Lithotomie,
Francois Tolet (Paris, 1708).

Jo Levine and Mark Levey use in performance. I was particularly interested in methods of surface decoration and detailing: ivory and mother of pearl inlay, 'parfling' (patterns scratched into the wooden surface), and use of colour.

As an extension of my work on *Viewing the Instruments*, I would like to collaborate with a contemporary, period instrument maker in designing a viol and harpsichord decorated with motifs and information drawn from our medical research.

Réflexions sérieuses —
Serious thoughts

PHILIP PARR The juxtaposition of musician and medic, and the contrasting ways of working and researching – both within the collaborating trio and in the wider group working on the project – has provoked a great deal of thought.

PETER ISAACS The collaboration has encouraged me to look again at the information given to patients pre-procedure and to plan a video recording as part of their preparation and consent. Reviewing audio records of patient responses to our questions also helped me to see (with Jane's prompting) my deficiencies as a listener, especially when patients are expressing gratitude. The interviews were a reminder of the essential nobility of our patients who are generally patient, humorous and grateful.

Fig. 9
Operating the sphinctero-
tome. Dr Isaacs and his team
during an ERCP session at
Blackpool Victoria Hospital.

These stories also led us to examine the stresses and reactions of the medical and nursing team during the surgical procedure. The nurses' concerns were mainly for the safety of the patient, especially in the face of apparently conflicting advice about the administration of sedative drugs. But the interviews and the visits of Philip, Jane, and the composers, Eleanor and Rachel, also helped them realize that what they did was unusual, valuable and exciting, as well as being stressful, boring and exhausting in various measure.

In giving my own reactions to carrying out ERCP, I reflected on the pressures that all doctors deal with – finding the right solution to the problem and delivering it safely and quickly. At the same time one must teach a trainee how to carry out fine and complex manoeuvres without seizing the instrument oneself. → Fig. 9

PHILIP PARR & JANE WILDGOOSE Alongside our contemporary research, we continued investigating the musical, medical and social background of Marais's 'Le Tableau'. In particular, we looked at Marais's continued musical output until his retirement, together with the lack of comment by diarists and letter writers (or rivals) at court on either his illness or any decline in his playing.

According to the viol player and researcher, Jonathan Dunford, Marais's will of 1709 was revoked in 1724.[ix] Given the high mortality rate associated with patients undergoing lithotomy at the time, it seems likely that, had Marais been considering surgery in 1720, this would have been the date he might have made (or revised) his will.

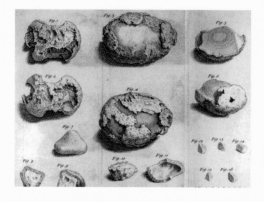

We considered the pain and symptoms of contemporary sufferers of the stone forced to submit to this harrowing procedure. Jo Levine, the bass viol player for our work-in-progress performance, told us that, in her opinion, it would be extremely difficult to maintain a high standard of playing when unwell, and especially if suffering from the localized pain and incontinence associated with a bladder stone. It therefore seems doubtful that Marais underwent the operation. However, we did find a number of diaries and other records from Marais's contemporaries at court that mention lithotomy and that illustrate how an important court musician such as Marais might have known about the procedure. → Fig. 8

Musicians and surgeons attached to Louis XIV's court occupied a similar social footing. Their origins were distinctly lower than those of the courtiers, yet they were closely involved in the intimate day-to-day life and gossip of court. Both professions were championed by the King, who took a personal interest in their achievements; these in turn reflected upon the importance of his court internationally, and his own power. Friendships may well have been made across the professions, and individual musicians or surgeons would also, perhaps, have taken an active interest in the work and reputations of their counterparts. Could Le Tableau have accompanied a demonstration of the surgery – these could be popularly attended – or might it have been an 'advertisement' for a new surgical procedure? Could Marais have written Le Tableau in response to an event at court?

Fig. 11

Urinary bladder stones.

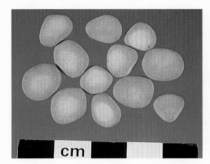 

One of the most significant developments in the history of lithotomy was initially demonstrated by an itinerant lithotomist known as Frère Jacques (born Jacques Beaulieu, 1651–1714) who was active at the court of Fontainebleau in 1698, where the progress of a patient – a shoe-maker's boy from Versailles – was reported daily to the Princes.[x] Another tantalizing story, told independently by two contemporary diarists (Marquis de Dangeau and Marquis de Sourches), describes the Comte de Toulouse (illegitimate son of Louis XIV by Madame de Montespan) undergoing the operation in 1711. The successful outcome was reported to the King at his levée (an event at which Marais may well have played regularly). De Dangeau relates that the stone was "as big as a large apricot, and so hard that it was not broken, though the King let it fall, while showing it to the courtiers".[xi] Extracts of this account are included in the *Viewing the Instruments* performance text. → Figs 10, 11

Entrelassement des soyes entre les bras et les jambes —
Tying the arms & legs with silk

JANE WILDGOOSE The phrase *entrelassement des soyes* encouraged us to think that the work referred to an aristocratic member of the court rather than to Marais himself. Louis XIV was renowned for the strict hierarchy of his court, symbolized by detailed and complicated codes of dress and behaviour. Even if the operation took place at court

and Marais had been the patient, it is likely that linen would have been chosen as a material more appropriate to his status. A son of the King, on the other hand, even an illegitimate one, may well have expected to be tied with nothing less than silk.
→ Fig. 12

PETER ISAACS While patients undergoing surgery for a bladder stone in the early eighteenth century did so without anaesthetic, and were therefore tied down on the operating table, today's patient is 'tied up' by drugs. All three composers seized on different aspects of the anaesthetic procedures used today. Rachel Stott was intrigued by the suspension of memory induced magically by the drug, midazolam, which, when given intravenously, has effect within one minute. Eddie McGuire also found inspiration in this 'forgetting the instruments', while Eleanor focused on the urgency of procedure.

Icy se fait l'incision —
Here the incision is made

Introduction de la tenette —
Introduction of the 'tenette' gripping device

Fig. 13
X-ray showing position of
bladder stone.

Fig. 14
Still from endoscope showing
small, faceted stone tumbling
down a patient's duodenum,
heading for oblivion in the
colon.

Fig. 15
Still from endoscope showing
sphincterotome wire (the
'string' of the 'bow');
the cut edge of the bile duct,
and the stone emerging.

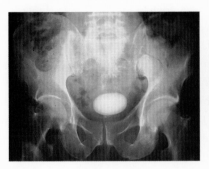 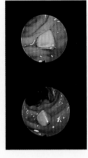 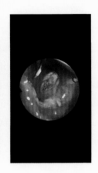

Icy l'on tire la piere —
Here one pulls the stone

Icy l'on perd quasi la voix —
Here one has almost lost one's voice

Écoulement du sang —
Flowing of the blood

PETER ISAACS Through contact with the artists and looking at photographs and video recordings, I also found myself re-examining the physical environment in which I work. The colours of the intestinal mucosa, bile, blood, gallstones are dramas when witnessed afresh through someone else's eyes. The odd darkened rooms and bleeping or humming equipment, the peculiar operating clothes (white gear for the patient tied loosely up the back, armour-like lead gowns for the operating team, starched white cotton for the radiographer perched behind the glass) began to lose their familiarity. If viewed through a haze of fever or drugs these could become terrifying. → Figs 13–15

JANE WILDGOOSE While researching in the Wellcome Library, I was fascinated to discover an eighteenth-century French medical text that advocated certain seasons and weather conditions for lithotomy.[xii] In particular, this text warned of the perceived dangers to patients operated on immediately prior to, during, or after storms. The writing had a nightmarish quality; fever (and death) was thought to have been aggravated by the fear and excitement brought on by thunder and lightning.

I also studied engravings of tableaux of human vessels, skeletal material and stones by the Dutch anatomist Frederick Ruysch (1638–1731). Their surreal quality seemed curiously similar to some of the French medical writing. The character of these engravings and the typographical style of the eighteenth-century medical texts have both informed my designs for written material accompanying the project. → Fig. 16

Icy l'on oste les soyes —
Here one unties the silk

PETER ISAACS Both Rachel Stott's and Eddie McGuire's compositions seemed to be about the amazing amnesiac effect of the midazolam sedation and its equally extra-ordinary reversal with flumazenil. To one habitually witnessing this and the equal astonishment of the patients, it was a stimulus to look with fresh eyes at the patient's experience, and to think about rewriting the information leaflet to emphasize amnesia as an expected effect. It also led to e-mail correspondence between Rachel and myself on the robbery of the patient's memory. Usually patients express nothing but gratitude that they have not felt (or do not remember) feeling anything, but after consulting my anaesthetist friends, I discovered that patients can be resentful of the memory loss. Discussions of memory and recall with Rachel continue, the subject being one central to composing music.

Icy l'on vous transporte dans le lit —
Here one takes you to bed

PETER ISAACS When the music, old and new, came together in the first performance at the Old Operating Theatre, new resonances arose for me between the old mendicant

Fig. 16
Table of injected vessels,
stones and infant skeletons,
*Thesaurus Animalium
Primus*, Frederik Ruysch,
(Amsterdam, 1744).

... FOR THE AIR BEEING HOT, AND LIKELY TO CAUSE THUNDER AGAIN
THE FOLLOWING NIGHT, SUCH ACCIDENTS MIGHT HAPPEN AS WOULD
OCCASION THE DEATH OF THE SICK PERSON.

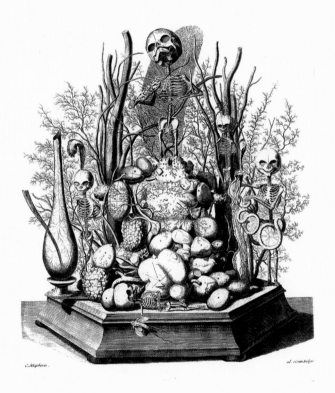

SOME GROW ONLY WEAK, AND HAVE A SMALL SWEAT, BUT OTHERS HAVE
BEEN FRIGHTED, THEIR PULSE IS IRREGULAR. BECAUSE THEY
HAD NO REST IN THE NIGHT, AND BECAUSE THEIR BLOOD IS IN
MOTION BY REASON OF THEIR FRIGHT.

friar surgeons – the ace lithotomists of London and Paris – their patients, famous and anonymous, and our work now. I now use stories of the surgeon, Frère Jacques, and patients like Samuel Pepys, to lead discussion with students on surgical risk and consent. The patients of 1725 may possibly have understood the risk of surgery better than modern-day patients. Certainly they would have placed their survival in the hands of God and would have been completely baffled by the performance league tables used today. The incentives to surgeons to enhance their performance were the same in the eighteenth century as they are in the twenty-first: humanitarian needs, fame, profit and the avoidance of infamy, loss of patients, erasure and, in the past, lynching that could result from bad practice.

JANE WILDGOOSE Medical practitioners (especially surgeons and pathologists) are often criticized for their specialized objectification of the patient's body. However, little attention is given to the patient's objectification of the doctor. As patients, we don't want to know that our doctor may have had a domestic row this morning, or is worried about patient waiting list numbers – factors that may well affect his or her performance on the day. We demand from doctors a level of professionalism that allows no margin for the type of human error that may naturally occur in other professions, but with less catastrophic results. While there is every reason to feel anger and outrage at medical mistakes, patients can also have disproportionate expectations of medicine, which are largely due to the remarkable medical results achieved regularly today.

Viewing the Instruments reminds audiences of the huge developments that have been made in medicine, and of the very real responsibilities and concerns of a modern medical team going about its day-to-day work. Eleanor Firmin's piece with its insistent refrain, "The next patient's outside", stresses the anxiety for doctors caused by today's conveyor-belt approach to medical procedures.

PHILIP PARR What we have achieved, and will continue to seek, is the use of these three minutes and 40 seconds of remarkable music, written nearly 300 years ago, as the starting point for new work and inquiry.

PETER ISAACS Celebrating our work with artists has yielded rich subjects for creativity within the field of sedation and endoscopy alone; there are no doubt many more to be found amongst the wider activities of the hospital. With a musician or poet in residence, looking at the experiences of both patients and the staff, we may be able to reach a new and better understanding of the many conflicts and dramas that occur. Understanding the stresses on personnel in the NHS is vital to recruitment and retention of staff. Currently there are major difficulties in getting newly qualified nurses to take up their careers and about one-quarter of GPs are considering early retirement.[xiii] A Department of Health initiative, entitled Improving Working Lives, seeks to make the NHS a more attractive work environment. Artistic perspectives could both limit environmental damage and bring clinical practice into the spotlight.

PHILIP PARR Following an application to the Performing Rights Society, and a successful concert at BVH in 2002 by Rachel Stott, *Viewing the Instruments* and the Hospital have now received funding for Rachel to be composer-in-residence there during 2003.

JANE WILDGOOSE We shall be touring the performance of *Viewing the Instruments* with associated workshops for musicians and medics (particularly students) in the UK, supported by a National Touring Programme grant from the Arts Council of England, in autumn 2003. I am now working on designs for a set for the tour that can be accommodated in hospital or university lecture rooms, medical museums and theatres.

Letter from M. F
Chirurgeon
M. Falconet, D
Medicine of l'A
Belles L

Work-in-progress perfor-
mance at the Old Operating
Theatre, Southwark, London,
November 2001.
Philip Parr as the Presenter
of Medical History;
Dr Peter Isaacs as himself;
Joanna Levine, bass viol;
Jonathan Tilbrook,
harpsichord; Rachel Latham,
baroque flute.

Text notes

i   Dougals J (1726) *The History of the Lateral Opération*. London p.26. Cited from Dionis (1708) *Cours d' Opérations* [sic] *de Chirurgie, demontrées* [sic] *au Jardin Royal*. Brussels p.170, and quoted in the *Viewing the Instruments* performance, Old Operating Theatre, Southwark, 22 November, 2001

ii   Marin Marais (1656–1728) was composer and player at the court of Louis XIV until his retirement in 1725. He studied viol with Saint-Colombe (d.c. 1700) and composition with Lully (1632–1687). Marais joined the royal orchestra in 1676 where he continued as conductor until around 1710, and was made *Ordinaire de la Chambre du Roi pour la Viole* in 1679. He published five volumes of *Pièces de Violes*, comprising some 500 compositions. 'Le Tableau de l'Opération de la Taille' was published in the fifth, and final, volume in 1725; it is the penultimate piece, no. 118

iii   Milliot S, de la Gorce J (1991) *Marin Marais*. Paris : Fayard, p.131

iv   Newton R (1952) Hommage à Marin Marais (1656–1728). *The Consort* ix : 18 June

v   Thompson, CH (1960) Marin Marais' 'Pièces de Violes'. *The Musical Quarterly* (New York) 46 (Oct): 482

vi   Keifer JH (1963) A lithotomy set to music; an histori-cal interlude. *Transcriptions of American Association of Genito-Urinary Surgeons* 55: 136

vii   Riches E (1967) The history of lithotomy and lithotrity. *Journal of the Royal College of Surgeons of England* (Jan): 185–198; Riches E (1977) Samuel Pepys and his stones. *Annals of the Royal College of Surgeons of England* 59 : 11–16; Ellis H (1979) A history of bladder stone. *Journal of the Royal College of Medicine* 72 (April): 248–251

viii   The composers were asked to follow Marais's instru-mentation of bass viol and continuo – in this case, harpsichord, as this was used on the first recording we heard of the piece by Paolo Pandolfo (2000) 'Le Tableau de l'Opération de la Taille, Le Labyrinthe & autres histoires', by Marin Marais. GCD929404, Glossa Music. Track 13. They were also given the option to have a speaker and one extra instrument. In the event, the baroque flute was chosen as the extra instrument.

ix   See http://mapage.noos.fr/dunford/new/html/pages/english/english.htm; Viol da Gamba Society of America: http://vdgsa.org

x   Douglas *History of the lateral operation*. pp 13–14

xi   Dangeau de. *Mémoires et Journal du Marquis de Dangeau*. Entry for 7 Nov : 1711

xii   Garengeot RJC, trans. André, St (1723) *A Treatise of chirurgical Operations*. London, which helped me identify the time of year when the Comte de Toulouse might have been operated on.

xiii   Findlayson B, Dixon J, Meadows S, Blair G (2002) Mind the gap: the extent of the NHS nursing shortage. *British Medical Journal* 325 : 538–641; BMA 2001 www.bma.org.uk

Acknowledgements

The patients, nursing and medical illustration staff, and radiographers of Blackpool Victoria Hospital, Mark Lambert for medical and historical material, Jonathan Dunford, Professor Richard Chew, Doug Bradley, Dr Ruth Richardson, The Old Operating Theatre Museum and Herb Garret, Southwark, London, The Wellcome Library for the History and Understanding of Medicine, Bibliothèque Nationale de France, and musicians: Joanna Levine (bass viol), Jonathan Tilbrook (harpsichord) and Rachel Latham (baroque flute).

References

Dangeau M de (1830) *Mémoires et Journal du Marquis de Dangeau.* Paris

Douglas J (1726) *The history of the lateral operation.* London

Ellis H (1979) A history of bladder stone. *Journal of the Royal College of Medicine* 72 (April): 248–251

Findlayson B, Dixon J, Meadows S, Blair G (2002) Mind the gap: the extent of the NHS nursing shortage. *British Medical Journal*, 325

Keifer Joseph H (1963) A lithotomy set to music; an historical interlude. *Transcriptions of American Association of Genito-Urinary Surgeons* 55: 132–137

Marais M (1686/R1972) five volumes of *Pièces de Violes* [1er livre]; (1701/R1972) 1, 2 viols [2e livre]; (1711/R1972) [3e livre]; (1717/R1972); 1, 3 viols [4e livre]; (1725/R1972) [5e livre]. No.108, '*Le Tableau de l'Opération de la Taille*' was published in the fifth volume in 1725

Milliot S, de La Gorce J (1991) *Marin Marais* Fayard Pandolfo P (2000) '*Le Tableau de l'Opération de la Taille, Le Labyrinthe & autres histoires*' by Marin Marais. GCD920404, Glossa Music, Track 13

Riches E (1977) Samuel Pepys and his stones. *Annals of the Royal College of Surgeons of England*, 59: 11–16

Riches E (1967) The history of lithotomy and lithotrity. *Journal of the Royal College of Surgeons of England*, Jan: 185–199

Sadie S (1980) *The New Grove Dictionary of Music and Musicians*. 20 vols. London: Macmillan

Sadie S (1984) *The New Grove Dictionary of Musical Instruments*. 3 vols. London: Macmillan

Newton R (1952) Hommage à Marin Marais (1656–1728). *The Consort* ix (June): 12–21

Pouchelle M–C (1990) *The Body and Surgery in the Middle Ages*. New Brunswick, New Jersey: Ruttgers University Press, p.38

Thompson CH (1960) Marin Marais' 'Pièces de Violes'. *The Musical Quarterly* 46 (Oct): 482–499

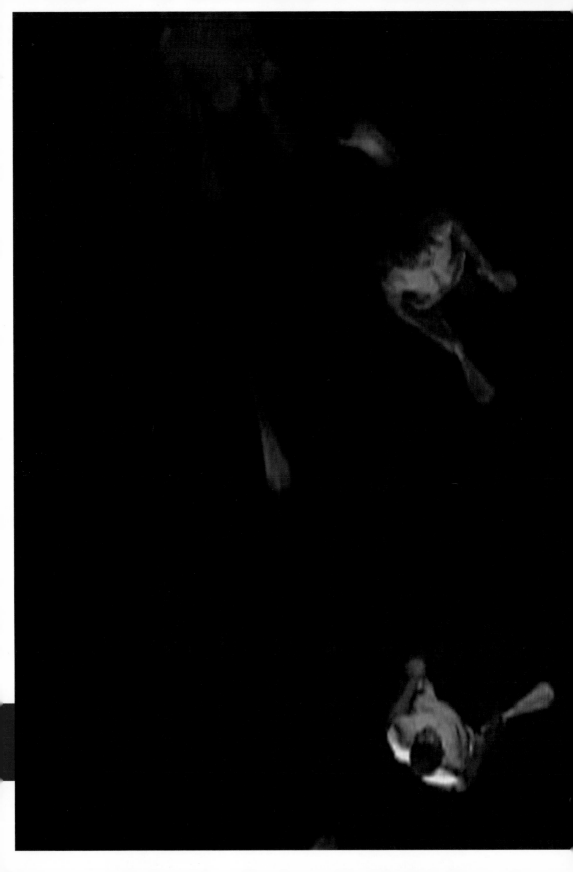

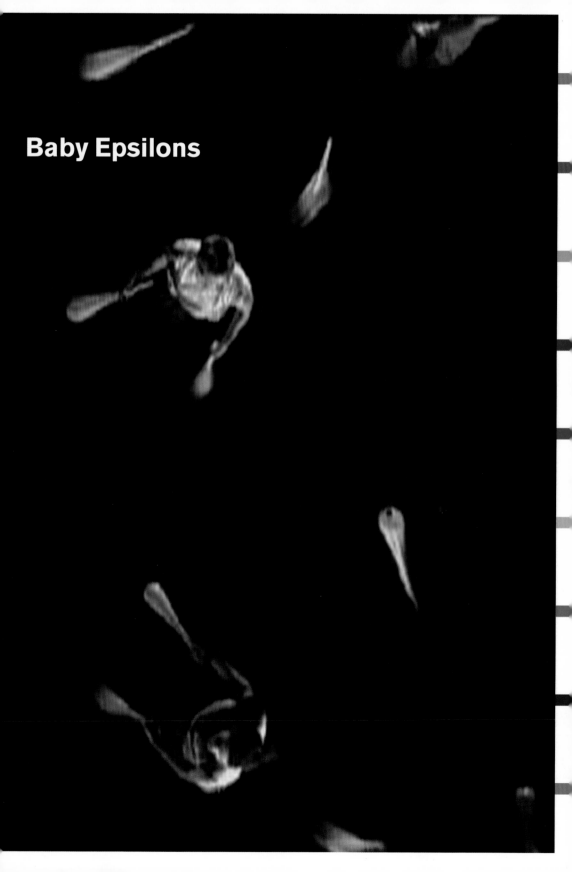

Baby Epsilons

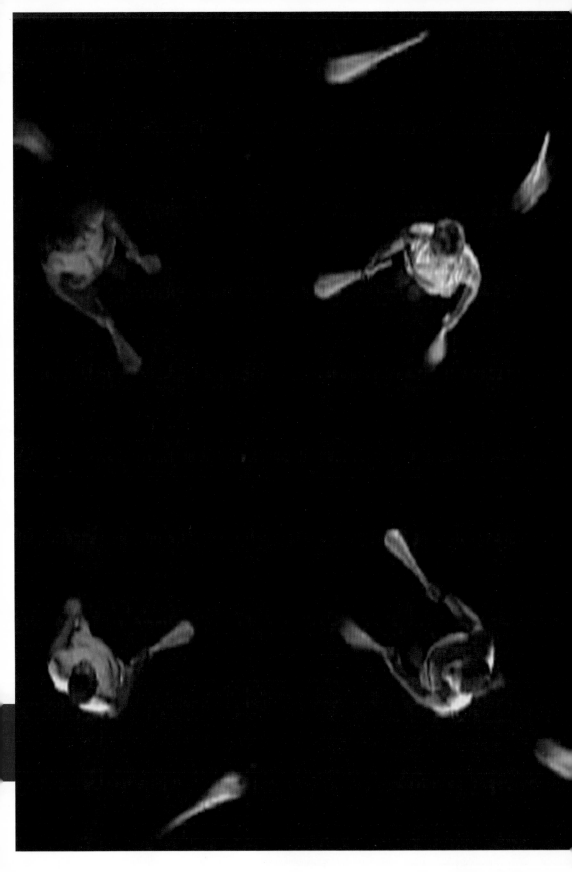

Baby Epsilons investigated the use of mathematics as practical and inspirational material in the making of a juggling-based performance. The research generated many new mathematical juggling patterns combining effects of geometry, colour, sound and rhythm, a collection of DVDs documenting juggling sequences, and ideas for virtual and non-juggling motion. The mathematical work was undertaken by Dr Norihide Tokushige and the juggling sequences designed and performed by Gandini Juggling.

Introduction

The term *cirque nouveau* was coined by the French in the 1980s and with it began the cross-over of circus skills with other contemporary performance arts: dance, theatre and music. Juggling was affected as all the circus disciplines were, and for a new generation of performers a fresh vocabulary was revealed, allowing the creation of new techniques and choreographic expression. In the UK, Gandini Juggling was at the forefront of this movement. For the past ten years, Sean Gandini and Kati Ylä-Hokkala (Gandini Juggling) have been researching, presenting and archiving the performance possibilities of juggling.

The mathematics behind juggling were also first exposed at this time. Highly influential in the UK was the work of Mike Day, a juggler and mathematician who was working with Sean and Kati on *siteswap* notation. In its simplest form, this notation system enables juggling patterns to be recorded as a string of numbers. Taken further, it allows the creation of brand new, never-before-seen patterns and clarifies many of the finer techniques of juggling: rhythm, relative heights, dwell times and landing sequences. Making the mathematics behind the juggling explicit rather than implicit allows what is happening on stage to be more fully experienced and understood. The hard science exposes the soft underbelly of the art and helps us to see the richness of the juggler's craft.

Fundamental to the material presented here is that the process feeds both ways. While the maths enriches the juggling, the juggling also brings fresh life to the mathematical principles explored. This path is seen clearly in the pictographical work: the clear and aesthetically pleasing representations of the numbers and geometries behind the sequences. Some of these images stand alone as miniature works of art.

Another area that has been directly nurtured by the research process is film production. Gandini Juggling has released a series of instructional videos and DVDs aimed at jugglers, which explain and demonstrate the huge variety of possibilities that can be achieved through the application of maths to juggling. In addition to promoting a more scientific approach, these productions encourage performers to go further in their search for complex and visually satisfying sequences. Included are many new juggling patterns that, until now, never existed.

In the work presented here, Gandini Juggling have aimed for clarity of ideas and presentation. Reading their explanations, watching the videos, and making the connections between throws, catches, numbers and graphics, it is possible to see the extent of what they have achieved: to enhance the scientific understanding of juggling and to illustrate the art within the numbers; to create a rich and dazzling range of mathematically based performances, and to inspire others to reach new heights.

Luke Wilson

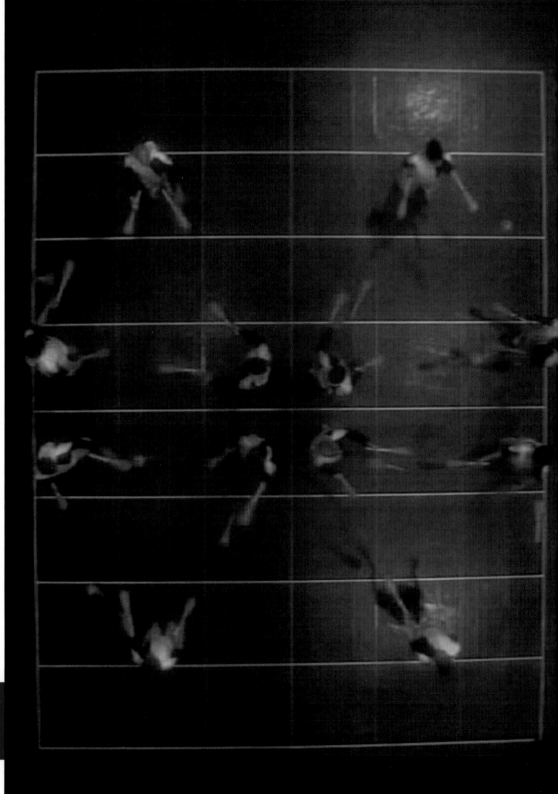

Baby Epsilons

Sean Gandini

On the surface of it, juggling seems very straightforward: a wrestle with gravity to keep a number of balls up in the air. There is something very Beckettian about this repetitive task: everything caught, everything thrown. And yet in the personal world of the juggler the act of dropping, or rather the fight to keep things in the air, is not primordial. The primordial is the pattern. The juggler's world is filled with the nuances of patterns: heights, orbits, rhythms, landing and throwing positions, hand-throwing orders, anatomical topologies and so on.

The last two decades have seen a dramatic growth in mathematical approaches to juggling patterns. Not all juggling performances are related to mathematics, but mathematics or mathematical thinking can be a very useful tool for juggling. How do mathematics and juggling relate, and why are mathematicians interested in juggling? One reason is that juggling, especially modern juggling, has a mathematical structure. If we can abstract a structure from juggling patterns, we can forget about juggling and analyse the patterns mathematically. This structure can then provide a means for describing patterns and generating new ones.

The improved understanding of pattern has mostly been confined to the rehearsal studio – an inward-looking process that swept through the juggling world, introducing and clarifying many patterns. Its repercussions on juggling performance have been relatively negligible. As jugglers, we became interested in finding ways of communicating the beauty of these patterns, of using the subtle variations between one pattern and another as swatches of colour with which to paint visual performances.

However, to call our project a collaboration between mathematics and juggling is slightly misleading. Most, if not all, of the collaboration involved the maths feeding the juggling. At best, our juggling illustrated ideas and concepts; it did not solve or contribute to mathematical hypotheses or conjectures. This is not to say that the dialogue between art and mathematics has always been unidirectional – indeed the original work on mathematics was inspired by juggling. Moreover, this relationship did not in any way diminish our excitement for the project. To us, juggling is a physical representation of mathematics. There is no borderline between the two; mathematics is part of the art. The patterns, 534, [54]24, (6x,4)(4,6x), far from being a soulless jungle of digits, are sequences with personalities, quirks, and idiosyncrasies.

The very practical transformation of sequences of digits into juggleable patterns, nevertheless, creates a conundrum: which came first, the pattern or its physical manifestation? Do juggling patterns have an autonomous existence if not juggled, and without juggling are they as interesting? Perhaps it is significant that Norihide Tokushige, a pure mathematician, was captivated by the practical implications of the project, whereas we were more interested in the theoretical.

One of our main concerns during the project was how to share complex juggling information in an accessible way. In their raw state, mathematical pattern sequences take time to be appreciated and differentiated; like good wine they cannot be grasped in a quick gulp. We were keen, though, not to lose complexity in order to gain accessibility and so adopted a number of strategies, most of them familiar from other art forms to help us; we began to think of juggling patterns as rich tapestries of colour and sound.

The summary below focuses on the graphical interpretation of juggling and the work we have done with complex patterns. Juggling is all to do with Newtonian motion, parabolic arcs ephemerally slicing space. This assembling and disassembling of patterns is very difficult to convey on the written page. We hope that what follows gives a glimpse of the excitement we have found in exploring mathematically generated juggling sequences.

Siteswaps

The centrepiece of a mathematical juggling sequence is called a *siteswap*. Siteswaps are elegant numerical notations that describe and generate all manner of interesting juggling patterns. To a mathematician, siteswaps are a periodic non-decreasing bijection on the set of integers; to jugglers they are just a rearrangement of the landing order of the objects thrown. While the basic mathematics of the siteswap notation is fairly well known, their translation into practical performance material is still relatively unexplored. A rudimentary understanding of siteswaps will be very useful in understanding our journey.

In siteswap notation, we only consider the landing order of balls, and patterns are specified by a sequence of numbers. If we think of a juggler as an airport, planes leave and planes arrive. Let's assume that the planes arrive and depart at even intervals and, for now, that the planes return to the same airport. Let's also imagine our airport only has three planes, each following the same route and then queuing up to land. We'll colour the planes in red, blue and green. So in our simplest possible scenario the planes depart:

red, blue, green, red, blue, green...

Now if we just focus on one of the planes, say the red one, we notice that it departs every third interval, i.e. every third take-off is a red one. The same can be said for the other two planes. What we do now is count how many times each plane re-departs. In this case we could describe the take-off sequence as 33333333, since it repeats simply as 3. If we have four planes, red, blue, green, yellow, the simplest sequence is 4, and so on.

For now the sequences are simple. Things get more complex if we start rearranging the landing order of the planes. So to return to our first example, if we change the landing order of the first two planes, we get a different, slightly more interesting, numerical sequence:

red, blue, green, blue, red, green

4 2 3 4 2 3, reducing to 423

Essentially this is siteswap juggling: two hands throwing a number of balls and playing with their landing schedules. The numerous ways of keeping these balls in

Figs 1, 2

Part of a limited set of
siteswap cards produced
as part of the *Baby
Epsilons* project.

Siteswap cards

0 – empty hand
1 – quick pass across from one hand to another
2 – held ball or a very small throw to the same hand
3 – throw to the other hand, as in the 3-object cascade
4 – throw to the same hand, as in the 4-object fountain
5 – throw to the other hand, as in the 5-object cascade

**Notice all odd throws cross and all even throws
return to the same hand.**   www.mediacircus.biz

The numbers in BLUE before the siteswaps, are the get-in
sequence from ground state, and the numbers after, again
in BLUE, the get out. Siteswaps with the same get in and
get out sequence can be strung together with no transition.

After a string of numbers means:
repeat, starting on the other side.

$a = 10$ $b = 11$ $c = 12$ $d = 13$

Synchronous
Because there are 2 throws at the same time, the throws
are represented in brackets. Only even throws work so
to distinguish crossing throws from same-hand throws we
add an x to the crossing throws.
Multiplex
Multiplex means to throw more than one ball at a time.
So once more we need to include more than one digit at
a time. This time we include the numbers inside square
brackets.

© Gandini Juggling 2002

the air are represented by strings of digits. → **Figs 1, 2** In fact, one can think of the
traffic controllers as celestial jugglers! Siteswaps can also be combined with other
juggling elements such as arm positions or the directions in which balls are thrown.
This means we can have many different realizations of the same siteswap.

A lot of research has been done on which sequences work and which don't –
gigantic lists of juggleable patterns produced by number-crunching home computers. It probably comes as no surprise that many recreational jugglers are mathematicians, physicists and computer programers.

Rhythm

In our quest to elucidate numerical patterns, we realized that sound and rhythm
were an excellent way of conveying a pattern's complexity. Each time an object
hits the hand it emits a thump, a metonymic tic tic tic. In a three-ball cascade this
sequence of beats is just a monotonous continuum (broken by the odd drop
or two). However, if we introduce different-sounding objects and different landing
sequences, we start to have slightly more interesting sounds. The area that we
focused on the most was removing objects from patterns; these are patterns with
zeros in them. The zero in a siteswap is sufficient time to slap part of the body and
make a percussive sound. So we can take any pattern with zeros in it and turn it

Period 2	Period 4	Period 4	Period 5	Period 6	other	Multiplex
42	4440	5 8130 22	52440	451512	4516131	41 [41]2
4 51 2	4512	6 9111 222	52512	461241	6316131	41 [43]0
45 60 12	4530	6 9300 222	55203	461511	4 6161601 2	41 [54]01
	5241	44 6051 1	56130	471231	4 7141404 2	521 [43]0
Period 3	5340	44 7041 1	62241	471312	5 5505051 2	2 4 [32]0 2 [32]
423	5511	45 8013 12	63051	525141	5 71701701 22	22 [41][11][11][32]
441	5520	45 8040 12	63141	526122	45 6050505 12	22 [41][22]0 [32]
522	6222		63501	526131	453053403	24 [63]00 [21]
531	6231	**Period 5**	64203	622512	451640164500	44 20 [43] 1
4 450 2	6312	34512	73131	631512	564006415041	
4 612 2	6330	45141	4 61251 2	722241	714014714700	**Synchronous**
5 711 22	6411	45501	4 61350 2	723141	741701740041	(4,2)
44 603 1	4 7131 2	46122	4 61611 2	731241	7330730370330	(4x,2x)
46 801 122	4 7401 2	46131		4 615600 2		(2x,4)(4,2x)
57 900 1122	5 5560 22	46302		4 713151 2		(4x,2x)(2,4)
	5 5700 22			4 913131 2		(4x,2x)(4,2x)(2x,4x)(2,4)

© Gandini Juggling 2002

into a rhythmic sequence. It then becomes possible to work this system in reverse to generate specific rhythmic sequences from siteswap patterns.

To achieve this, we needed a better understanding of rhythm. We decided to organize some sessions with two leading percussionists: Simone Rebello from the chamber percussion group, Back Beat, and Afro-Cuban percussion expert, Christian Weaver. The exhilaration of learning new percussion was counter-balanced by the double complexity of trying to juggle complex patterns whilst keeping time with each other. Many hours were spent trying out new co-ordinations.

Colour

Since siteswaps are essentially variations on the landing order of a series of balls, colouring them individually clarifies and amplifies structural nuances. The pattern 534 is one of the cornerstones of siteswap juggling. It is both wonderfully simple and sneakily complex. Essentially, it involves three throws: a big crossing throw, a little crossing throw and a same-hand throw. Yet within this apparently simple pattern lie all kinds of fascinating permutations. One piece we made is based entirely on the pattern 534.

Fig. 3
Colour sequences of
a selection of siteswap
patterns.

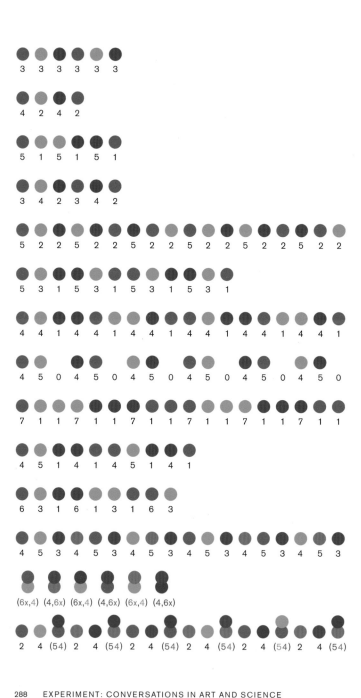

Fig. 4
Colour illustrations
of juggling pattern 534
with balls removed.

Fig. 4 Colour illustrations of juggling pattern 534 with balls removed.

All the balls

| 4 5 3 4 5 3 4 5 3 | 4 5 3 4 5 3 4 5 3 | 4 5 3 4 5 3 4 5 3 | |

Minus one ball

0 5 3 4 0 3 4 5 3	0 5 3 4 0 3 4 5 3	0 5 3 4 0 3 4 5 3	053403453
4 0 3 4 5 3 0 5 3	4 0 3 4 5 3 0 5 3	4 0 3 4 5 3 0 5 3	403453053
4 5 3 0 5 3 4 0 3	4 5 3 0 5 3 4 0 3	4 5 3 0 5 3 4 0 3	453053403
4 5 0 4 5 0 4 5 0	4 5 0 4 5 0 4 5 0	4 5 0 4 5 0 4 5 0	450

Minus two balls

0 0 3 4 0 3 0 5 3	0 0 3 4 0 3 0 5 3	0 0 3 4 0 3 0 5 3	003403053
0 5 3 0 0 3 4 0 3	0 5 3 0 0 3 4 0 3	0 5 3 0 0 3 4 0 3	053003403
4 0 3 0 5 3 0 0 3	4 0 3 0 5 3 0 0 3	4 0 3 0 5 3 0 0 3	403053003
0 5 0 4 0 0 4 5 0	0 5 0 4 0 0 4 5 0	0 5 0 4 0 0 4 5 0	050400450
4 0 0 4 5 0 0 5 0	4 0 0 4 5 0 0 5 0	4 0 0 4 5 0 0 5 0	400450050
4 5 0 0 5 0 4 0 0	4 5 0 0 5 0 4 0 0	4 5 0 0 5 0 4 0 0	450050400

Minus three balls

4 0 0 0 5 0 0 0 0	4 0 0 0 5 0 0 0 0	4 0 0 0 5 0 0 0 0	400050000
0 5 0 0 0 0 4 0 0	0 5 0 0 0 0 4 0 0	0 5 0 0 0 0 4 0 0	050000400
0 0 0 4 0 0 0 5 0	0 0 0 4 0 0 0 5 0	0 0 0 4 0 0 0 5 0	000400050
0 0 3 0 0 3 0 0 3	0 0 3 0 0 3 0 0 3	0 0 3 0 0 3 0 0 3	003003003

Minus four balls

| 0 0 0 0 0 0 0 0 0 | 0 0 0 0 0 0 0 0 0 | 0 0 0 0 0 0 0 0 0 | 0 |

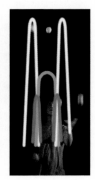

Archiving and DVDs

We decided to archive some of the fascinating families of patterns that we were finding. We filmed hundreds of patterns that had never been filmed and, in many cases, juggled before, resulting in a series of DVDs that document the mathematical notation of juggling. 'Notations' contains over 500 numerically categorized patterns for two, three and four jugglers and in-depth interviews with jugglers and mathematicians. 'Madison Variations' is a collection of club-passing patterns inspired by geometrical tessellations, set to the music of J.S. Bach.

Passing

There is a fascinating branch of juggling that involves multi-handed juggling. As the term implies, this involves juggling with more than two hands and is one of the most interesting structurally, but also one of the most difficult. *Baby Epsilons* generated a lot of intriguing multi-handed ideas, a number of which helped build the rhythm and colour pieces.

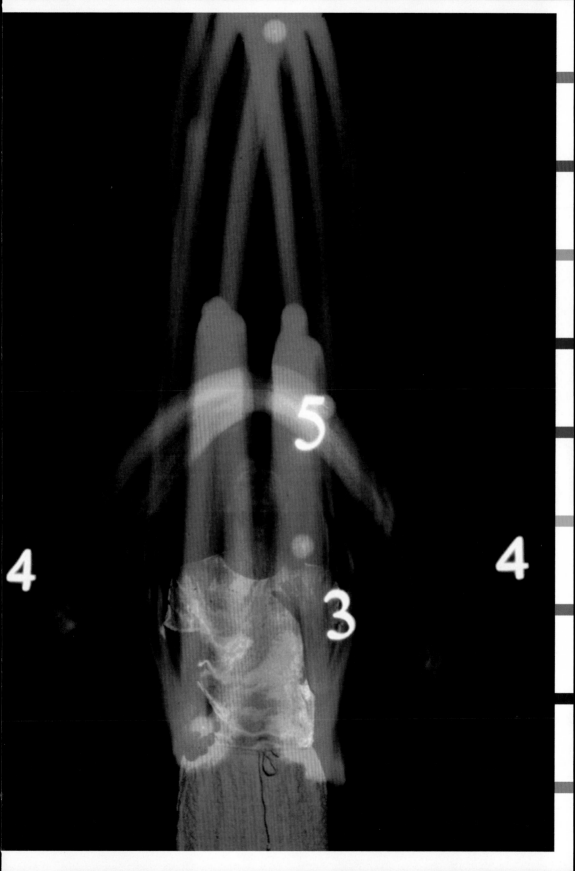

↑ Fig. 7
Performance after the
Concerto in f major, rv 98,
part 1, 'La Tempesta di
Mare', by Antonio Vivaldi,
juggled by Sean Gandini,
Manu Laude and Kati
Ylä-Hokkala. Filmed live
at the International Mime
Festival, 2002.

Fig. 8
Design proposal by
Michelle Weaver to create
a staircase of revolving
circular platforms for the
passing and placing of
siteswaps.

Performance works

i These pieces were
premièred at the
London International
Mime Festival, 2002.

Three short pieces were made as a tribute to the Italian composer Antonio Vivaldi.[i]
These involved mapping a selection of Vivaldi's chamber concertos with juggling
patterns and are performed in total darkness with the aid of illuminated juggling
equipment. This equipment is the latest and most exciting advance in juggling
technology and uses light-emitting diodes (LEDs) to light balls and clubs.

Following the music, we worked meticulously on note-to-throw correlation,
synchronizing the heights of the jugglers' throws, and using a number of musically
derived strategies: counter-pointing, inverting, translating and canoning. Particular
attention was paid to colour coding. We assigned each piece of music a colour,
then applied the mathematical procedures described earlier to trace the pathway
of any one colour at a given moment. In one piece, we used blue balls to follow
the music but needed transition throws for all the blue balls to come back into
unison without the jugglers stopping. Siteswap diagrams placed beneath the
music score were used to generate the transition.

Fig. 9

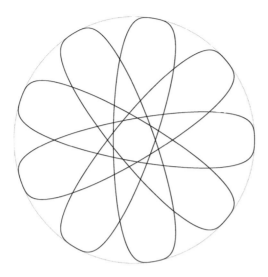

Future work

The research period opened numerous doors for future projects as well as contributing to existing pieces. We are in the process of developing further film ideas based on research into filming patterns. Mathematical description of juggling doesn't specify the direction of times or, indeed, the direction of gravity; film makes it possible to play with both of these elements.

We are also very interested in three-dimensional simulations of complex juggling patterns, which are physically impossible to perform, but interesting as patterns. This includes the possibility of no gravity, multiple gravities and multi-dimensional (3D) space.

One of the central ideas of the original project was to look at ways of translating pattern information from throw and catch juggling into non-juggling motions. We spent a lot of time with circus designer, Michelle Weaver, discussing ways of doing this. The results can be seen in Michelle's prototype sketches, some of which are very beautiful but too complex to build, and others that we hope to make in some form in the future. → Fig. 8

In the field of ball-rolling alone, the potential for 3D geometry is enormous: cylinders, toruses, hemispheres… One of Norihide's most lovely designs involved

Fig. 10

a program that simulated the pathway of balls rolled on a hemisphere. This is called a spherical pendulum and can be described using the elliptic functions – a set of equations with solutions that give the patterns illustrated. → Fig. 9 gives the top view of one of the loci of the balls.

If balls are released on a hemisphere from certain positions at timed intervals, assuming that each ball travels on the same locus as above, they can make infinitely beautiful moving curves. → Fig. 10 These diagrams look like trochoids, but are actually more interesting since an algebraic structure is contained among the curves. The balls in the final and most complicated diagram describe more than one curve. Other variations on this pattern are illustrated in → Fig. 11.

We attempted to replicate some of these patterns on a 2-metre wide, transparent satellite dish, but gradually realized that the more interesting patterns needed a hemisphere about 10 m in diameter – too big to be practical. The hemisphere was donated to French juggler, Dennis Pumier, who is currently researching it as a performance shape.

Another option is to explore simple surfaces with complex objects, such as robotic or computer-generated vehicles that roll in complex pathways, or pendulums that release traces. It would be intriguing to create drawings illustrating

Fig. 11

↓ Fig. 12
Triple-layered sandwich,
performed during the
Lille Masterclass, 2001.

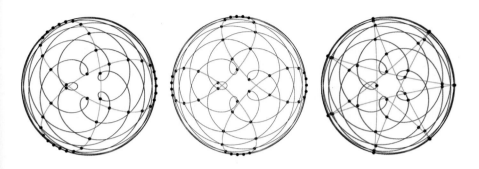

what patterns look like and compare these with different graphical interpretations.

The dialogue between mathematics and juggling is an extremely fertile one; there are still many conversations to be had. We hope in future to find links between topology and the weaves of group passing, between ball bouncing and the geometry of polyhedra. In many ways the relationship between maths and juggling is only just beginning.

Acknowledgements

Jugglers: Kati Ylä-Hokkala, Manu Laude, Ben Beaver.
Mathematician: Norihide Tokushige.
Prop designer: Michelle Weaver.

Further sources

Beek P, Lewbel A, The science of juggling.
    www.its.caltech.edu/papers/~juggling/science.html
Boyce J, The longest simple siteswap patterns.
    www.sonic.net/~boyce/juggling/simple/simple.html
Boyce J, www.juggleanim.sourceforge.net/doc/
    notation.html (for articles on notation)

Buchler J, Eisenbud D, Graham R, Wright C, Juggling
    drops and descents. www.cecm.sfu.ca/organics/
    papers/buhler/paper/html/nodel.html
Carstens E, Mathematics of Juggling.
    www.juggling.org/papers/carstens
Gandini Juggling. www.gandinijuggling.com;
    www.mediacircus.biz
Polster B, (2002) *The mathematics of juggling.*
    Springer Verlag, New York
Prechac C, www.pogo5.free.fr/juggling/mhn&causal.html
Westerboers W, www.koelnvention.de/software/index.html

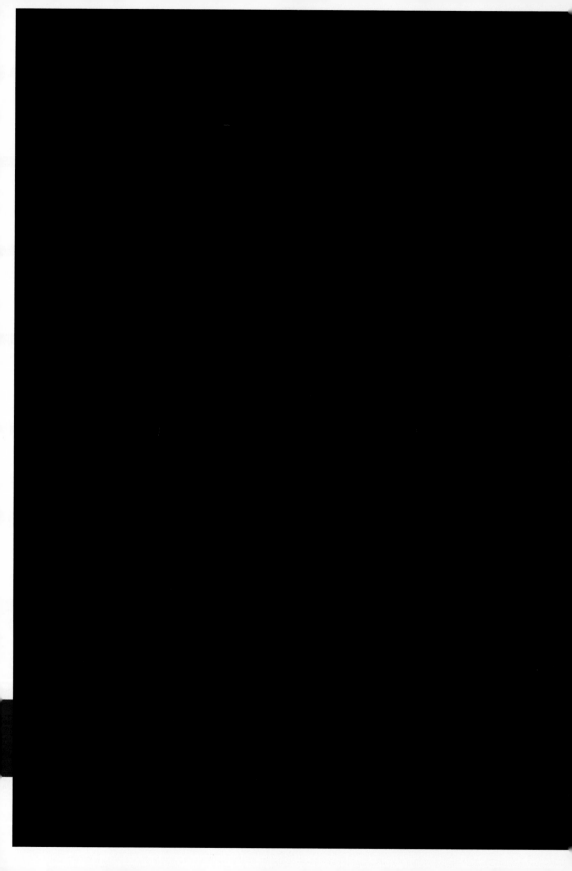

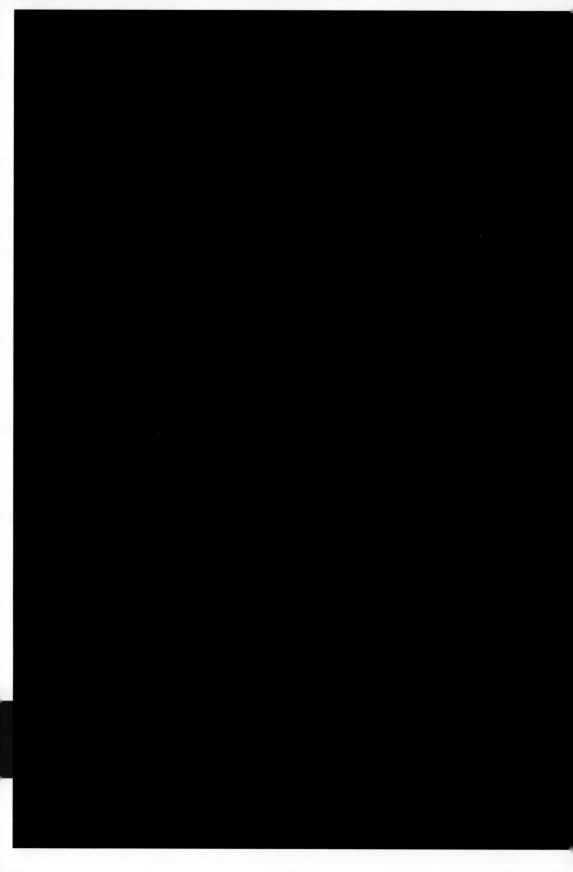

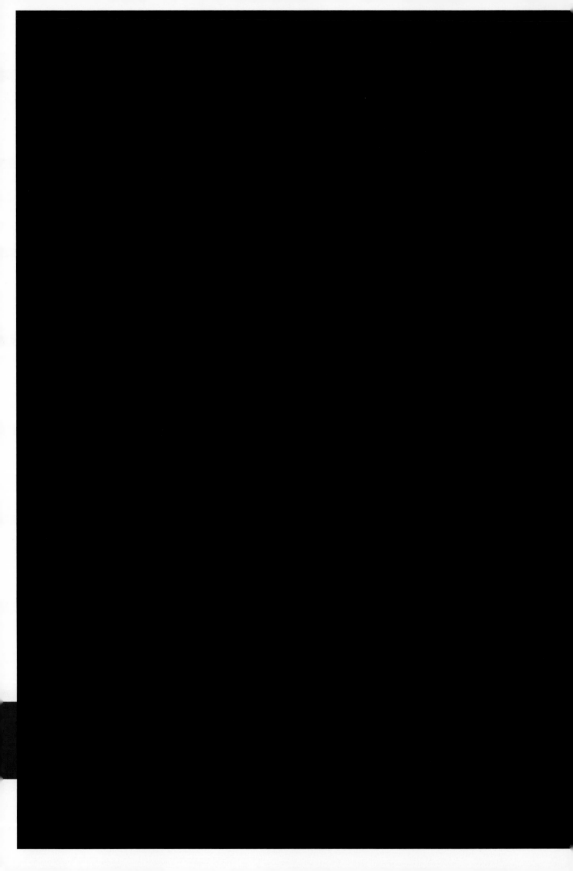

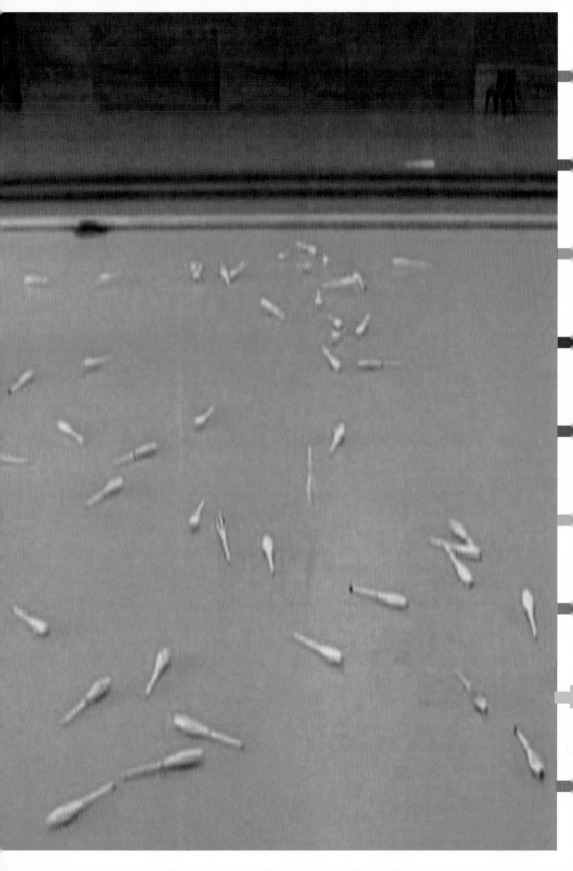

Projects 2000–2002

Between 2000–2002, the sciart Consortium provided resources and encouragement for individuals from different disciplines to meet in fruitful exchanges. The following are summaries of all projects awarded grants during this period.

AgainAndAgain

Jacqueline Donachie, artist / Professor Keith Johnson, Head of Division of Molecular Genetics, Institute of Biomedical and Life Sciences, University of Glasgow / Dr Darren Monckton, Research Fellow, Lister Institute, University of Glasgow

AgainAndAgain was a research project that looked at ways of visualizing the gene mutation and associated clinical symptoms of myotonic dystrophy (DM) as an aid to a wider understanding and recognition of the disease.

The symptoms of DM can be quite obvious to anyone with a working knowledge of the condition, but it remains acutely underdiagnosed. As it is one of the most prevalent forms of inherited genetic illness, affecting approximately one in 5000 people in the UK, and the most common form of muscular dystrophy in adults, this situation could easily be remedied by a greater level of public awareness. In 1992 the defect that causes DM was proved by Professor Johnson and others to be a region of unstable genetic material (DNA) on chromosome 19. This unstable sequence can show an expansion that varies from slight to very large in different people, and which can now be used as a specific test for the disorder, both for detecting gene carriers and in prenatal diagnosis.

The project came about following the diagnosis of DM in the artist's family after the birth of her sister's second child in 1999. DM is characterized by an increase in the severity of the symptoms and a decrease in the age of onset as the disease is passed from one generation to the next, as has happened in Jacqueline Donachie's family. The core of the project involved a visit by the team, accompanied by the artist's sister, to the Saguenay Lac St Jean region of Quebec, Canada, which has a high incidence of DM; there they met families severely affected by the DM gene across several generations. The outcome was an artist's book, entitled *DM*. Images and text address DM on many levels – cell samples, laboratory environments, patients, scientists and the various manifestations of the disease in the artist's family.

Artificial Rockpools

b consultants / Dr Michael Burrows, Project Leader, Biodiversity group, Dunstaffnage Marine Laboratories / Nicola Holmes, artist / Dr Iain McFadzen, Research Ecotoxicologist, Plymouth Marine Laboratory

Occupying a shifting zone between land and sea, rockpools play host to a kaleidoscopic micro-world of animals, plants and minerals. These minute lifeforms are often acutely sensitive to toxins in the environment. In stretches of coast that have been contaminated by industrial waste, mussels have been found with genetic mutations and chromosomal defects.

Situated on the once heavily polluted north east shore between Redcar and Tyne Mouth, N.E. England, *Artificial Rockpools* aims to create a series of habitats that will encourage colonization and breeding by hundreds of healthy marine species. Artist Nicola Holmes is working with a team of scientists and environmental consultants to produce a sustainable ecology that harnesses an array of biological, temporal and material processes. The sites chosen will take into account local community and access issues and provide a resource for schools and scientists. In time it is hoped that other artists will contribute to the pools' diversity, gradually adding new layers to their structure and evolution.

Baby Epsilons

Sean Gandini, Gandini Juggling / Dr Norihide Tokushige, mathematician

Juggling has undergone considerable developments in recent decades. New technologies have expanded the range of potential objects with which to juggle (such as illuminated objects that can be thrown in the dark), while the introduction of notation systems has clarified and made explicit the many techniques of the juggler's craft. Juggling notation is largely the invention of mathematicians who began to analyse juggling sequences as strings of numbers and patterns. These systems have in turn allowed for the creation and recording of more complex and sophisticated juggling routines.

In *Baby Epsilons*, Sean Gandini worked with mathematician Norihide Tokushige to develop a series of juggling patterns that combine effects of geometry, colour, rhythm and sound. Some of these will remain theoretical while others have been translated into performances presented to the public or recorded on video and CD. Gandini Juggling is committed to developing the expressive effects that can be achieved through juggling and to expanding their own performance repertoire. Their collection of films and CDs are designed to help train new generations of jugglers and to encourage today's performers to broaden their range.

Cell

Dr Jane Prophet, Senior Research Fellow, Centre for Arts Research, Technology and Education (CARTE), University of Westminster, London / Peter Ride, Curator, DA2, University of Westminster / Dr Neil Theise, Associate Professor, Department of Pathology, New York University School of Medicine

Cell brings together two individuals whose work addresses how we conceptualize human biology. Neil Theise's research has stimulated a major paradigm shift in the understanding of cells. Jane Prophet produces work using artificial lifeforms and virtual ecological environments, in which code and algorithms are treated as devices for suggesting boundless complexity and a sense of the technologically sublime. Together, Theise and Prophet have a common interest in finding new languages to propel forward their respective practices; their collaboration is as much about nature of discovery and how philosophies change as it is about specific research.

DA2, which is curating the project, is a digital arts agency committed to exploring new areas of practice, asking how we define and value them as 'new', and how to evaluate creativity and understand audiences.

Connections in Space: from the quantum to the cosmos–visual representation of space in art and science

Professor John D Barrow, Professor of Mathematical Sciences, Cambridge University / Richard Bright, Interalia Centre, Bristol / Professor Martin Kemp, History of Art, Oxford University

What is the 'shape of space'? Is atomic space the same as cosmic space? How do you visually represent theoretical or complex mathematical spaces? And how is form related to space through varying degrees of size? In the last few years there has been a growth of interest in the representation of space. Images of space play a role in understanding the structure of the universe on its smallest and largest scales.

Perspective has provided a fundamental tool for the representation of space and has served as an aid to visualization in almost every field of science and technology. But are we trapped in our perspectival box, with the limitations it has for visualizing complex spaces currently being theorized in science? Artists and scientists are inclined to use drawing systems traditional to their own fields without considering how useful a particular system may be in solving a particular problem. Can different artistic systems of representation be used to create a greater understanding of space for scientists, and can scientific systems be helpful to artists?

Connections in Space explores these questions by examining the use of different methods for representing space in contemporary art and science, from the very small to the very large. The primary aim of the project is to provide a visual language for space that integrates the concerns of physics, chemistry, mathematics and biology with those of the visual arts, examining both the similarities and differences in spatial representation that these subjects have uncovered.

Contemporary Poetry–Contemporary Science
Robert Crawford, Professor of Modern Scottish Literature,
University of St Andrews

The aim of this project was to explore some of the differences separating the
scientific and literary cultures and to encourage greater communication and understanding between the two. At its heart were ten 'scientifically commissioned
poems'. Ten scientists were each invited to read a collection of poems by one of
ten contemporary poets and to provide the poet with a 'provocative object', such
as a test tube, robot, or tour of a laboratory. Each scientist met the poet to talk
about the object further and exchange ideas about working methods, philosophies
and specific concerns. The poet then created a poem and the scientist wrote a
short response.

The project has generated a wide range of associated events. Five artists or
artist pairs – Anne Bevan, Dalziel and Scullion, Will MacLean, Kathryn Maxwell and
Wilhelmina Barns-Graham – were commissioned by Dundee Contemporary Arts
(DCA) to produce a set of prints in response to the poems. These were exhibited
alongside the texts at DCA in March 2003. A book on the poems with an essay by
each poet and the scientists' response is due to be published by Oxford University
Press in 2004, readings of the poems have taken place at venues across the
country (the Natural History Museum, London; the Scottish Poetry Library; StAnza
at St Andrews, Newcastle and Durham Universities), and several workshops for
school groups were held at the Sensation Science Centre in Dundee in 2003.

Designing a Play Kit to Nurture the Sensory Development of New-born Premature Babies

Dr Elvidina N. Adamson-Macedo, Lecturer, Division of Psychology, University of Wolverhampton / David Henley, Lecturer, School of Art and Design, University of Wolverhampton / John Myers, Lecturer, School of Art and Design, University of Wolverhampton

The new-born baby, whether full-term or pre-term (born under 36 weeks' gestational age), needs an appropriate environment and level of care to maintain and facilitate psycho-neurological development. Particularly for the pre-terms in intensive- or special-care units (ICUs/SCUs), the incubator is a necessary, but unfriendly and unstimulating environment in which babies may remain for many months.

Touch, far from being a 'lower sense' is one of the first to attain complex development. This project aimed to reassess a hypothesis proposed in 1983, which suggested that cross-modal texture discrimination would be impossible before the age of six months. Preliminary research, however, suggests that both full-term and pre-term babies under six months of age may well be able to use touch to discriminate texture if the stimulus is appropriate to their age and size. They may be also capable of matching texture information cross-modally. In this research, pre-term neonates are viewed as active, 'sensory-competent', unique human beings capable of interacting with care-givers and their environment.

Progress in studying psycho-neurological development in premature babies requires a combination of science-based infant research and the design of suitable artefacts, particularly those for use in incubators. The three members of the team are currently working to produce and test a series of interactive artefacts that will be appropriate to the development of babies in the pre-term age group.

The Eternal Artefact?

James Putnam, Curator, Contemporary Arts and Culture Programme, The British Museum / João Penalva, artist / Susan Bradley, Head of Conservation Research Group, The British Museum / Gillian Roy, conservator and Head of Organic Materials Group, British Museum

Museums strive obsessively to preserve artefacts. The scientific role of conservators is to slow down processes of decay to enable artefacts to be preserved for posterity. However, many ethnographic artefacts are made from organic materials and were intended to be ephemeral. For conservators, diagnosis and cure, and the dilemma of when restoration is acceptable, is an ongoing debate that involves scientific and aesthetic criteria and a respect for the beliefs of other cultures. Such issues hold intriguing conceptual possibilities for artists who can offer a challenging view of the scientific rationale of the conservation process.

The artist João Penalva worked in collaboration with the conservation department at the British Museum to examine the art and science of organic materials. Adopting the role of objective observer, Penalva documented in narrative and visual images the scientific analysis carried out on artefacts at the Museum. As well as recording the curiosity and methodology inherent in the conservator's investigations, the artist was able to create new insights into this process for visitor and scientist.

Eye Control

**Dr John Tchalenko, Research Fellow, Camberwell College of Art, London /
Dr Guang-Zhong Yang, Head of Visual Information Processing,
Imperial College, London**

In normal life, our eyes move in rapid jerks (or saccades) from one point to another about 150 times/minute. However, there are some remarkable exceptions, both amongst painters who draw regularly from life, as well as in medics. In both drawing and medicine, training and practice can result in controlled patterns of eye movements optimized for the task in hand.

Could this eye control factor be assessed objectively and used for training and monitoring purposes? Could painters who draw from life assist radiologists searching for signs of lung disease in X-ray or CT scans? Could research into the movements of a painter's eyes be applied to detect fatigue in surgeons performing lengthy operations? These are some of the questions that Dr John Tchalenko, Head of Drawing and Cognition at Camberwell College of Arts, and Dr Guang-Zhong Yang, Head of Visual Information Processing at Imperial College investigated in *Eye Control*, using an eyemouse. With this instrument the computer cursor is controlled with the eyes, allowing the operator to follow a curve, draw a picture or sign a name on the monitor with the eyes alone. Artists and medics, particularly surgeons working in keyhole surgery, were tested on the eyemouse to explore the potential applications of this approach. Guang-Zhong observed in consultant radiologists a clearer and more economical pattern than in the novice.

Material from the project has been presented in several exhibitions and conferences in the UK and abroad, and the overall conclusions are discussed in a publication, *The Mind's Eye: cognitive and applied aspects of eye movements* (Hyönä J, Radach R, Deubel H [2002]: Amsterdam, Elsevier Science).

From Code to Code

Nick Skaer, biologist, Department of Zoology, Cambridge University /
Lucy Skaer, artist

Nick and Lucy Skaer investigate pattern and its meaning in their respective fields
of developmental genetics and contemporary art. Their areas of research have a
central theme in common: the relation of the visible to underlying structures. In
Nick's work this is the relationship between genetic information and its expression
as visible traits in neuronal patterning; in Lucy's, it is pattern as a cultural signifier
in objects and in images.

The initial aim of the project is to clone the coding sequence of the gene
(*Actias selene*) responsible for the characteristic wing marking of the Indian
Moon Moth. The Moon Moth is a large, pale green member of the Lunar Moth
family (*Saturniidae*) that bears a striking motif of four crescent moons on its wings.
Due to the belief in numerous cultures that they represent the souls of the dead,
and the deeply superstitious attitude held towards them in general, moths are
often endowed with profound cultural significance. Once cloning is complete,
the project will focus on establishing correspondences between genetic pattern
sequencing in the Moon Moth and patterns in art – specifically, the rhyming
sequences of Elizabethan sonnets. The outcome of the research will be a voice-
over film that illustrates the development and lifecycle of the moth, structured
according to a four-part sonnet. The film aims to offer new insights into the use of
pattern in art and a highly innovative way of visualizing and communicating gene
sequencing.

Gravity Zero

Dr Anthony Bull, Mechanical Engineering Department, Imperial College, London / Dr Nicholas Davey, Department of Neurophysiology, Imperial College School of Medicine, London / Dr Kitsou Dubois, dancer / Dr Alison McGregor, Lecturer in Physiotherapy, Imperial College School of Medicine, London / Dr Alexander V. Nowicky, Lecturer in Human Biology, Middlesex University / Dr Olga Rutherford, Imperial College School of Medicine, London / Professor Robert Schroter, Head of the BioDynamics Group, Imperial College, London / Nicola Triscott, Director, The Arts Catalyst, London

Choreographer and movement researcher Kitsou Dubois collaborated with scientists from the Biodynamics Group at Imperial College and The Arts Catalyst, to investigate movement in zero gravity. Dr Nick Davey leads a neurophysiological study aimed at understanding the corticospinal control of movement in varying gravitational conditions. Their research took place on a series of parabolic flights where a specially designed aircraft undertook a series of diving manoeuvres to create the effects of zero gravity. The project examined dancers' and other physical performers' awareness of and ability to control the extremities of the body when weightless. The full experiment into postural controls was performed on a flight in April 2003.

During the project Dubois gave masterclasses in London and Paris for dancers and physical performers. Demonstrations of transcranial magnetic stimulations (TMSs) took place at the Art Space at Imperial College as part of an installation, *Altered States of Gravity*, for the Creating Sparks festival of 2000. Dubois's film *Fluid Trajectories* from the Russian flight, and her ground-based work in water and on trampoline, was premièred at the Lilian Baylis Theatre, Sadlers Wells, London, in April 2002, and a four-screen installation by Dubois was shown in the exhibition *Space Design: Life in Space*, Zürich Museum of Design, Switzerland, in 2001/2002.

How To Live
Bobby Baker, performance artist / Dr Richard Hallam, psychologist,
St Ann's Hospital, Haringey, London

In recent years there has been an explosion of interest in therapeutic 'self-help' strategies. No longer the unique preserve of the specialist, therapy is now a mass-market industry, generating annually dozens of publications and films dedicated to teaching people techniques for dealing with emotional and life problems. Cognitive behavioural therapy (CBT), which focuses on cultivating skills for dealing with unwanted emotions, has been particularly amenable to this approach. One method advocated by CBT involves 'acting opposite' to a particular emotion or behaviour by cultivating the opposite tendency. The benefits of CBT are now widely recognized, but attempts to explain CBT techniques through training manuals and videos have often been culturally skewed and patronizing, suggesting that there is scope for these to be designed in a more thoughtful and imaginative way.

How To Live set out to create and compare two CBT training videos – one explaining a CBT technique, the other a comparison condition – and to test their effectiveness under controlled conditions. The videos were made and performed by Bobby Baker, with advice from Dr Richard Hallam, and then screened to an invited audience before taking part in a carefully staged tea party. The aim was to assess reactions to an emotionally provocative event and to gauge whether these had been influenced by the technique suggested. *How To Live* forms part of a larger project by Baker due to be launched at the Barbican Centre, London, in September 2004.

Makrolab Research Station for Antartica

Rob La Frenais, Curator, The Arts Catalyst, London / Marko Peljhan, artist, Projekt Atol / Martin Price, Perth College, University of the Highlands and Islands / Nicola Triscott, Director, The Arts Catalyst

Makrolab is a living experiment – a high-tech, art–science project devised and run by Slovenian artist Marko Peljhan. The Makrolab itself is a temporary sustainable laboratory – a hexagonal, silver, cylindrical pod, bristling with antennae – designed to support up to six artists and scientists working and living together in isolated, fragile environments. *Makrolab* includes the work of many people from many different disciplines and cultures. No specific brief is given to participants – all pursue independent research interests and are given the opportunity to share in and discover each other's work. Inside the pod, researchers study telecommunications, environment, migration and weather patterns. Most of the work conducted on the Makrolab is public; the results are published in electronic form and are freely available on the Internet.

The *Makrolab* project is planned to take ten years, its ultimate goal being a permanent research station in Antarctica. During summer 2002 Makrolab was installed in Perthshire, Scotland, as part of the International Year of Mountains, hosting crews of artists and scientists developing its operations and systems. Before transferring to Antarctica the lab will need to undergo considerable technical development. In the meantime it will be exhibited at the Venice Biennale, in the USA and in South Africa during 2003–2005. It is expected to reach Antartica in 2007.

Mapping Perception

Andrew Kötting, filmmaker / Giles Lane, Director, Proboscis, London /
Dr Mark Lythgoe, neurophysiologist, Institute of Child Health, London

Mapping Perception is a four-year collaboration to examine the limits of human perception, blending art, science and technology.

At the heart of the project is Eden, Andrew Kötting's daughter. Eden was born in London in 1988 with Joubert syndrome – a rare genetic disorder that leads to severe neurological complications and causes problems with speech, motor coordination, eye movements and breathing. Eden participates both as subject and catalyst for an investigation into how we see the world and perceive difference.

Through an exploration of impaired brain function and its effects on perception, the project set out to achieve a deeper understanding of mind–body interaction and our relationship with disability. Probing what is seen and what courses unseen beneath the surface brings us to the core of what we perceive in ourselves and others, and reveals the thin membrane that exists between the able and disabled. By drawing on a range of source material, the project also aimed to make visible the connections and differences between scientific and artistic explorations of the human condition.

Mapping Perception has resulted in a variety of outcomes: a 37-minute 35-mm film, an audio-visual installation, a book, CD-ROM and website (www.mappingperception.org.uk).

Medusae

Dorothy Cross, artist / Dr Tom Cross, Associate Professor of Zoology, Ecology and Plant Science, National University of Ireland, Cork

Jellyfish, which include some of the most dangerous animals on earth, exert a powerful fascination. Throughout history they have provided a focus for myth and superstition, and their delicate beauty has often been an inspiration for artists. In the nineteenth century, several extraordinary collections of decorative objects were produced based on jellyfish forms, and early attempts at scientific research also began during this period. An important contribution to jellyfish science was made by Maude Delap, an amateur naturalist living in Ireland at the turn of the twentieth century. Delap collected jellyfish specimens and bred them in bell jars at her home on Valentia Island.

   Medusae revived this mutual interest of art and science, bringing to it the benefits of contemporary scientific understanding and modern technology. Digital technology, in particular, has greatly facilitated the study of animal movement by enabling detailed examination of video footage. While Tom Cross investigated the biomechanics of *Chironex fleckeri* – a fast-swimming and deadly Australian species – his sister, the artist Dorothy Cross, researched the life and work of Maude Delap who had lived near her in Ireland. The collaboration resulted in a series of moving images: a digital analysis of the swimming movements of *C. fleckeri* and two work-in-progress videos: *Come into the garden Maude* and *Jellyfish Lake*. A final film, *Medusae*, which combines aspects from both sides of the project, received its first public screening on Valentia Island, Ireland, in April 2003.

Membracidae: the art and science of treehopper disguise

Mark Fairnington, artist and acting Head of Painting, Ruskin School,
Oxford / Dr George McGavin, entomologist and Assistant Curator
at the Hope Entomological Collections, Oxford

Mimesis is the basis for illusion in western art. Mimesis also exists in the natural
world, where its primary function is to conceal, camouflage or deceive predators,
thereby ensuring survival of the species. The purpose of *Membracidae* was
to study the treehopper's (*Insecta membracidae*) use of mimesis from these
two viewpoints. The project is a continuation of a previous collaboration that took
place at the Hope Entomological Collections in Oxford University Museum:
Mantidae, a series of paintings of specimens exhibited at the Museum in
August–September 2000.

Adult treehoppers often have a large and sometimes weirdly shaped pronotum
that extends backwards and sideways to cover the abdomen and sometimes
the whole bug. In tropical species, these unique pronotal extensions can assume
incredible, branched or inflated forms. Little fieldwork has been done on these
intriguing insects and even basic data on biology, behaviour and associated para-
sitoids are lacking. Few, if any, artists since the early part of the twentieth century
have painted these subjects.

The outcomes of *Membracidae* included a series of large-scale paintings and
scientific publications dealing with the taxonomy and ecology of the insects in their
centre of greatest diversity – the forests of Central America. The collected material
is now available to taxonomists and researchers at the University of Natural History
in Oxford, and the work is discussed in a book, *Dead or Alive* (2002, Black Dog
Publishers Ltd.), by the art historian, Mark Gisbourne.

Memory and Forgetting

Dr Tom Shakespeare, Director of Outreach, Policy, Ethics and Life Sciences Research Institute (PEALS), Newcastle upon Tyne / Anna Wilkinson, Senior Executive, Northern Print, Newcastle upon Tyne

The hard science of neuroscience and psychology appears to run counter to the intangible poetic allusions of identity and history. Memory is what defines us as individuals, while neuroscience explores what we have in common. Yet concepts such as sensory memory, childhood amnesia and dementia are fecund with potential for scientific inquiry, as well as carrying associations of personal experience and culture.

Four artist–scientist teams worked together to explore how each could contribute to the other's practice, discover ways to conceptualize memory, represent memory deficiencies and communicate with people with brain conditions. The teams comprised scientist Anya Hurlbert and artist Daniel Sturgis, artist Shona Illingworth with scientist Martin Conway, artist Ashley McCormick with scientist Julian Hughes, and artist Louise K. Wilson with scientist Madeleine Eacott. The research aimed to produce new models of memory and forgetting, richer and more comprehensible research data and a deeper understanding of mental disorder.

The collaboration culminated in an exhibition at Newcastle's Hatton Gallery in spring 2003, coinciding with DANA European Week of the Brain. The show presented paintings, prints, videos and sound installations by the artists, details of the scientists' research with images of the brain, and work by schools and community groups.

Mental

Professor Helen Storey, artist / Dr John McLachlan, School of Biology,
University of St Andrews / Caroline Coates, Project Manager,
Helen Storey Foundation

Mental explored the emotions that occur during the creative process. The project was 'a walk through one woman's mind', a visualization of the emotional elements that influence and inform creativity.

Helen Storey created a series of figures that acted as visual depictions of emotions and creative states, and incorporated explanations by John McLachlan of their scientific cause and effect. *Whisper*; *First, Last, Everything*; *Death Dresses*; and *Amygdala* addressed issues such as: how do we express our individuality and what gives it meaning? Does sexuality inform creativity? What does death look like? Where is your place of refuge? The figures also included a number of interactive elements designed to promote a unique experience for the viewer.

An installation of the figures was held at Oksnehallen, Copenhagen, and at the ICA, London, in 2001, and the exhibition has since toured to a number of venues in the UK. As the result of the collaboration, Dr McLachlan has constructed over 20 3D computer models of the human brain, indicating emotional signalling pathways, from sensory inputs to hormone-mediated outputs.

Mesh

Gavin Baily, artist / Dr Jonathan Mackenzie, computer programer

Mesh was a project that explored self-organizing neural networks, which have been employed with great success in the fields of artificial intelligence and computational neuroscience. Neural networks are determined by the formation and behaviour of agents, which in turn depend on the relationship developed between an agent and its environment.

Mesh sought to gain insight into this process by creating a cognitive agent capable of adapting to and learning from its information environment. During the course of the project a number of prototypes were developed; these were governed by two main components: a system to load structured image data, and a self-organizing algorithm that determines dynamic relationships between image data in a 3D environment. The partnership also experimented with ways to collect material from sources such as the Internet. Next steps include the development of user-friendly interfaces to the prototypes to allow easy experimentation for a general audience.

Midge Bait
Dr Alison Blackwell, scientist / Alison Hayes, artist / David Mackenzie, filmmaker

The Highland midge (*Culicoides impunctatus*) has gained a folklore reputation for its viciousness and persistency of attack. For three to four months each year, the incredible midge biomass dominates vast areas of the Highlands of Scotland, producing a significant impact on mankind's outdoor activities. To date, no detailed photographic/film documentation exists of this phenomenon.

Midge Bait explored the swarming patterns and attacking behaviour of the infamous biting midge and for the first time captured some visually spectacular images of this movement on film. The research resulted in a number of outputs – a body of scientific data, a collection of large-scale photographs, five video installation works and a short documentary film – that have made an important contribution to the scientific understanding of the midge.

Navigating Memories

Jennie Pedley, artist / Dr Laura Camfield, anthropologist / Professor Nigel Foreman, Department of Psychology, Middlesex University, London / Camden Arts Centre, London / Action for Kids

The development of spatial awareness depends on the ability to explore space freely and independently. In disabled people with poor mobility, this understanding may fail to develop properly or be impaired. As time is also 'spatial', these individuals may also have difficulty in appreciating sequential events, which in turn affects their ability to order their past and plan for the future.

Navigating Memories set out to assess and improve chronological and spatial thinking in a group of young adults with a range of physical disabilities. Laura Camfield and Jennie Pedley worked with the group members to create stories and drawings illustrating their life stories. These were then assembled by Professor Foreman and staff at Middlesex University into 3D virtual environments (VEs) that enabled each participant to travel through and navigate their autobiography. As well as enhancing spatial and temporal perception, VEs also have potential for teaching history to children.

An exhibition featuring the work of Jennie Pedley and an interactive virtual reality projection of the group's stories will be held at Camden Arts Centre, London, from April to June 2004.

Pentland Moon

Tom Barker, Director, b consultants / Juliet Dean, Director, PACE /
Dr M R Taghizadeh, Reader in Physics, Heriot-Watt University / Marcus Taylor,
artist / Ian J Young, Project Officer, Midlothian Council

In 2000, Midlothian Council chose Hillend Country Park near Edinburgh as the site for a contemporary landmark to celebrate artistic and scientific creativity and to act as an information and educational resource. An international competition was organized to select an artist and a shortlist of three was invited to develop proposals in collaboration with the physics department of Heriot-Watt University. The artists were asked to explore the history of the site, ecological issues of sustainability, notions of public art and the critical debate surrounding landmark artworks.

Marcus Taylor's winning design, *Pentland Moon*, proposed a circular screen set into the hillside, on which to display images of the moon and its prevalent phases. The moon image would occasionally be replaced by others, such as satellite pictures of weather patterns on Earth, an eclipse moving across the Earth's surface and sunspot activity on the face of the Sun. The work would also have an interactive link with the Internet, enabling a viewer (a school, university, space research centre or weather station) to download images to the screen which could then be seen in the artwork and on a dedicated website.

The Power of the Image

Neil Murray, Director, Northern Stage / Professor Pamela Briggs, Department of Psychology, University of Northumbria

It is a common belief that insanity results from an individual's inability to distinguish between what is real and what is imagined or hallucinated. Yet psychological research into 'reality monitoring' and 'false memory' demonstrates that, given certain circumstances, everyone can potentially confuse fact and fabrication. When recalling events, people are not always able to discriminate between memories derived from experience, and those that are generated by imagination, dreams and fantasy.

The Power of the Image combined visual theatre and elements of psychological research into 'reality monitoring' and 'false memory' to examine the mutability of memory and perception, and the degree to which they can be influenced by suggestion. The project aimed to stimulate debate about new ways of creating theatre, to raise awareness amongst scientists of the power of theatre to communicate ideas, and to enhance understanding amongst arts practitioners of new research and thinking in psychology. The outcome, a work-in-progress performance entitled *Stone, Paper, Scissors*, was performed to an audience of psychologists, students, art practitioners and members of the public at the Gulbenkian Studio Theatre, Newcastle upon Tyne, in January 2003.

The Psychology of Magic

**Professor Richard Wiseman, psychologist, University of Hertfordshire /
Peter Lamont, Research Associate, Department of Psychology, University
of Edinburgh / Mac King, magician**

For thousands of years magicians have used psychology to create a sense of
wonder in the minds of their audiences. However, magic is a highly secretive
business and little is known about the psychological techniques employed in this
branch of the performing arts. In August 2001 the collaborators travelled to Las
Vegas to work with some of the world's leading magicians, to discuss some of the
theories developed in previous research, and to explore how academic psychology
can influence a magician's performance. Las Vegas has more resident magicians
than any other part of the world and is the home of many of the world's top
conjurors. In addition, one of the world's largest magic conventions was taking
place in Las Vegas at the time, which provided an opportunity to work with many
highly skilled magicians. In doing so, the project team identified areas that were
of interest to both psychologists and magicians.

The project team explored various notions such as the 'psychology of lying'
(the degree to which magicians control their behaviour when performing sleight
of hand to avoid arousing the audience's sense of suspicion). Their research
was presented to professional and lay audiences to survey reactions and encourage discussions about how these ideas could enhance performance. The project
team are continuing with their research and plan to explore further connections
between psychology and magic.

Red and Wet on the Iron Air

Dr Tony Holder, Division of Parasitology, National Institute for Medical Research / Zarina Bhimji, artist

Malaria is a disease that affects hundreds of millions of people in tropical regions of the world. Of all deaths due to malaria and acute cases of the disease, 90 per cent currently occur in sub-Saharan Africa, mostly amongst children. Despite concerted attempts during the twentieth century to limit the spread of the disease by eliminating mosquitoes, the main vector, the *Anopheles* mosquito, has grown increasingly resistant to insecticides; at the same time traditional drugs, such as chloroquine, are now largely ineffective against the malaria parasite.

In December 2002 Tony Holder and Zarina Bhimji travelled to Kenya and Uganda in East Africa to investigate the conditions surrounding malaria, and to develop a deeper understanding of the human and environmental factors that contribute to its transmission. Their journey put many issues into perspective and highlighted the numerous problems that will need to be addressed before a successful solution can be found. In future, a multi-faceted approach to cure and prevention will be needed, in which laboratory and clinical research is married to economic and social programmes, cultural traditions and community care. Much of the research material yielded by the project has yet to be distilled and a collection of photographic work by Zarina is currently still in progress.

Scents of Space

Josephine Pletts, Pletts Haque Architects, London / Usman Haque, Pletts
Haque Architects / Dr Luca Turin, olfactory specialist and Senior Lecturer,
Physiology Department, University College London

Smell can have a powerful effect on the experience of space. Smell and temperature work together to influence how we perceive space, its scale, character and
intimacy. Although understanding of the human olfactory system has progressed
rapidly in recent years, architects and designers have tended to ignore its potential
for enriching spatial environments. If architecture can be 'tuned' with scent, it
might be possible to create new ways of experiencing space to fit or alter the
mood and lifestyle of its inhabitants.

In *Scents of Space,* the collaborators set out to develop a prototype of an environment defined by ambient scent. Using new technologies and delivery systems,
a 'smell installation' made of polycarbonate sheets was filled with a variety of
smells, synthetic and natural, released at different heights, combinations and intervals. By moving through the space and blending air currents, visitors were able to
influence scent streams creating individual olfactory paths and triggering personal
associations and memories. The prototype structure has been exhibited in a
number of venues. As the project evolves and more responses are recorded, it
will yield increasing information on the interaction of environment, fragrance and
human activity and how these factors can be harnessed in the interests of more
evocative and memorable design.

Soundless Music

**Sarah Angliss, composer / Ciarán O'Keefe, parapsychologist / GéNIA,
pianist / Professor Richard Wiseman, Department of Psychology,
University of Hertfordshire / National Physical Laboratory**

Infrasound – sound that occurs below the threshold of human hearing – is present all around us in the natural, animal and man-made worlds. Although we cannot hear it, we may, under certain conditions, be able to sense it, physically and psychologically. Infrasound has been known about for centuries and has often been added to musical performance to strengthen and enrich an instrument's tone and resonance. Because of its unusual properties, it has also been associated with strange sensations – peripheral vision, cold shivers, feelings of discomfort and so on – and has occasionally been implicated in paranormal phenemona and hauntings. However, little scientific research has been conducted into infrasound and its impact on people, and it is not known how infrasound affects our response to music.

Soundless Music is an experiment, staged as a series of multimedia concerts, to explore the effects of infrasound on audiences. Each concert features a programme of live music by a range of contemporary and modern composers (Sarah Angliss, Roddy Skeaping, Philip Glass, Arvo Pärt, Hayden Parsey, Howard Skempton and Karen Tanaka, and Steve Watson) played by the pianist GéNIA, a video installation by Ravi Deepres, and occasional deep-bass frequencies supplied by an infrasonic generator. While they experience the concert, the audience is asked to take part in a series of subjective tests conducted by psychologists, Ciarán O'Keefe and Richard Wiseman. The first *Soundless Music* concert (titled *Infrasonic*) took place in the Purcell Room, London, on 31 May 2003.

Sounds of Prehistory

Deborah Long, Research Manager, Kilmartin House Trust / Murray Campbell, Department of Physics and Astronomy, University of Edinburgh / Dr John Purser, musicologist, writer, broadcaster and composer / Rod Cameron, maker of historical woodwind musical instruments / John Creed, metalworker and Lecturer, Glasgow School of Art / Fraser Hunter, Curator, National Museums of Scotland / John Kenny, musician / Simon and Maria O'Dwyer, Bronze Age Horns

Archaeology has long been silent; we have assumed that the sounds of prehistory were lost in the depths of time. *Sounds of Prehistory* shows otherwise. The project team, which included archaeologists, craftsmen, musicians and physicists, collaborated to reconstruct and test four bronze and wooden instruments dating from the Iron and Dark Ages, and by reproducing them, to analyse the sounds of prehistoric times.

The collaborators produced replicas of the Ard Brin Horn, the Bekan Trumpet, the River Erne Horne and the Loch Tay Whistle. The recreation of these instruments has enabled us to hear and explore mankind's earliest attempts at music making and to shed light on the history and science of instrument construction. The research has resulted in a number of performances, lectures and academic papers, and the musicians involved in the project continue to use the instruments as part of their repertoires.

The STI Project: the search for terrestrial intelligence

Mike Phillips, STAR, University of Plymouth / Dr Guido Bugmann, School of Computing, University of Plymouth / Dr Angelo Cangelosi, School of Computing, University of Plymouth / Geoff Cox, Department of Media Arts, University of Plymouth / Laurent Mignonneau, artist / Christa Sommerer, artist / Chris Speed, School of Computing, University of Plymouth / Dr Nick Veck, Technical Director, National Remote Sensing Centre

STI turned the technologies that search space for alien intelligence back to planet Earth in a quest for 'evidence' of terrestrial intelligence. The project brought together artists, scientists and technologists to explore a collective knowledge of remote sensing, imaging technologies, autonomous agents (artificial intelligence and neural networks) and online interaction. Using satellite imaging and remote sensing techniques similar to those employed by the Search for Extraterrestrial Intelligence (SETI), STI scoured the Earth, while autonomous software agents processed the resulting data into images, animations and audio material made publicly accessible through the STI website.

The project also produced a short video documenting the thought processes provoked by the collaboration, and the research has been presented at a number of conferences and symposia at home and abroad. Disseminating the work has encouraged debate about the collaborative and transdisciplinary production of digital interactive media and highlighted the dynamics of artistic and scientific inquiry.

Viewing the Instruments

Jane Wildgoose, artist and writer / Philip Parr, opera director and musician / Dr Peter Isaacs, Department of Gastroenterology, Blackpool Victoria Hospital

In 1725 the French composer and viol player, Marin Marais, published a composition for bass viol and continuo – 'Le Tableau de l'Opération de la Taille' ('The scene of the operation of the cut'). The work, which has a performance time of four minutes, describes in music and accompanying text an operation to remove bladder stone. Jane Wildgoose, Philip Parr and Dr Peter Isaacs undertook a detailed investigation of the medical, social and musical history surrounding Marais's work and commissioned three new pieces of music from contemporary composers, Eleanor Firman, Rachel Stott and Eddie McGuire. At the same time, the team researched the feelings of patients, doctors and nurses towards an equivalent modern procedure – endoscopy under sedation. The three new scores, which had the same performance time and used similar instruments to the Marais work, aimed to respond musically to aspects of this present-day surgical technique.

The project culminated in a work-in-progress performance of the four compositions, accompanied by accounts of the two surgical operations, at the Old Operating Theatre in London in November 2001. The performance, with workshops for musicians and medics, will be touring the UK in autumn 2003.

Visualizing Complementary Shapes: a photographic view of molecular recognition

Catherine Yass, artist / Dr William James, Sir William Dunn School of Pathology, Oxford

Visualizing Complementary Shapes took the form of a year-long residency in which artist Catherine Yass worked alongside Dr William James and his team at the Sir William Dunn School of Pathology.

Yass explored the similarities between her own practice, the use of colour as a tool and metaphor, and the scientific research that takes place at the School. Dr James's work is based on 'shape recognition' and focuses on how antibodies and viruses recognize their counterparts in the body's cells. Science uses metaphors such as colour to explain phenomena; the way a 'string' of nucleotides fits together may be described in terms of colour even though the colours ascribed to the nucleotides are arbitrary. Photography is also a language with its own references and history in relation to colour; if a photographic image is put through the wrong process, the colours will be 'wrong' and seem to be unrelated to the original. In both cases it is the relationship between colours that makes the image coherent. The collaborators explored these cross-overs: how visual metaphors could provide research tools for scientists and offer new ways of considering photographic practice.

The residency resulted in a series of photographic works entitled *Double Agent*. These are now on permanent display at the Sir William Dunn School of Pathology.

A Visual Language for Chronic Pain

Deborah Padfield, artist / Dr Charles Pither, consultant pain specialist, St Thomas's Hospital, London

Pain is intangible and invisible. For the patient, attempting to describe pain can be enormously difficult, leading to feelings of isolation and helplessness. Moreover, pain itself is often poorly understood and in many cases proves unresponsive to treatment. The medical challenge may not be to cure in a conventional sense, but to help patients understand, manage and come to terms with their pain. Communication in both instances is key. Helping patients to express what they feel, either physically or psychologically, can create a more beneficial relationship with medical teams and improve the outcome of care.

A Visual Language for Chronic Pain attempted to address these issues by using photographic images to communicate individual experience of pain. A programme of workshops led by artist and chronic pain sufferer, Deborah Padfield, in collaboration with pain consultant Dr Charles Pither, was conducted with patients attending the INPUT Pain Management Unit at St Thomas's Hospital, London. By exploring the photographic gaze and finding evocative visual images to represent their symptoms, patients were encouraged to take greater control of their pain and become partners in its diagnosis and management. The work produced has been exhibited in a variety of arts and medical contexts and on leaving the programme, participants were encouraged to continue developing their visual ideas.

Biographies

Baby Epsilons

Sean Gandini is considered one of the world's most adventurous jugglers. His work ranges from juggling choreography to films and articles that explore the nuances of this often-neglected art form.

For the last decade Gandini and his partner Kati Ylä-Hokkala have run Gandini Juggling, a constantly changing group of virtuoso jugglers. As well as performances in contexts that include Buckingham Palace, circuses, art galleries, football stadiums and the streets, their work investigates the more formal aspects of juggling. In the year 2000 the company expanded to 12 performers, forming the largest juggling company in the world.

Sean is a regular teacher at The Circus Space and Circomedia in the UK, and gives annual masterclasses abroad.

Dr Norihide Tokushige is Associate Professor at the Department of Mathematics, University of the Ryukyus, Okinawa, Japan. He specializes in extremal set theory, Ramsey theory, graph theory and combinatorial geometry, and has a keen interest in juggling.

Luke Wilson is a professional juggler and performer, a part-time theorist, and an ex-student and collaborator of Gandini Juggling.

How To Live

Bobby Baker is one of Britain's leading performance artists. During the past three decades she has produced an extensive repertoire of work, ranging from *An Edible Family in a Mobile Home* in 1976, when she made a life-sized family out of cake, to *Drawing on a Mother's Experience*, a show that has been performed over 200 times around the world. In 1991 she began her *Daily Life* series, a domestic quintet commissioned by London International Festival of Theatre (LIFT). During the first part, *Kitchen Show*, Bobby opened her own kitchen to the public and has since toured to 'guest kitchens' in Britain, Europe, Australia, Canada and South America. *How To Shop* in 1993 took the form of a lecture on supermarket shopping and has toured to festivals and cities worldwide and in the UK, including Australia, the USA and Scotland. *Take A Peek!* in 1995 was Bobby's inimitable interpretation of the healthcare system, and *Grown-Up School*, the fourth in the series, took the audience back to the classroom for a special lesson in a London primary school. *Box Story* is the culmination of this series. A version of *Box Story* was broadcast on BBC Radio 4 in November 2002. *Housework House* (2001) led to the creation of an interactive web-based performance. Her new work, *How To Live*, is in development for 2004.

Dr Richard Hallam is currently Visiting Professor in Clinical Psychology at the University of Greenwich and has spent most of his working career in London, where he has taught, researched and practised psychotherapy. He has published extensively in the field of cognitive behavioural therapy, specializing in anxiety and problems of hearing and balance. With a background in philosophy and anthropology, he is also interested in the influence of psychology on cultural practices, in particular the growth of self-analysis and self-management of psychological problems. *How To Live* is the first project on which he has collaborated with an artist.

Jeni Walwin is an independent curator, writer and researcher.

Medusae

Dorothy Cross is an artist, working largely with sculpture and the moving image, who trained at Leicester Polytechnic and the San Francisco Art Institute. Her work has been shown at the Venice Biennale in 1992, where she represented Ireland, the Istanbul Biennial in 1997 and the Liverpool Biennial in 1999. Other exhibitions include those at the ICA, Philadelphia, PA (1991), Arnolfini, Bristol (1997) and *Cry* at Artpace, San Antonio, TX (1996). Future projects include an opera, Pergolesi's 'Stabat Mater' in conjunction with the Opera Theatre Company, which will be held in a cave on Valentia Island, Ireland, in 2004. She is represented by Kerlin Gallery, Dublin and Frith Street Gallery, London.

Dr Tom Cross is an Associate Professor in Zoology at University College, National University of Ireland, Cork (NUIC). After receiving his PhD on the genetics of hybrid fish from NUIC in 1975, he worked as a postdoctoral fellow in the Canadian Department of Fisheries and Oceans, and in the Department of Genetics at Swansea University before being appointed Assistant Director at the Salmon Research Trust of Ireland in 1980. He was appointed to the NUIC faculty in 1983. He received the Bennsinger Liddell Salmon award in 1987, which was used to visit fish genetics laboratories in Scandinavia and North America, a sabbatical fellowship from the Salmon Genetics Programme of the North American Atlantic Salmon Federation in 1991, and a two-month EC Leonardo-funded placement in the Institute of Marine Biology Crete in 1996. He was also one of the experts used by the EC to formulate updated aquaculture research programmes. He has received 11 EC grants on fisheries and aquaculture genetics, has published over 80 papers in international journals and has been Assistant Editor in Genetics for the *Journal of Fish Biology*.

Marina Warner is a novelist, historian and critic.

Navigating Memories

Dr Laura Camfield is a social anthropologist who investigates the experiences of people with disabilities using a combination of qualitative and quantitative techniques. In particular, she likes to contrast the richness of individual narratives with processes of quantitative measurement that fragment experience and reduce it to generalizing categories. Her interest in measurement and 'labelling' was reinforced by her experience following a major accident when she had to adjust to altered physical function, visual perception, and body image. She has also had experience of participatory research and is a trained counsellor, which helps her to deal with the emotions evoked by this topic.

Professor Nigel Foreman is a psychologist based at Middlesex University who has been working in spatial cognition since 1988 and is the co-author of the two-volume *Handbook of Spatial Paradigms and Methodologies* (Psychology Press, Hove, UK, 1997–1998). He was one of the first to use VR technology to examine spatial navigation and perception, and has been awarded several grants to study spatial awareness of environments such as schools and public buildings in disabled and able-bodied individuals. His research has already demonstrated the value of VR technology for pupils with disabilities; its extension to time–space relationships in the current project has potential to provide these groups with many benefits, including new forms of education and training.

Jennie Pedley trained as a physiotherapist before studying painting and printmaking. She now creates three-dimensional (3D) virtual environments and works part-time as a paediatric physiotherapist. Jennie's physiotherapy work with young people with disabilities inspired her to work with similar groups on an art project. In 2000–2001 with the help of Professor Roy Kalawsky, an expert in virtual reality (VR) at Loughborough University, she created a fly-through virtual environment based on the lives of teenagers from the Vale Resource Base in Tottenham, London. This on-going project has received support from The Year of the Artist,

London Arts, and currently the Arts and Technology Partnerships and the National Endowment for Science Technology and the Arts (NESTA).

Action for Kids is a registered charity based in Hornsey, north London, which provides an exciting work community and environment where people with a range of disabilities can develop office skills in preparation for later employment.

Camden Arts Centre is a contemporary visual art venue in north London, independent in spirit and pioneering in practice, that enjoys a distinctive and successful role as a place where art is seen, made and discussed. The Centre offers integrated exhibitions, community and education projects and an innovative programme of arts and science residencies. Following a substantial refurbishment programme, it is now fully accessible to people with disabilities.

Colette Conroy is Lecturer in Drama at the University of the West of England. She writes about disability and representation and has extensive experience as a director of theatre, especially disability theatre.

Red and Wet on the Iron Air

Dr Tony Holder, Head of the Division of Parasitology, National Institute for Medical Research, Mill Hill, London, trained as a biochemist at the University of East Anglia and obtained a PhD in genetics at Leeds University. Following a postdoctoral fellowship in Copenhagen in 1978 he became a staff scientist at the Wellcome Foundation. He took up his current position in 1988. His interests in parasitology started in 1978 with African trypanosomes, but from 1980 onwards his main focus has been malaria. Particular research interests have been protein structure and glycosylation, and the application of molecular and cell biological methods to the study of malaria parasite invasion of erythrocytes and subsequent intracellular development. Current research is focused on the structure and function of malaria proteins involved in red blood cell recognition, and the importance of host immunity in interfering with these functions. Potential applications of this research include vaccine development and the identification of targets for therapeutic intervention.

Soundless Music

Sarah Angliss works independently as an exhibit maker, composer and author.
After acquiring a degree in electroacoustics (1989) and a diploma from the Royal
College of Music (1996), and spending a short spell in the building industry,
Sarah worked for four years at the Science Museum, London (1991), firing her
enthusiasm for obsolete electronic musical instruments.

In 1995 Sarah authored and co-edited a number of prize-winning children's
books and multimedia titles, and became involved in the practical side of exhibit
creation. She now enjoys employing all her skills – engineering, music, multimedia,
curatorship and writing – but her main interest is in composing her own sounds
and music and using them to create immersive visitor experiences. Recent
examples of Sarah's soundtracks can be heard in the *Booth of Truth* (Southwold
Pier, 2002), *Science in the Dock* (Glasgow Science Centre, 2000), *The Globe*
(original version, Eden Project, 1999), *The Gene Forecaster* and the *Fear Room*
(The Museum Of, 1999–2000).

At the end of the 1990s Sarah worked with other exhibit makers under the
umbrella name Mongrel Media. She now works independently and in collaboration
with others under the name Spacedog (www.spacedog.biz). In parallel with the
Soundless Music project, Sarah co-created a video and performance piece
in 2002, *Old Dog New Trick,* London International Festival of Theatre (LIFT), and
embarked on building a time machine for the Cheltenham Science Festival.

GéNIA is a virtuoso pianist with a highly eclectic repertoire that embraces
mainstream classics, new music and multimedia projects.

A student of the distinguished Ukrainian teacher, Regina Horowitz, she holds
six instrumental diplomas, including the prestigious Premier Prix from the Guildhall
School of Music. After receiving exceptional reviews for her debut at the South
Bank Centre (London) in 1998 in the PLG Young Artist Series, GéNIA toured
the UK, Europe, the USA and the Middle East. In London she has played at the
Wigmore Hall, the Barbican, St John's Smith Square and St Martin in the Fields.

She has recorded two albums of twentieth-century music, *GéNIA:Unveiled* and *Transformations* on the Black Box label, and appeared as guest soloist on soundtracks for the films *Paradise Grove* and *Bookcruncher*.

GéNIA regularly commissions new music and collaborates with innovative artists, including the Brodsky Quartet; the Ensemble Bash; the composers Howard Skempton, Sarah Angliss, and John Richards; and the film-maker Ravi Deepres. Alongside a busy artistic career she also undertakes educational work, giving masterclasses and lectures. She has taught at Trinity College of Music (London), Dartington Summer School, De Montfort University (Leicester) and Lewis University (Peoria, IL, USA).

Professor Richard Wiseman began his working life as an award-winning professional magician and was one of the youngest members of The Magic Circle. He obtained a first-class honours degree in psychology from University College, London, a doctorate in psychology from Edinburgh University and was awarded a prestigious Perrott-Warrick Scholarship from Trinity College, Cambridge. He now heads a research unit based within the Psychology department at the University of Hertfordshire and carries out scientific research into a range of unusual topics, including the psychology of ghosts and miracles, magic, lying and intuition.

Professor Wiseman's research has been widely reported in many of the world's leading science journals, including *Nature*, *Science* and *Psychological Bulletin*. He has presented his findings at many national and international academic conferences, and given invited public talks about his work at The Royal Society, The Royal Society for the Arts and The Royal Institution. He has featured in hundreds of radio and television programmes, and articles about his work have appeared in *The Times*, the *Daily Telegraph* and the *Guardian*. He has also devised several large-scale experiments involving thousands of people. Many of these have been carried out in collaboration with the *Daily Telegraph* and the BBC science programme, *Tomorrow's World*.

Ciarán O'Keeffe is currently employed at Liverpool Hope University College, lecturing in criminal psychology and parapsychology. His research interests include twentieth-century Japanese music, which culminated in a stage presentation about Toru Takemitsu, and aspects of music psychology, including performance anxiety and emotional responses to music. He is currently completing a PhD in parapsychology, focusing on paranormal claimants at the University of Hertfordshire. His expertise in this area has resulted in a number of publications and consultations on mediumship and psychic cases.

In conjunction with his PhD sponsors, Ciarán is keen to promote a critical, responsible, scientific point of view towards parapsychology and to disseminate factual information about the results of parapsychological inquiries to the scientific community and the public. This is reflected in several projects that he is actively involved in, including the use of dowsers in criminal investigations, the psychological examination of psychic readings, dream imagery and precognition.

Dr Susan Hallam is an educational specialist, musician and author based at the Institute of Education, University of London.

Viewing the Instruments

Dr Peter Isaacs trained in medicine in Manchester (qualified 1967) and thereafter worked in hospitals in Manchester (1967), Lancaster (1968–1969), Aberdeen (1969–1970), and Nigeria (1970–1971). His specialist interest in gastroenterology first developed during a Wellcome research scholarship with Professor Turnberg in Manchester (1971–1973). He completed his specialist clinical training at Guy's Hospital, London (1976–1984) and later undertook a one-year research fellowship at the University of California, San Francisco (1981–1982).

Peter has been a consultant physician at Blackpool Victoria Hospital for 17 years and clinical tutor at the University of Manchester for eight years. He is responsible for all medical teaching programmes at BVH and has particular teaching interests in consent for operative procedures and problem-based learning. His research interests include oesophageal disease and family-history-directed colon cancer screening. Scientific papers include Electrolyte Transport in Human Intestinal Mucosa in Vitro (MD thesis, University of Manchester, 1979), and over 60 papers published in *Nature*, The *Lancet*, *Clinical Science*, *Gut*, *Gastroenterology*, and *Gastrointestinal Endoscopy*.

Philip Parr was born in New York City and educated in Australia at Sydney University and the University of New South Wales. He has worked as an actor, singer, musician, dancer, composer and puppeteer and is now a theatre and opera director. He is currently director of the Swaledale Festival in Yorkshire, which presents chamber music of all genres.

Philip's work has taken him from small touring opera in Scandinavia to the Millennium Dome, and from community theatre in a decaying Yorkshire seaside town to the Sydney Opera House. He was responsible for the building of Spitalfields Market Opera, stage-managed and performed in a stunt show in Sydney and has taught theatre in numerous places. He has commissioned over 50 new works of music and opera.

Jane Wildgoose trained in fashion and textiles at Winchester School of Art, subsequently working as a designer/maker for stage and film. She has worked in collaboration with numerous arts professionals: with the writer Clive Barker (costume designer, five productions, the Dog Co., 1979–1982; special-effects costume designer, *Hellraiser*, New World Films, 1987); as costume and production designer with the writer/director Alasdair Middleton (nine productions ranging from classical theatre to performance/installation at London venues including Battersea Arts Centre, Rebecca Hossack Gallery, the Arts Theatre, 1989–1996); and with art director Simon Costin (props and textiles for Miss Havisham's breakfast table, *Great Expectations*, BBC television 1988), and on three productions with Philip Parr (Spitalfields Market Opera, 1997; Millennium Festival, 2000). Associated research for these and other performance works – into representations of the body in dress, literature and medical illustration – has led to articles and reviews in publications including The *Independent*, The *Guardian*, The *Daily Telegraph*, The *New Statesman* and The *Lancet*.

Other recent work includes two 'Year of the Artist' projects in 2000–2001: a residency with sculptor Mary Hooper at Bexhill Museum of Costume and Social History, and an exploration of collectors and collecting on the banks of the River Thames with artist Sally Hampson (exhibition, Trinity Hospital, Greenwich, 2001). In 2002 she was co-host with Dr Ruth Richardson of a conference entitled *The Business of the Flesh: Art, Science & Access to the Human Body*, in association with the Ruskin School of Drawing and Fine Art, Oxford; in 2003 she was associate producer, with radio artist Gregory Whitehead and producer Neil MacCarthy, of *On One Lost Hair* (BBC Radio 4). She is a visiting lecturer at Winchester School of Art.

Professor Brian Hurwitz is D'Oyly Carte Professor of Medicine and the Arts, King's College, London.

Editors

Bergit Arends Since graduating in Visual Arts Administration: Curating and Commissioning Contemporary Art from the Royal College of Art in 1997, Bergit Arends has initiated and run a visual arts programme at the National Institute for Medical Research, London, working with, among others, Marc Atkins, Lucy Orta, and Zarina Bhimji.

In 1998/1999 as associate of Art Project Management, she co-ordinated the Inshore Sites arts programme in Medway.

Her interests have also focused on recent German history. She initiated and managed the first international symposium on WWII air-raid bunker architecture in Europe within the context of twentieth-century architecture and urbanism in Emden, Germany, in 1999.

She is a freelance art consultant and has been based part-time at the Wellcome Trust since 1999 where she manages the sciart programme.

Davina Thackara trained in history of art at Sussex University and the Courtauld Institute of Art, specializing in twentieth-century painting and sculpture. She worked for many years as a lecturer and course leader on the BA and MA programmes of the Faculty of Art and Design, Kingston University, and contributed as a visiting lecturer to undergraduate and postgraduate courses elsewhere in public art, site-specific sculpture and art and architecture. She has written and published numerous articles on these same topics and from 1999–2002 was Managing Editor of *Public Art Journal*. Recently she co-authored catalogues on a contemporary British sculptor, and on the public sculpture of south west London for the Public Monuments and Sculpture Association (PMSA).

She now works mainly as an editor, researcher and project manager.

Image List

Medusae
→ **Intro**
Courtesy of Dorothy Cross
→ **Intro, page 21**
Courtesy of The Bridgeman Art Library
→ **Figs 1–13, 19, 22–28, 48–56**
Courtesy of Dorothy Cross
→ **Figs 14, 15, 29–47, 57**
Courtesy of Tom Cross
→ **Figs 17, 20, 21**
Courtesy of Paul Sutherland
(www.sutherlandstock.com)
→ **Figs 16, 18**
Courtesy of Jamie Seymour

How To Live
→ **Intro, Figs 2, 3**
Courtesy of Bobby Baker
→ **Intro pages 68, 69, Figs 1, 4, 6, 7, 9, 10, 11**
Courtesy of Andrew Whittuck
→ **Fig. 5**
Courtesy of Deborah May
→ **Fig. 8**
Courtesy of Behavioural Tech, LLC

Red and Wet on the Iron Air
→ **All images**
Courtesy of Tony Holder
→ **Map on page 102**
Courtesy of Dr Evasius Kaburu Bauni
→ **Pages 98, 114**
Courtesy of The Wellcome Trust Sanger Institute

Soundless Music
→ **Intro, Figs 9–11**
Courtesy of Professor James Russell
→ **Fig. 1**
Courtesy of The Schubert Club Museum
of Musical Instruments, St Paul, Minnesota, USA
→ **Fig. 2**
By permission of the British Library
→ **Fig. 3**
Courtesy of Atlantic City Convention Hall Organ Society
→ **Fig. 4**
Courtesy of Tom Hunkin

→ **Fig. 5**
Courtesy of Martin Birchall and Liverpool Post
→ **Fig. 6**
Courtesy of Dr Richard Lord and Dan Simmons, NPL
→ **Figs 7, 8, 12**
Courtesy of Sarah Angliss

Navigating Memories
→ **All images**
Courtesy of Jennie Pedley and
the workshop participants

Viewing the Instruments
→ **Intro**
By permission of the British Library;
Courtesy of the Trustees of The Wellcome Trust
→ **Figs 1, 3, 4, 6, 8**
Courtesy of Jane Wildgoose
→ **Fig. 2**
By permission of the British Library
→ **Page 256**
Courtesy of The Encyclopaedia of Illustration
→ **Figs 5, 7, 9, 11, 15, 16**
Courtesy of The Trustees of the Wellcome Trust, London
→ **Figs 10, 12**
Courtesy of Mark Lambert
→ **Figs 13, 14**
Courtesy of Peter Isaacs
→ **Fig. 17**
Courtesy of Katie Isaacs

Baby Epsilons
→ **Intro pages, Figs 1–4, 7, 12**
Courtesy of Gandini Juggling
→ **Figs 5, 6**
Courtesy of Guy Bellingham
→ **Fig. 8**
Courtesy of Michelle Weaver
→ **Figs 9–11**
Courtesy of Norihide Tokushige

Cover image
Me, experiencing DBT, 2002
Courtesy of Bobby Baker

Experiment: conversations in art and science

Edited by Bergit Arends and Davina Thackara

Texts © 2003 the artists, scientists and authors

Images © 2003 the artists and scientists
(unless otherwise stated)

Designed by Nanni Goebel
at Clarendon Road Studio

Printed by B.A.S.

sciart is a Wellcome Trust scheme that was funded
2000–2002 by a consortium comprising: Arts Council
of England, British Council, Calouste Gulbenkian
Foundation, National Endowment for Science, Technology
and the Arts (NESTA) and The Wellcome Trust.

The Wellcome Trust is a registered charity, no. 210183.
Its sole Trustee is The Wellcome Trust Limited, a company
registered in England, no. 2711000, whose registered
office is 183 Euston Road, London NW1 2BE.

Published by The Wellcome Trust
Distributed by Cornerhouse Publishing

ISBN 1 84129 043 2
Price £16.99

Acknowledgements

We would like to thank: The artists, scientists and authors.
The members of the sciart Consortium: Ken Arnold,
Lloyd Anderson, Gareth Binns, Siân Ede, Bronaç Ferran,
Denna Jones, and Claire Lovett.
The sciart judges: Paul Bonaventura, Richard Gregory,
Nancy Lane, Janna Levin, Francis McKee, Richard
Wentworth, Michael Greenhough, and Richard Brown.
Laurence Smaje, Terry Trickett and all those involved
in the early phases of sciart.

We especially thank Verity Slater for her contribution
to the sciart programme and the publication.

We are grateful to the following for their support:
Paul Chapman
Kelly Chorpening
Clare Cohen
Rachel Collins
the late Jo Colston
Clive Coward
Nanni Goebel and Peter B. Willberg
Mike Page
The Publishing Department, The Wellcome Trust
Ellen Clarke
Louise Simon
Lucy Shanahan

The Wellcome Trust